Partisan Hearts and Minds

The Institution for Social and Policy Studies at Yale University

The Yale ISPS Series

Partisan Hearts and Minds

Political Parties and the Social Identities

of Voters

Donald Green
Bradley Palmquist
Eric Schickler

Yale University Press

New Haven & London

306. 26
G 821 p OCT 18 2018

Set in Adobe Garamond and Stone Sans type by The Composing Room
of Michigan, Inc., Grand Rapids, Michigan.

Printed in the United States of America.

The Library of Congress has cataloged the hardcover edition as follows:
Green, Donald P., 1961–
    Partisan hearts and minds : political parties and the social identities of voters /
Donald Green, Bradley Palmquist, Eric Schickler.
        p.   cm. — (Yale ISPS series)
Includes bibliographical references and index.
    ISBN 0-300-09215-6 (cloth : alk. paper)
    1. Party affiliation.   2. Voting.   3. Party affiliation—United States.
4. Voting—United States.   I. Palmquist, Bradley, 1953–   II. Schickler, Eric,
1969–   III. Title.   IV. Series.
    JF2071   .G74 2002
    306.2'6'0973—dc21

                                                        2002002242

A catalogue record for this book is available from the British Library.

The paper in this book meets the guidelines for permanence and durability
of the Committee on Production Guidelines for Book Longevity of the Council
on Library Resources.

ISBN 0-300-10156-2 (pbk. : alk. paper)

10 9 8 7 6 5 4 3 2

Contents

Preface

This book is the culmination of a circuitous intellectual journey. In 1987 we first tried to make sense of the new arguments and evidence purporting to show that voters continually adjust their party affiliations in response to changing political and economic conditions. A welter of books and articles seemed to be eating away at what an earlier generation of scholars took to be a fundamental truth about electoral politics: Voters who feel a sense of attachment to a political party seldom embrace another party. Which was right, the old canon or the new?

Intrigued by the fact that our mentors, Christopher Achen, Jack Citrin, and J. Merrill Shanks, staked out different positions on the question, we began to retrace the steps of previous scholars. We discovered that the evidence for partisan change hinged on subtle and often dubious modeling assumptions. With encouragement from Harold Clarke, David Rohde, and Robert Erikson, we published our first paper, "Of Artifacts and Partisan Instability," in the *American Journal of Political Science* (Green and Palmquist 1990). That essay, which took on a host of important works on party identification, planted our flag in the sand, expressing our skepticism about both the new view of party identification and the statistical methods used to bolster it. In a nutshell, we argued that survey measures of party identification are often imprecise, and models that fail to account for measurement error will overstate the instability of party attachments.

We wrote several companion essays shortly afterward to explain and develop our statistical argument. An essay in *Political Analysis* (Green 1991) offered a detailed defense of our simultaneous equations results. We grappled with the special complications introduced by nonrandom measurement error in a note written for *Psychometrica* (Green and Palmquist 1991) and canvassed methods for separating trait stability from measurement error in an essay for *Sociological Methodology* (Palmquist and Green 1992). An essay in *Public Opinion Quarterly* (Green and Schickler 1993) showed that the results we obtained from panel surveys, which track a group of individuals over time, were consistent with findings from a survey that repeatedly quizzed respondents about partisanship in the course of a single interview. In an essay for *Political Behavior* (Green and Palmquist 1994), we demonstrated that our initial findings of partisan stability generalized to an assortment of American panel surveys. In 1995, we circled back to simultaneous equations models purporting to show how party identification adjusts to respondents' ideological proximity to the parties. In a second *Political Analysis* essay (Schickler and Green 1995), we explained why these models are biased. Finally, thanks to the encouragement of Richard Johnston, in 1997 we demonstrated in *Comparative Political Studies* (Schickler and Green 1997) that our individual-level results generalize to countries other than the United States.

To that point, all of our work had centered on individual-level survey data. The field of electoral studies, however, had grown increasingly interested in aggregate data, specifically, the manner in which the balance of Democrats and Republicans changed over time. Our work moved in a similar direction, and, perhaps predictably, we found ourselves far less convinced than other scholars of partisanship's responsiveness to economic conditions and presidential popularity. In an exchange written for the *American Political Science Review* (Green, Palmquist, and Schickler 1998) and later embellished in Kent Jennings and Richard Niemi's *Controversies in Voting Behavior* (Green, Palmquist, and Schickler 2001), we argued that the partisan balance changes far less than other analyses of aggregate time series seemed to suggest. This foray into time-series analysis shaped the way we looked at individual-level panel data, and Chapter 4 of the present book grows out of a synthesis of individual and aggregate evidence in an essay in *Political Analysis* coauthored with David Yoon (Green and Yoon 2002).

Accompanying these empirical refinements was the development of an increasingly distinctive theoretical perspective on party identification. An important turning point was an essay published in the *American Journal of Political Science* (Gerber and Green 1998), written in collaboration with Alan Gerber. This article took issue with both newer conceptions of partisanship, which characterize party identification as a voter's running tally of evaluations of the parties' competence and ideological appeal, and older conceptions, which claim that party identification functions as a perceptual screen. Both arguments, it seemed, understated the extent to which party attachments may endure even when people give low marks to the party with which they affiliate.

Having lain the empirical groundwork in the form of journal articles, the final step was to produce a book-length treatment that joined the strands of argument into a coherent thesis. Readers familiar with our earlier work will nonetheless find a great deal of new material herein, chief among which is our discussion of the nature and significance of party identification. Most of our journal articles began by alluding to the importance of party identification for those who study electoral politics, without bothering to discuss whether this reputation is warranted. The present work, on the other hand, devotes a great deal of attention to the question of what partisanship is and why it merits our attention.

The centerpiece of this book is the claim that party identification is a genuine form of social identification. Citizens have an enduring sense of what sorts of people belong to various parties and whether they identify with these social groups. To make our case and to rebut competing theoretical claims, we marshal an unusually broad array of survey evidence. Much of this book relies on the stalwart American National Election Studies dating back to the 1950s, but we also make ample use of polls conducted in other countries and by private organizations. Where necessary, we have also filled in some gaps by commissioning our own surveys. For example, we worked with the Roper Starch organization, one of the last commercial polling firms that uses face-to-face interviews, to assess partisan group stereotypes (Chapter 1) and social identification with parties (Chapter 2). Thanks to Renato Mannheimer and Gianluca Galletto, we also commissioned questions about party identification on an Italian panel study to examine the nature of partisan attachments in an unstable political environment. Thanks to Kent Jennings and Laura Stoker, who in 1997 reinterviewed respondents originally surveyed in 1965, we are able to present new evidence on the long-term stability of party, class, and religious identifications and the extent to which they are passed from parents to children. We are grateful also to researchers at the University of Essex, who furnished information from British election surveys.

Yale's Institution for Social and Policy Studies has supported our research unstintingly since 1989. The Social Science Statistics Laboratory, under the direction of Ann Green, and UC Data at Berkeley, under the direction of Ilona Einowski, have lent countless hours meeting our requests for data. We have also benefited from the work of many able research assistants over the years, among them Jon Cowden, Joel Fetzer, Matt Green, Eric McGhee, Barry McMillion, Melissa Michelson, David Nickerson, Kathryn Pearson, John Sides, Jenny Smith, Dara Strolovitch, Janelle Wong, and David Yoon. Special thanks goes to David Mayhew, Larry Bartels, Jack Citrin, and Alan Gerber for their many helpful comments and suggestions, and to Pam LaMonaca, who provided invaluable assistance in preparing the manuscript.

Last, we are grateful to Ann Green, Liz Jeff, and Terri Bimes for their support, encouragement, and patience throughout.

Partisan Hearts and Minds

Chapter 1 Introduction

In the context of public opinion research, the term *partisanship* is something of a double entendre, calling to mind both partisan cheering at sports events and affiliation with political parties. Both meanings, as it happens, comport with what those who study elections typically have in mind when discussing partisan attitudes. Ask a sample of ordinary citizens to assess the president's integrity, policy initiatives, or performance in office, and one finds sharp disagreement between Democrats and Republicans. Indeed, Democrats and Republicans offer contrasting views not only on party leaders and their programs but also on their family, friends, pets—anything that has become emblematic of a political party.

Of course, it is hardly news that Democrats and Republicans disagree about politics. Early survey researchers noted in 1936 that 83% of Republicans believed that Franklin Delano Roosevelt's policies were leading the country down the road to dictatorship, a view shared by only 9% of Democrats (Key 1961: 246). What makes partisanship interesting, and what was not apparent to researchers until the 1950s, is the fact that voters who call themselves Republicans at age thirty-two will most likely continue to do so at age eighty-two. Recessions, wars, and dramatic swings in the political fortunes of the parties tend to leave a shallow imprint on the partisan affiliations of adults, just as doctrinal and organizational disputes within Christian sects typically have little effect on the religious affiliations of churchgoers. To be sure, one generation may be more enamored of the Republican Party or the Lutheran church than the last, but the pace at which adults change their group attachments tends to be slow.

This degree of persistence is surprising because identification with political parties is a minor part of the typical American's self-conception. Race, sex, ethnicity, religion, region, and social class come immediately to mind as core social identities; political party does not. The core identities suffuse nearly all of our day-to-day interactions with others; it is difficult to imagine a social gathering in which people fail to take notice of accents, skin color, or secondary sexual characteristics. Partisan stereotypes and self-images, by contrast, are called to mind sporadically, when one glances at the newspaper or discusses politics with friends. It is not unusual for people to be unaware of the party affiliations of their friends, even when these friends' other group identities are known in minute detail. The political self is for the most part eclipsed by other selves—cultural, economic, spiritual, sexual, familial, athletic, artistic. In those instances when our attention turns to politics, however, partisan attachments become highly influential, whereas more fundamental social identities, such as sex, religion, or social class, tend to have less predictive power.

A simple example drawn from the classic Youth-Parent Socialization Panel Study (Jennings, Markus, and Niemi 1991) illustrates the point. In this survey, a national sample of 728 parents of high school students were interviewed in 1965 and reinterviewed in 1982. In 1965, respondents were asked the canonical question about their political partisanship: "Generally speaking, do you usually think of yourself as a Republican, Democrat, Independent, or what?" On the basis of this question, respondents were classified as Democrats (45.5%), Republicans (30.0%), or Independents (24.0%) or as "apolitical" (0.5%). In 1982, these respondents reported which presidential candidate they had voted for in 1980. Ronald Reagan received votes from 89.5% of those who in 1965 had labeled themselves Republicans but from just 33.8% of those who had earlier labeled themselves Democrats. Independents fell in the middle, at 65.1%. It is remarkable to think that identities formed before the rise and fall of Richard Nixon, Gerald Ford, Jimmy Carter, bell-bottoms, disco, stagflation, and gasoline shortages could so powerfully shape presidential preferences seventeen years later.

Remarkable, too, is that these sharp partisan differences eclipse correspond-ing sex, class, or religion effects. For example, in this survey, Reagan received 57.8% of the male and 58.6% of the female parents' votes. He garnered the sup-port of nearly identical proportions of Protestants and Catholics (58.2% and 60.7%, respectively). A mere sixteen-point gap separated Jews (41.9%) from Protestants. Even class differences pale compared with the predictive power of party identification: 63.9% of those identifying as middle class in 1982 voted for Reagan, whereas 47.1% of those identifying as working class voted for this conservative Republican. It is notable that sex, religion, and class were weaker predictors of the vote for Ronald Reagan than was party identification mea-sured during the Johnson administration.

Of the seemingly "fundamental" social identities, only race is a powerful predictor of electoral choice. The relationship between race and voting, how-ever, is largely traceable to the fact that since the early 1960s, a preponderance of African Americans have identified themselves as Democrats. Seldom have black voters since that time offered much electoral support to black Republi-cans or Independents running against white Democrats. Tellingly, groups with less sharply defined partisan proclivities, such as Chinese Americans, are less prone to vote in distinctive ways. Our point is not that race is unimportant but rather that its influence on electoral choice is mediated largely by partisan affil-iation.

The persistence and motive power of partisan identities vis-à-vis other sorts of social identities are all the more remarkable given that political party organi-zations have almost no detectable presence in Americans' everyday lives. In many ways, political parties in the United States have declined since the 1950s, as urban political machines, patronage jobs, party levers in voting booths, and backroom nominating procedures have waned or disappeared. As campaigns have grown more reliant on direct mail, commercial phone banks, and televi-sion, the role of party activists has receded. As the percentage of adults who work for or with parties has dropped (Putnam 2000), the level of personal con-tact with party activists has diminished accordingly. To be sure, the parties have access to a great deal of money. But the so-called soft money that courses through the veins of the political parties, although justified politically as a means of "party building," tends to fund candidates' advertising campaigns that, ironically, seldom bother to mention political parties (Krasno and Seltz 2000). Given these changes in institutional structure and campaign style, it is tempting to assume that partisan identities have become a thing of the past and hold little sway over voting decisions in what has increasingly become a candidate-centered, rather than party-centered, political environment. It turns out, however, that the decline of party institutions has not rendered party attachments irrelevant, nor has it diminished the influence of party attachments on vote choice. Parties are not what they used to be, but partisan *groups*—Democrats and Republicans—remain important objects of social identification.

This book builds a case for the continuing theoretical and political significance of party identities. Because we do not view party attachments as a product of how voters evaluate party leaders or party platforms, our view of party identification differs from that of other leading interpretations. Currently in political science the prevailing way of thinking about partisan identities emphasizes the extent to which they are shaped by rational evaluations of party platforms and performance in office. Following in an intellectual tradition founded by Anthony Downs (1957), many scholars contend that partisanship reflects a citizen's level of policy agreement with the two parties. Voters with more conservative views gravitate toward the Republican Party; liberals, to the Democratic Party. Over time, the relative attractiveness of the two parties may change, as leaders in each party maneuver left and right in an effort to garner electoral support. Another prominent argument concerns the manner in which people adjust their party identification as they assess the incumbent administration's management of domestic and foreign affairs. Morris Fiorina (1981) argues that partisanship constitutes a "running tally" of performance evaluations, as citizens accumulate information about each party's capacity to govern. Whether people focus on policies or performance in office, the characterization of partisan identification is similar. Voters, like consumers in the marketplace, form loyalties based on their evaluations of what parties deliver.

Our view, which hearkens back to earlier social-psychological perspectives on partisanship, draws a parallel between party identification and religious identification. Partisan attachments form relatively early in adulthood. To be sure, party issue positions have something to do with the attractiveness of partisan labels to young adults, much as religious doctrines have something to do with the attractiveness of religious denominations. But causality also flows in the other direction: When people feel a sense of belonging to a given social group, they absorb the doctrinal positions that the group advocates. However party and religious identifications come about, once they take root in early adulthood, they often persist. Partisan identities are enduring features of citizens' self-conceptions. They do not merely come and go with election cycles and campaign ephemera. The public's interest in party politics climbs as elections draw near, but partisan self-conceptions remain intact during peaks and lulls in party competition.

These are strong empirical claims, and all of them have been challenged at one time or another in the enormous corpus of research on party identification. Our aim is therefore to reevaluate the evidence on partisan stability and change. Much of the research on partisanship suffers from a simple but nonetheless debilitating weakness: Scholars tend to look at only one type of data. Some researchers work exclusively with panel surveys; others, with aggregate data (for example, the percentage of Democrats recorded in successive surveys). Or they tend to focus attention on one country, one time period, or just one survey. This book pulls together a wide array of survey data—aggregate, individual, U.S., comparative—dating back to the 1950s. This approach enables us to develop a synoptic account of the nature of partisanship and the sources of partisan change.

Another distinctive feature of this book is its attentiveness to methodological nuance. Many previous analysts of party identification have overlooked measurement problems in the survey data they analyzed. The standard measures of party identification, although more reliable than most survey questions, are nonetheless fallible. Respondents, interviewers, and data coders make mistakes. As a result, quantitative ratings derived from surveys do not always reflect respondents' true levels of identification with political parties. Of course, differentiating mistakes from true changes in attitude is a complicated matter, and in the chapters that follow we devote a great deal of attention to this complex but important issue. Recognizing that some readers may be reluctant to wade through the arcane technical details, we intersperse our mathematical discussions with summaries of the substantive results. Suffice it to say that standard survey assessments of party identification contain enough measurement error to distort statistical findings, and unless one makes specific allowances for measurement error, one risks overstating the malleability of party attachments.

The most important contribution of this book, however, is theoretical. Few subjects in political science have received as much attention as party identification. Yet it is very difficult to find a single work that offers a clear explanation of what it is and why it behaves as it does. Those who return to *The American Voter* (Campbell et al. 1960) for guidance find its discussion of party identification terse and a bit vague. Party identification is characterized as a "psychological orientation," an "enduring attachment," but there is little discussion of self-conceptions, and one must read between the lines to work out the implied analogy between party identification and class identification.[1] Subsequent works on partisanship have generally used *The American Voter* as a foil; as a result, the "traditional" view of party identification has not been fully articulated and defended empirically.

IDENTIFICATION VERSUS EVALUATION

To highlight our interpretation of partisan attachments, we return to the analogy between parties and religious denominations. Like members of political parties, members of a religion or religious denomination comprise an identifiable social group, cleave to distinctive underlying doctrines, and maintain (to varying degrees) an adversarial relationship toward other religions. And like party identification, religious identification is often acquired early in life as a product of one's family environment or early adult socialization. As a member of a religion, one is indoctrinated into that religion's precepts, much as partisans learn the slogans and nostrums of their party. To be sure, some adults choose their religion by canvassing various sects' theological positions, selecting the one that best fits their personal values. But these people seem to be a minority, for among adults over thirty years of age, religious affiliation, once established, tends to remain intact. A more common avenue for shifting religious affiliation is a changing small-group environment, in particular, marriage to a person of another faith. In such instances, people may commit themselves to their new faith for reasons that have little to do with its overall doctrinal attractiveness, or they may alter their perception of the new religion as they come to see it through their spouse's eyes. Parallel observations may be made about partisan identities, which also change as regional and occupational mobility put adults into contact with new friends and social groups, some of which may have different partisan coloration (Brown 1981; Gimpel 1999).

The analogy between partisan and religious identification has an implication that many political scientists find disconcerting: Partisan change among adults often has little to do with unfolding political and economic events. Scholars who study politics like to think that politics matters. They are right for certain limiting cases, such as the party realignment precipitated by the Great Depression or the advent of two-party competition in the South after the Voting Rights Act of 1965. Seldom, however, do political events alter the stereotypes of partisan *groups*, and that is why most reversals of political fortune—scandals, diplomatic crises, economic news, legislative outcomes—leave little imprint on the partisan attachments of the adult electorate. To the extent that they alter the partisan balance, it is because they shape the newly forming partisan attachments of young adults and immigrants.

Why do changing political and economic circumstances not have a bigger effect on party attachments? The answer offered by the authors of *The American Voter* is that partisans ignore or deflect information that is inconsistent with their party attachments. Echoing a theme originally set forth by Berelson, Lazarsfeld, and McPhee (1954), Campbell et al. (1960: 133) argue that "identification with a party raises a perceptual screen through which the individual tends to see what is favorable to his partisan orientation. The stronger the party bond, the more exaggerated the process of selection and perceptual distortion will be." Rational updating based on new information is undone by "subtle processes of perceptual adjustment by which the individual assembles an image of current politics consistent with his partisan allegiance" (Stokes 1966: 127). This biased processing of information functions to insulate party attachments from political events.

This argument goes hand in hand with another recurrent theme in *The American Voter:* the public's inattentiveness to politics. The general public, it is argued, follows politics in only the most cursory fashion and shows a dim awareness of newsworthy names, places, and points on the globe. Thus, it should not be surprising to discover that partisanship persists in the wake of changing political events. These events remain largely unknown to all but the most attentive, who also tend to possess the deepest partisan attachments and thus the greatest propensity toward perceptual bias.

Although this book is on the whole sympathetic to the propositions advanced by early theorists of partisanship, we disagree about how partisans attend to and retain information about party performance. Like those scholars who emphasize the rational underpinnings of public opinion, we are skeptical of the notion that partisans ignore or reinterpret discordant information. We find that although citizens often lack specific information about day-to-day political events, they do update their overall assessments of national conditions and the capacities of the parties to handle important problems. Moreover, partisanship does not seem to prevent people from assimilating new information. As party fortunes shift due to changes in economic performance, Democrats, Republicans, and Independents change their evaluations of party competence, often dramatically. Thus, for example, when the economy soured between 1991 and 1992, Democrats, Republicans, and Independents each became less sanguine about the Republican Party's capacity to manage the economy. To be sure, Republicans have more faith in the party's economic stewardship than Democrats, but the process by which the two partisan groups update their evaluations is similar. These patterns of voter learning, we argue in Chapter 5, suggest that partisan stability cannot be traced to biases in the way citizens gather and retain information.

Evaluations of party capabilities are distinct from partisan identities, both conceptually and empirically. People may assimilate new information about the parties and change their perceptions of the parties without changing the team for which they cheer. We find, for example, that when a Democratic administration presides over a long period of economic prosperity, Republicans may become more impressed with Democratic economic management, but they tend not to reconsider whether they think of themselves as Republicans. It is also telling in this regard that electoral landslides do little to alter the balance of partisan attachments. Indeed, this is the central insight that the authors of *The American Voter* derived from their observation of the Eisenhower era. One may vote for a Republican candidate and yet feel part of a Democratic team.

To explain the stability of partisan attachments, we must focus on the special characteristics of social identities. How do people define themselves in relation to political groups? To what extent are perceptions of these groups susceptible to change?

PARTISAN IMAGES

The occasional disjuncture between what voters think of the parties and the degree to which they identify with partisan groups suggests the need to reconsider the motivational assumptions of revisionist models. The underlying premise of such models is that voters attach themselves to the party that offers the most attractive platform, able leaders, and charismatic candidates. The attachment is hollow, scarcely more than an expression of beliefs about which party will best pursue one's interests. The contrasting view, which we explore in this book, focuses instead on identification with social groups. Social identification involves comparing a judgment about oneself with one's perception of a social group. As people reflect on whether they are Democrats or Republicans (or neither), they call to mind some mental image, or stereotype, of what these sorts of people are like and square these images with their own self-conceptions. In effect, people ask themselves two questions: What kinds of social groups come to mind as I think about Democrats, Republicans, and Independents? Which assemblage of groups (if any) best describes me?

Not many surveys have addressed the first question, but those that have attest to the remarkable persistence of stereotypes over time. In 1953, Gallup asked a national sample of adults, "When you think of people who are Democrats, what type of person comes to your mind?" Respondents could offer multiple responses (though few did so), and these were assembled into broad group categories. The groups "working class," "common people," and "poor" accounted for 34% of the responses and "union person" and "middle class" an additional 4%. Just 1% fell under the rubric "rich, wealthy, high class." When next asked about Republicans, respondents painted the opposite picture. Just 6% of the responses fell under the headings "working people," "average person," or "middle class." On the other hand, "rich, wealthy, people of means," "business executive," "capitalist," and "high class" accounted for 31% of all responses. In 1997, some four decades later, the Roper Starch organization conducted face-to-face interviews with a national sample of adults. This time respondents were presented with a card containing a variety of words and phrases; their task was to choose those words that described Democrats and Republicans (respondents could choose as many descriptors as they liked). When asked about Republicans, 55% selected the descriptor "big business" and 52% "rich people." Only 18% chose "middle class" and just 6%, "minorities." By contrast, over 40% of the sample selected the terms "middle class" and "minorities" to describe Democrats; less than 20% chose the terms "rich people" or "big business." The partisan stereotypes of the New Deal are alive and well. The only innovation seems to involve minorities, which pollsters and respondents neglected to mention in 1953.[2]

It should hardly be surprising that stereotypes persist over a long time. Studies of racial tolerance have documented again and again the notorious stubbornness of mental images of various ethnic or racial groups. Moreover, these studies indicate that even those people who may be ideologically predisposed to reject negative group stereotypes (for example, Jews are stingy) are nonetheless familiar with them and struggle to resist their influence (Devine et al. 1991). Although not as elaborate or as emotionally charged as racial stereotypes, partisan group images are coherent, widespread, and influential (Lodge and Hamill 1986).

Stereotypes concerning social groups are not only powerful, they are also pervasive. It has long been recognized that even those who are on the losing end of a negative stereotype often fall under its spell. One interesting but seldom mentioned fact about partisan stereotypes is that they are held in more or less equivalent form by Democrats, Republicans, and Independents. Ask whether phrases such as "forward looking" or "able leadership" describe Republicans, and naturally Democrats will say "no" and Republicans, "yes." Yet Democrats and Republicans do not differ much in the associations they draw between partisan groups and "minorities," or "big business."[3] Granted, Republicans are somewhat less likely to select a loaded term such as "rich people" when describing Republicans, but to a remarkable extent Democrats and Republicans operate with similar group stereotypes.

What differentiates Democrats and Republicans is how they think of themselves in relation to these group stereotypes. Both may associate "minorities" with Democrats and not Republicans, but are "minorities" an aversive or attractive group? How one orients oneself vis-à-vis certain key social groups has a profound influence on one's party identification. In 1996, respondents to the American National Election Study (NES) were presented with a list of social groups and were asked to indicate which ones they felt "particularly close to."[4] To reflect the dominant stereotypes associated with the two parties, we focus our attention on working- and upper-class groups (the poor, blacks, union members, working class, and Hispanics on one hand; business people on the other), although we could just as easily have chosen more evocative political groups (for example, feminists, liberals). Suffice it to say that even this rather limited inventory of groups provides an effective means by which to sort Democrats from Republicans. Of those who feel close to business people but not minority or working-class groups, 62.1% identify as Republicans and 15.3% as Democrats. Of those with the converse pattern of group affinities, 65.7% are Democrats, and 6.5% are Republicans. Citizens whose group attachments conflict or do not involve these social categories split more or less evenly between the parties, with a plurality calling themselves Independents.[5] The terms *Democrats* and *Republicans* clearly call to mind different constituent groups, and how people feel about these social categories has a great deal to do with whether they identify with a partisan group and, if so, which one.

The matching process by which people examine the fit between their self-conceptions and what they take to be the social bases of the parties tends to evolve rapidly in young adulthood and slowly thereafter. One reason is that young people are still learning to sort out which groups "belong" to each party. Another is that the self-conceptions of young people evolve rapidly.

Compared with their older counterparts, younger voters tend to experience much more significant and frequent changes in their social surroundings. They leave home, launch careers, start families, and make new acquaintances. By their early thirties, however, rapid change in primary social groups has begun to subside, and partisanship, along with many other sorts of social identifications, becomes much more deeply entrenched. From this point, partisanship changes gradually. In short, partisanship tends to be stable among adults because both stereotypes and self-conceptions tend to be stable.

Our perspective on social identification, it should be stressed, differs from what is commonly termed *social identity theory* (Hogg, Terry, and White 1995). The latter emphasizes an individual's drive to achieve positive self-esteem. People attach themselves to socially valued groups, and those who are trapped in low-status groups either disassociate themselves or formulate a different way of looking at groups, such that this group is more prized than others. This depiction is very different from ours. We focus on how people categorize themselves and remain agnostic about the underlying psychological motives that impel people to form social identities such as party attachment. Indeed, it seems to us unlikely that the pursuit of self-esteem drives the formation and adjustment of party attachments. One would think that esteem-seeking voters would climb aboard the victorious party's bandwagon after a landslide victory, yet we do not see citizens severing their party attachments in the wake of scandals or electoral defeats. Nor do we see adherents to the losing party resisting these bandwagon pressures by demonizing the victorious party and finding new virtues in their own. Instead, we find party identification to be stable amid changes in party fortunes, and we find that Democrats' and Republicans' assessments of the parties' merits change in similar ways over time. Conceiving of party identification as the solution to a strategic problem of esteem-maximization seems to lead down a blind alley. At most, voters can be said to be maximizing the fit between their social mores and their self-conceptions, but even here, we must be careful not to overstate the degree to which people switch their attachments when the party's platform or performance goes awry. To paraphrase Lyndon Johnson, our party may be led by jerks, but they're *our* jerks.

PARTISAN CHANGE

The discussion thus far has tended to downplay the causative role of party politics in favor of social-psychological influences. To argue that political events seldom affect partisan identities is compatible with the claim that events do matter under certain conditions. Party platforms and performance in office from time to time touch on these partisan self-conceptions. During the early 1980s, mobilization of Christian fundamentalist leaders on behalf of a conservative social agenda altered both the platform of the Republican Party and how

Republicans as a social group were perceived. Similarly, evidence of widespread corruption throughout Italy's Christian Democratic Party robbed this partisan group of its social respectability as an object of identification during the early 1990s, leading to the party's rapid collapse after four decades of dominance. But such dramatic and highly publicized instances in which partisan stereotypes are altered occur infrequently. Seldom does a scandal run so deep as to impugn the character of a political party from top to bottom. Watergate and the Iran-Contra Affair, to say nothing of less-memorable scandals, had faint effects on party identification, even though these events grabbed headlines for long periods of time. Generally speaking, parties' efforts to attract groups of potential supporters do little to alter partisan stereotypes and are therefore incapable of loosening the bonds of identification. Scarcely an election goes by without an announcement by the Republican Party that it intends to reach out to minorities or by the Democratic Party that it seeks to appeal to business leaders. Such gestures are generally too short-lived and transparently strategic to be taken seriously. Interestingly, experiments designed to change party identification by altering (randomly) the ideological stances of the Republican and Democratic candidates confirm the stubbornness of party attachments (Cowden and McDermott 2000).

The stability of partisanship in the wake of party maneuvering is well illustrated by the campaign of 1948, during which Harry S. Truman announced his plan to desegregate the armed forces. Both commentators of that day and political historians tended to regard this announcement as a watershed event that precipitated both a revolt among Southern white Democrats and a secular realignment that brought blacks into the Democratic Party. Although Truman's actions proved to be much more profound and long-lasting than most election year gestures, their short-term effects on partisanship were subtle at best. Daniel Dowd's (1999) careful analysis of public opinion polls during this era reveals that black partisanship did not shift appreciably during 1948 and moved only gradually in the Democratic direction until the late 1950s. As for whites, Truman's policies triggered an election day bolt to the Dixiecrats in Alabama, Mississippi, South Carolina, and Louisiana but did not set off widespread changes in party identification. And with the exception of Louisiana, the Deep South did not exhibit Republican voting during the landslide presidential victories of the 1950s. Republican voting, which occurred only at the presidential level, was instead confined to the border states of Florida, Texas, Tennessee, and Virginia. Truman's executive order was doubtless a turning point in race relations in the United States, but partisan ties were not easily broken.

By stressing how difficult it is to alter the partisan balance, we do not mean to suggest that parties are altogether incapable of producing change. From time to time, a party alters the social group composition of its leadership and, by extension, its public persona. For example, the Republican Party in the 1980s began to put Southerners into top party positions, and by the 1990s Southerners such as Phil Gramm, Newt Gingrich, Haley Barbour, Trent Lott, and Dick Armey ranked among the party's most prominent public figures. The Southern face of the Republican Party has, as we will see in Chapter 6, made the party more congenial to young Southerners entering the electorate. In effect, gradual changes in perceptions about which regional and racial groups "go with" each party caused a sea change in the way Southerners and blacks defined themselves in relation to the parties.

At the same time, one cannot but be impressed by how slowly this partisan transformation occurred. In 1966, Philip Converse (p. 220) observed that since the election of 1948, pundits had been predicting the Republicanization of the South, an event that never seemed to materialize. In Converse's estimation, the slow pace of partisan change meant that the North and South could be expected to have the same partisan complexion by the early 1980s. With the benefit of hindsight, we see that this cautious forecast actually overestimated the pace of partisan change. Despite several Republican landslides in national and regional elections, whites in the North and South achieved parity only at the century's end. Party images can and do change, but the accompanying change in party identification unfolds gradually.

The psychology of group attachments works in conjunction with institutional incentives to slow the pace at which party systems change. Parties (or, more specifically, politicians and staff who inhabit and depend on parties) institute rules, such as ballot qualifications and provisions for public subsidies, that create barriers to entry for new parties. Moreover, parties create platforms, some of which eventuate into government action, that solidify their interest group coalitions. As Lipset and Rokkan (1967) point out in their description of how preindustrial party systems shaped politics after industrialization, these coalitions may endure long after the political conditions that forged the coalition have changed. Finally, the psychology of party attachment dovetails with the parties' interest in maintaining their distinctive and widely recognized brand labels, to use Aldrich's (1995) metaphor. The psychological processes of self-categorization and group evaluation are therefore most apparent in established party systems, in which parties have cultivated symbols and group imagery.

EXAGGERATED RUMORS
OF PARTISANSHIP'S DEATH

Since the late 1960s, students of electoral behavior have been fed a steady diet of skepticism about party identification. Party identification has lost its sway over voting decisions; voters feel a sense of indifference about the parties; split-ticket voting runs rampant. It would scarcely make sense to write (or read) a book in defense of partisanship if its effects on electoral choice were weak or diminishing, so before proceeding, we must address the notion that partisanship has ceased to be influential.

Table 1.1 shows the distribution of political partisanship over time. Using data gathered by the NES, we find that the partisanship of the population has evolved gradually. In 1952, 48.6% of voting-age adults called themselves Democrats and only 23.3% Independents. By 1978, the Independents category had grown to 38.5%, at the expense of both parties. The 1980s saw a resurgence of the Republican Party, and the 1990s saw a gradual decline in the proportion of Independents. By 1996, the balance of partisans to Independents had returned to pre-Watergate levels. Indeed, the distribution of partisanship in 1996 looks very much as it did in 1972. The oft-repeated thesis of the 1970s that the American political system was teetering toward a "dealignment" in which most citizens identified with neither of the two major parties now seems overdrawn. There are still more than enough partisans to make partisanship a viable topic of study.[6]

This point is underscored when we confine our analysis to the American *voting* public. Restricting our attention to survey respondents who actually went to the polls, we find even less support for the view that the death of partisanship has given rise to unattached voters. Table 1.2 shows that 71.4% of those voting in 1996 identified with the two major parties. The corresponding figure for 1956 is 75.9%. From these figures, it would appear that the partisan character of the de facto electorate is similar to what it was several decades ago.

But are today's partisans as loyal as the partisans of decades ago? Table 1.3 presents a cross-tabulation of vote choice in presidential elections since 1952. In each year, the NES conducted a postelection interview in which voters were asked for which presidential candidate they had voted. For ease of comparison over time, entries in this table are the percentage of respondents in each partisan category (Democrats, Republicans, Independents) who reported having voted for the Democratic contender. The numbers provide compelling evidence against the claim that party loyalty in elections isn't what it used to be. In

Table 1.1. Distribution of Partisanship, 1952–98

	Democrat (%)	Independent (%)	Republican (%)	N
1952	48.6	23.3	28.1	1,729
1954	49.3	22.7	28.0	1,088
1956	45.3	24.4	30.3	1,690
1958	51.0	20.2	28.9	1,737
1960	46.4	23.4	30.0	1,864
1962	48.3	22.1	29.7	1,237
1964	52.2	23.0	24.8	1,536
1966	46.2	28.7	25.1	1,263
1968	46.1	29.5	24.5	1,531
1970	44.0	31.3	24.7	1,490
1972	41.0	35.2	23.8	2,656
1974	39.7	37.5	22.8	2,433
1976	40.1	36.4	23.5	2,824
1978	40.3	38.5	21.1	2,224
1980	41.7	35.3	23.0	1,577
1982	45.1	30.6	24.4	1,383
1984	37.7	34.8	27.6	2,198
1986	40.9	33.5	25.6	2,120
1988	35.7	36.3	28.0	1,999
1990	39.8	35.3	24.9	1,935
1992	35.9	38.6	25.5	2,447
1994	34.0	35.9	30.1	1,769
1996	38.2	35.1	26.7	1,692
1998	38.1	35.2	26.7	1,256

Source: American National Election Studies.
Note: Cases are weighted by sample weights. Data from presidential election years were taken from preelection surveys.

1952, Adlai Stevenson won 72.6% of the Democrats' votes, 33.5% of the Independents', and just 3.8% of the Republicans'. Forty years later saw another contest between nonincumbents following a long stint of one party's control of the presidency. In 1992, Bill Clinton won 82.4% of the votes cast by Democrats, 42.3% by Independents, and 8.9% by Republicans. The magnitude of the chasm between those who identify with different parties remains as wide as ever.

The same conclusion emerges when we compare 1956 and 1996, both years in which popular incumbents won decisive reelection victories. Stevenson re-

Table 1.2. Distribution of Partisanship among Voters, 1952–98

	Democrat (%)	Independent (%)	Republican (%)	N
1952	45.5	23.2	31.3	1,187
1956	44.0	24.1	31.9	1,278
1958	50.2	17.7	32.1	1,032
1960	45.4	21.9	32.7	1,421
1962	46.9	19.3	33.8	776
1964	52.4	20.0	27.6	1,119
1966	46.6	24.1	29.3	788
1968	45.3	27.6	27.1	1,052
1970	44.0	26.1	29.9	884
1972	40.8	30.8	28.3	1,651
1974	40.1	32.1	27.8	1,317
1976	39.2	33.6	27.2	1,711
1978	40.1	33.9	26.0	1,248
1980	41.2	32.0	26.8	1,000
1982	48.8	24.1	27.1	845
1984	38.3	31.2	30.5	1,454
1986	44.5	28.1	27.5	1,136
1988	36.5	30.2	33.3	1,231
1990	44.8	27.1	28.0	921
1992	36.9	35.2	27.9	1,689
1994	35.6	30.5	33.9	997
1996	40.1	28.6	31.3	1,092
1998	41.2	28.1	30.7	665

Source: American National Election Studies.
Note: Cases are weighted by sample weights. Data from presidential election years were taken from preelection surveys. Samples were restricted to those respondents who reported having voted.

ceived votes from 74.5% of Democrats and 3.7% of Republicans. Clinton won 90.4% of the Democratic votes and 12.3% of the Republican votes. (Note that if one were to gauge the size of these partisan effects using logistic regression, so as to account for the fact that it is in some sense harder to move from 85% to 95% than it is to move from 75% to 85%, one obtains almost identical coefficients for these two races.) With the exception of the Nixon-McGovern election, the gap between Democrats and Republicans in presidential elections has remained marked over the past four decades. Indeed, Bartels's (2000) detailed analysis of presidential elections since 1952 suggests that partisanship's effects

Table 1.3. Party Identification and the Presidential Vote, 1952–96

	Republican	Independent	Democrat	Total
1952	3.8	33.5	72.6	42.0
	(370)	(269)	(536)	(1,175)
1956	3.7	26.4	74.5	40.3
	(403)	(303)	(554)	(1,260)
1960	6.8	45.6	80.8	49.0
	(459)	(298)	(640)	(1,397)
1964	27.5	66.2	89.3	67.6
	(306)	(219)	(581)	(1,106)
1968	6.7	26.3	70.8	40.9
	(283)	(281)	(462)	(1,026)
1972	6.3	33.8	58.2	35.8
	(458)	(474)	(648)	(1,580)
1976	13.5	45.3	82.0	51.0
	(451)	(532)	(644)	(1,627)
1980	4.6	27.5	72.7	39.9
	(263)	(295)	(396)	(954)
1984	4.4	34.0	78.5	41.7
	(427)	(421)	(521)	(1,369)
1988	8.4	46.6	84.0	47.1
	(404)	(358)	(430)	(1,192)
1992	8.9	42.3	82.4	47.8
	(462)	(574)	(613)	(1,649)
1996	12.3	47.9	90.4	54.0
	(332)	(288)	(427)	(1,047)

Source: American National Election Studies.

Note: Entries are the percentage of each partisan group voting for the Democratic presidential candidate, with the number of observations in parentheses. Party identification was measured in preelection surveys. Vote preference was measured in postelection surveys. Samples were restricted to those respondents who reported having voted for president, regardless of whether they voted for a major party candidate.

have grown steadily since 1972, to the point that partisanship is now more influential than ever.

What about split-ticket voting? Hasn't voting for one party for president and another party for Congress become more commonplace, suggesting a decline in party attachments? Although ticket splitting is widely cited as evidence of party decline, voting is an inadequate measure of self-conception. Party identification is by no means the sole determinant of vote preference. Changes in the

Table 1.4. Party Identification and Congressional Voting, Open
House Seats, 1956–98

	Republican	Independent	Democrat
1956	8.7	41.2	93.3
	(23)	(17)	(30)
1958	10.2	69.6	91.0
	(49)	(23)	(67)
1960	8.3	35.3	82.1
	(36)	(17)	(56)
1964	37.5	60.9	96.7
	(32)	(23)	(61)
1966	5.6	28.6	72.7
	(18)	(7)	(22)
1968	14.8	54.5	84.8
	(27)	(22)	(33)
1970	17.4	44.4	83.3
	(23)	(18)	(30)
1974	15.6	56.1	84.6
	(64)	(41)	(52)
1976	17.9	55.2	87.3
	(39)	(58)	(79)
1978	18.8	42.9	83.1
	(32)	(35)	(65)
1980	20.0	26.1	63.2
	(15)	(23)	(19)
1982	11.5	35.0	88.9
	(26)	(20)	(36)
1984	7.0	31.7	59.3
	(43)	(41)	(27)
1986	36.0	41.4	71.1
	(25)	(29)	(38)
1988	3.6	70.0	76.2
	(28)	(20)	(21)
1990	17.9	24.0	84.6
	(28)	(25)	(26)
1992	25.3	46.9	77.9
	(79)	(81)	(104)
1994	12.8	27.5	79.0
	(47)	(40)	(62)
1996	6.3	64.0	90.0
	(16)	(25)	(50)
1998	12.5	46.7	90.0
	(24)	(15)	(20)

Table 1.4. (*Continued*)

Source: American National Election Studies.
Note: Entries are the percentage of each partisan group voting for the Democratic candidate, with the number of observations in parentheses. The NES cumulative file was used for elections dating back to 1970. For years before 1970, open seats were classified using King (1994). Party identification was measured in preelection surveys during presidential election years. Vote preference was measured in postelection surveys. Samples were restricted to those respondents who reported having voted. Although these data are weighted, the resulting sample is a nationally representative cluster sample, which may or may not be representative of the population of open-seat districts.

nature of electoral competition distort assessments of partisan motivation.[7] Strong incumbents in the House and Senate frequently scare off serious challengers, leaving voters to choose between a popular, well-known incumbent and an obscure challenger. It should hardly be surprising that under such conditions, proincumbent voting tends to occur, creating a pattern of split-ticket voting in many districts. More telling is how voters behave when a seat is vacated and two challengers square off. Table 1.4 shows that partisan attachments come to the fore, regardless of whether one looks at data from the 1950s or 1990s. In the 1960s, Democrats running for open seats won 87% of the votes cast by Democrats and 18% by Republicans. The corresponding percentages for 1990–98 are 82% and 18%. Partisanship is by no means a weak predictor of vote choice in congressional races, and rates of party loyalty in the late 1990s do not differ markedly from those of the late 1950s (see Bartels 2000).

Perhaps voters still vote their partisan sympathies but do not bring any partisan passion to the voting booth. One of the most prominent critiques of party identification contends that citizens nowadays view political parties with indifference, as politics becomes increasingly candidate-centered (Wattenberg 1994). Although this argument enjoys wide currency, it is deficient in at least two respects. First, when we look at responses to survey questions going back to the early 1950s asking people whether they care about which party wins the national election, we find very little movement over time. The most recent NES surveys to ask this question occurred in 1984 and 1988, when 64.8% and 61.0% claimed to care. These figures are higher than the 56.6% and 55.9% registered in 1976 and 1980 but scarcely different from the 66.8% and 63.0% obtained in 1952 and 1956. Second, although it is true that survey respondents today are less likely than respondents in the 1950s to report that they "like or dislike something" about the two political parties, they are hardly awash in indifference. Fully 71.9% of the NES respondents to surveys conducted during the 1990s claimed to like or dislike something about the parties. In sum, people continue to identify as partisans, continue to vote on the basis of these identifications, and seem to cheer for one of the parties. Although lacking the partisan zeal of elected officials and interest group leaders, ordinary citizens do not look upon party competition with indifference.

PARTISANSHIP OUTSIDE THE UNITED STATES

Although this book draws many of its examples from American politics, our arguments apply to other political systems as well. For a variety of reasons, analysts of other countries have tended to resist party identification as an explanatory concept. Some have argued that party identification is less stable outside the United States and therefore less compelling as a putative cause of electoral choice. Others have argued that class, linguistic, or religious attachments are simply more predictive of electoral choice than party attachments, especially in electoral systems in which parties emerge to voice the concerns of particular social groups, such as farmers or regional separatists.

These are important hypotheses that may be addressed by using data from other countries. As we point out in Chapter 7, a wide-ranging synthesis of panel survey data from other democracies indicates that party identification in those democracies functions in much the same ways as it does in the United States. Provided that one allows for the special difficulties of measuring party identification in countries with several parties, one finds that partisan attachments both persist over time and exert great influence over electoral choice. Our point is not that party attachments matter to the exclusion of other factors but rather that a common explanatory framework—one that focuses on identification with social groups—can be usefully applied across very different political settings.

For example, the period 1974–79 in Britain saw major swings in party popularity, yet party identification remained remarkably stable and continued to be an extremely strong predictor of the vote. Amid labor unrest and the first international oil crisis, the Labour Party secured enough seats to oust the Tory government of Edward Heath in 1974. But the Labour government's popularity fell precipitously during its term—in part because of continuing economic troubles—and the party was soundly defeated in May 1979 by Conservative leader Margaret Thatcher. The five-year period thus spans two changes of government and a dramatic reversal of party fortunes. Yet just 9% of those respondents who identified with the Labour Party in February 1974 voted for the Tories in 1979, and just 4.5% of Labour identifiers from 1974 called themselves Tories five years later. Of the Tory identifiers in February 1974, just 3% voted Labour in 1979, and only 1.5% considered themselves Labour identifiers that year. Fully 86% of Labour identifiers and 90% of Tory identifiers continued to identify with the same party after five turbulent years.

Placing party identification in comparative perspective highlights what is distinctive about the American case. For decades, there has been relatively little change in America's core political institutions—the rules governing how representatives are elected, how different branches of government interact, how laws are enforced, and the like. In this respect, the United States and Great Britain are similar. The situation is different in Italy, where waves of scandal and the fall of Soviet communism led to the abrupt dissolution of several long-standing political parties in the early 1990s. The emergent party system featured an array of new parties that continually split and entered into coalitions. Meanwhile, electoral rules have changed, and the prospect of further constitutional change hovers over the party system. Italy therefore presents an interesting contrasting case in which the objects of partisan attitudes have passed out of existence. Old attachments to partisan groups tend to shape new identities, but the pace with which the parties fracture or coalesce has prevented these incipient identities from solidifying. The result is a fluid party system that makes for an apt contrast to the United States.

PLAN OF THIS BOOK

The chapters that follow critique the myriad attempts to depict party attachments as unstable, ineffectual, or epiphenomenal. At the same time, we develop and test a set of propositions about the conditions under which partisan change does occur. The evidence suggests that partisan affiliation is best understood as a form of social identity and that partisan stability is traceable to constancy in citizens' primary group environment and their mental images of partisan groups, which in turn reflects stability in the structure of party competition within the electoral system.

The next chapter discusses the conceptual underpinnings of party identification and delves more deeply into survey evidence. Both Chapters 2 and 3 make the case for the distinctiveness of party identification, as against other kinds of attitudes and evaluations. Attention is devoted to the definition and measurement of party identification, concerns that bear directly on the question of how much party attachments change over time, which is the central question addressed in Chapter 3. Chapter 3 marshals evidence from a variety of sources and statistical approaches to demonstrate the persistence of individuals' partisan identities. In Chapter 4, we track the partisan balance of the electorate as a whole, a quantity often termed *macropartisanship*. Both in absolute terms and in comparison with other types of political evaluations, macropartisanship changes slowly. The partisan balance gently sways with the prevailing political winds but afterward returns to its long-term equilibrium.

What stable attachments mean for the understanding of party identification is taken up in Chapter 5. Many scholars have stressed the "rational" character of partisanship, contending that voters adjust their attachments based on the performance of the parties when in power and the stances that they take on the leading issues of the day. This interpretation has a variety of testable implications. As assessments of party competence change, so too should party attachments. As party platforms change or as new issues arise, party identities should gravitate toward the party that has the most ideological resonance. It turns out, however, that the process of partisan adjustment is so gradual that it often escapes detection, even when survey respondents are tracked over long periods.

In the face of such findings, proponents of these hypotheses sometimes argue that rational partisans might update their evaluations very slowly, particularly if they receive little novel information about what the parties stand for or how they conduct themselves. In other words, the banality of American political competition draws rational updating to a standstill. But this revised position is untenable because perceptions of the parties often shift abruptly while party attachments remain unchanged. If rational partisanship is stable under these conditions, it is arguably because perceptions of partisan groups—as distinct from the quite variable assessments of party leaders—tend to remain intact.

Although we claim that partisanship is typically stable and unresponsive to environmental forces, we are quick to acknowledge that this need not be the case. The central question animating this book is not simply "Is partisanship stable?" but rather "Under what conditions is partisanship stable?" In Chapters 6 and 7, we explore several instructive cases in which the party system changes in ways that induce shifts in party attachments. As mentioned above, these include the revitalization of the Republican Party in the South after the Voting Rights Act and the transformation of the Italian party system following the collapse of the Christian Democrats and Socialists, the reorganization of the Communists, and the emergence of new regional and center-right parties. We shall argue that these kinds of political changes alter the public's mental image of the parties' followers. Few people associated middle-class Southerners with the Republican Party in 1948; by 1998, this had become a plausible association. The so-called Red and White cultural groups of Italy were readily associated with Communist and Christian Democratic constituencies; the breakup and division of the old parties brought about more diffuse partisan stereotypes. Finally, at the individual level, we have evidence that party attachments change as people migrate from one political environment to another. Examples such as these, although by no means definitive, suggest that large-scale partisan change may take two forms. In cases such as Italy, the sudden collapse of a party dislocates partisan attachments. In cases such as the South, the creation or resuscitation of a party gradually alters existing identities, as partisan stereotypes take root and begin to attract people who take a genial view of these stereotypes. The fact that residential mobility affects partisanship further attests to the social dimension of party attachment.

Although most of the book focuses on developing and testing our social identity model of partisanship, the final chapter turns to the implications of partisan ties for electoral competition. We demonstrate partisanship's profound influence on both individual-level vote choice and the structure of electoral competition more generally.

As the title of the book suggests, our thesis is that partisan identities reflect a blend of cognition and affect. People know who they are and where they fit in the matrix of prominent social groups. Citizens' group attachments shape the way that they evaluate political candidates and the policies they espouse. These evaluations change as new information becomes available, but seldom does the political environment change in ways that alter how people think of themselves or their relationship to significant social groups. For this reason, voters' attachments may remain firm even as their voting preferences shift. Thus, the basic structure of electoral competition remains intact even as the personae and policies that dominate politics change.

Chapter 2 Partisan Groups

as Objects of Identification

The term *identification* is commonly used in two ways. One use is synonymous with empathy, as when a person identifies with a sympathetic social group. The groups in question may be real or imaginary, contemporary or historical. When we read *The Peloponnesian Wars*, for example, we typically identify with the Athenians in the sense that we side emotionally with Athenian culture and institutions. Athenians are our kind of people; they are humane, articulate, and high-minded, if a bit fractious. Their Spartan adversaries are coarse and cruel. We identify with them only in those passages when their battlefield misfortunes elicit our sympathies.

Another usage of identification is synonymous with self-conception, as when a person labels himself or herself an ancient Athenian. Membership in the social group "ancient Athenian" is a necessary condition for identification of this sort. Pericles identified with ancient Athenians: He lived in ancient Athens and clearly regarded himself as an Athenian. Absent some sort of delusion, this form of identification is unavailable to modern people because we cannot *be* ancient Athenians.

As this example makes apparent, the two meanings of identification, affinity and self-categorization, need not be conterminous. A person may identify with a group but perceive no membership in it. Conversely, people may perceive themselves to be members of a group but feel no affinity for it or its members. Disaffected group members may recognize an identification *as* without feeling an identification *with*.

Although it is important to keep these two meanings of identification distinct for purposes of defining party identification, they will often overlap empirically. For one thing, members of social groups, particularly groups that the broader society accords great significance, tend to view the group and its members in a positive light. By and large, Jewish people display more positive feelings toward Jews as a group; attorneys give higher ratings to lawyers as a group; those who describe their class status as "lower" or "lower-working" class offer more favorable ratings of "poor people"; self-described gay men express much more positive evaluations of homosexuals than do the rest of the public. Although members of unpopular groups tend to harbor some of the same negative stereotypes about these groups as nonmembers, members' overall evaluations of these groups tend to be positive.

A second reason why affinity and self-categorization tend to go hand in hand is that the criteria by which one judges membership in a social group are often vague and indeterminate. No formal or widely shared standards exist for determining whether a person is a feminist, a baseball fan, a member of the underclass, or a patriot. Most Americans, for example, seem to think of themselves as environmentalists even though they do not belong to any formal environmental organization or, indeed, engage in any readily identifiable environment-friendly behavior (Guber 1998). Criteria for membership in the social category "environmentalist" are sufficiently porous to allow anyone who identifies with environmentalism (or its proponents) to identify as an environmentalist. One need only be an environmentalist at heart.

Murky standards of group membership are of special importance to the conception of party identification in most political systems. Although some parties have official membership lists (for example, the Chinese Communist Party and Britain's Conservative Party), American parties and many mass-based parties elsewhere have formal standards for membership that vary from meager to venal. Any citizen willing to part with a few dollars may visit the Web sites of the Republican or Democratic parties and become a member of one or both. Some U.S. states have party registration, but this, too, is membership of the most minimal kind. Party registration in a (diminishing) number of states is a prerequisite for voting in a party primary, but Democrats and Republicans who seek to vote against candidates they detest may freely switch their registration. Indeed, anyone willing to put up with the annoyance of filling out forms is entitled to change party registration without fear of being purged for disloyalty. Party membership may have some formally defined meaning, but this meaning is much more diffuse than for other organizations, such as the Rotary Club or the American Civil Liberties Union.

The diffuse nature of mass-based parties creates a puzzle: If *identification as* presupposes some form of membership, to what do partisan identifiers belong? The ingenious answer supplied by Angus Campbell et al. in *The American Voter* (1960) is that voters frequently (but by no means invariably or to any great degree) see themselves as belonging to partisan groups, Democrats or Republicans. The group in effect is suspended by the psychological image it conjures. It exists as a stereotype in the minds of voters, who in turn harbor a sense of attachment toward this group image. Democrats, for example, are people who think of themselves as Democrats.

This solves the puzzle of how a public that is traditionally skeptical of parties, has little information about their activities, and virtually no contact with them as organizations could identify themselves as partisans. The conceptual focus is not on identification with the parties per se but with Democrats and Republicans as social groups. Valid measures of party identification must focus attention on these social groups and invite respondents to define themselves using these group nouns. Scholars have sometimes lost sight of this definition when studying party identification. Merely asking respondents whether they like a political party, support it, vote for it, feel close to it, believe it to be effective in office, or find its ideas attractive is not the same as asking about self-definition and group attachment. As James Campbell et al. (1986) point out, these distinctions are central to the conception of party identification laid out in *The American Voter*:

> Partisanship was conceptualized as a psychological identification with a party. . . . As thus conceived, partisans are partisan because they think they are partisan. They are not necessarily partisan because they vote like a partisan, or think like a partisan, or register as a partisan, or because someone else thinks they are a partisan. In a strict sense, they are not even partisan because they like one party more than another. Partisanship as party identification is entirely a matter of self-definition.

In the same vein, we would argue that to appreciate the special properties of party identification, it is essential to maintain a clear distinction between it and other sorts of attitudes, beliefs, and behaviors. To make this case, we must address two related questions: What *isn't* party identification? How do we know that party identification is genuine?

To be sure, party identification tends to be correlated with a variety of political attitudes, particularly those directly related to parties. People who think of themselves as Democrats tend to like the Democratic Party (and not the Republican Party). Consider, for example, how self-described Democrats, Independents, and Republicans rated their feelings of "warmth" about the parties on scales ranging from zero ("cold") to 100 ("very warm") in the 1996 NES. Democrats on average assigned the Democratic Party a score of 77, compared with 41 for the Republican Party. A similar gap in evaluations was evident among Republicans, who on average rated the Democratic Party a 37 and the Republican Party a 73. Independents fell in the middle, assigning average evaluations of 53 and 54 to the Democratic and Republican parties, respectively. The correlation between partisan identification and partisan opinions remains high as we move from rather diffuse feelings of "warmth" toward more focused assessments about which party can better handle foreign affairs or manage the nation's economy. Only 2% of the Republicans polled believed that the Democratic Party does a better job of handling the economy; 71% believed the Republican Party to be superior. Among Democrats, 56% gave the Democratic Party the edge, and only 7% endorsed the Republican Party's economic stewardship. As usual, Independents fell in between, with 21% preferring the Democratic Party and 27% the Republican.

Finally, partisanship is correlated with opinions on questions of public policy. On most political issues, Democrats stand to the left of Independents, who in turn stand to the left of Republicans. One must be cautious when interpreting this correlation, however. As Gregory Markus (1982) has noted, the direction of causality flows in two directions. On the one hand, citizens occasionally drift toward parties that take ideologically appealing stances on the issues of the day. On the other hand, parties also instruct partisan supporters on how right-thinking Democrats or Republicans view these issues. Classic examples of this phenomenon are Richard Nixon's decision to open diplomatic relations with China in 1972, which produced a dramatic transformation of Republicans' views about how the United States should deal with this Communist regime. Another is Ronald Reagan's proposal to cut taxes during the 1980 campaign. Reagan contended that his tax cut would stimulate the economy to such an extent that the government would experience no loss of tax revenue. This idea went from a relatively controversial campaign plank (derided as "voodoo economics" by Reagan's primary opponent, George Bush) to the centerpiece of the Republican legislative agenda in 1981 and a key article of faith among Republicans in the turbulent years that followed.

Another point to bear in mind is the fact that the correlation between party identification and stances on issues is often weak. Consider, for example, the relationship between partisanship and views on the question of whether civil rights leaders are "pushing too fast," an NES question that dates back to 1964. This item has attracted special attention because it is often argued that racial issues have played a central role in disrupting the Democratic coalition forged during the New Deal. Carmines and Stimson (1989) contend that racially conservative white Democrats became alienated by policies such as affirmative action and school desegregation, which increasingly became identified with the Democratic platform. Although the civil rights question typically ranks among the most reliable measures of racial attitudes in the NES, Table 2.1 shows that it tends to be weakly correlated with party identification. In any given year, a greater fraction of Republicans than Democrats expressed the view that civil rights leaders are "pushing too fast," but the gap between them is not large, often just a few percentage points. Although racial issues have profoundly altered party coalitions at the congressional level (Carmines and Stimson 1989), it is by no means clear that the same has been true of the mass public (Abramowitz 1994).

A stronger correlation emerges when we shift attention to questions concerning the scope of the welfare state. The NES has traditionally asked respondents whether "the government in Washington should see to it that every person has a job and a good standard of living" or instead whether government "should just let each person get ahead on his own." As shown in Table 2.2, the gap between Democrats and Republicans has been fairly marked since 1972 when the question was first asked in its current format. In 1996, one-third of all Democrats supported job guarantees, compared with one in ten Republicans. Orientations toward the welfare state do not coincide exactly with party affiliation, but the two are certainly related.

Stronger still is the relationship between party identification and ideological self-categorization (Table 2.3). Ideological self-categorization differs in subtle but important ways from ideology itself. It taps not what the respondent thinks about various issues but rather the ideological label he or she finds most suitable. In that sense, it bears a certain similarity to party identification: One need not be a card-carrying conservative to call oneself a conservative. It is hard to tell from available data whether survey respondents are primarily describing

Table 2.1. Partisan Identification and Opinions about Civil Rights

	Democrats	Independents	Republicans
1964	62	62	71
1966	63	63	71
1968	57	70	65
1970	44	48	56
1972	44	44	52
1974	39	43	43
1976	38	40	41
1980	29	34	41
1984	23	31	38
1986	23	22	28
1988	20	25	31
1990	24	29	30
1992	29	25	31

Source: American National Election Studies, 1964–92.
Note: Entries are the percentage of each partisan group saying that civil rights leaders are pushing too fast. Note that the civil rights question does not appear in certain NES surveys. The question reads: "Some say that the civil rights people have been trying to push too fast. Others feel that they haven't pushed fast enough. How about you: Do you think that civil rights leaders are trying to push too fast, are going too slowly, or are they moving about the right speed?"

their intellectual orientation or their opinions of the social groups known as liberals and conservatives. As Converse (1964) points out, many survey respondents have difficulty supplying adequate definitions of liberalism and conservatism, and ideological self-categorization is only moderately correlated with stances on issues such as the death penalty, abortion, and defense spending.[1]

We will revisit the nexus between issues and partisanship in Chapter 3. For now, our point is that although party attachments tend to coincide with partisan evaluations and other political orientations, identification with political parties is both conceptually distinct and empirically quite different in character. The statistical association between partisanship and issue stance, although often strong, is far from exact; partisans need not and do not invariably agree with the leaders of their party. This point takes on special importance with re-

Table 2.2. Partisan Identification and Opinions
about the Scope of Government

	Democrats	Independents	Republicans
1972	43	27	17
1974	31	23	14
1976	33	20	13
1978	23	17	7
1980	37	22	12
1982	32	24	14
1984	35	31	18
1986	33	22	14
1988	34	23	14
1990	38	30	19
1992	37	25	14
1994	37	27	16
1996	34	23	10

Source: American National Election Studies, 1972–96.
Note: Entries are the percentage of each partisan group
saying that government should guarantee jobs. The
question reads: "Some people feel that the government
in Washington should see to it that every person has a
job and a good standard of living. Others think the government should just let each person get ahead on his
own. And, of course, some other people have opinions
somewhere in between. Where would you place yourself
on this scale, or haven't you thought much about this?"
Entries are the percentage of respondents placing themselves at points one through three on the seven-point
scale.

gard to voting preferences. Nothing in the definition of party identification
precludes Democrats from voting for Republican candidates. (Whether doing
so in fact erodes the Democrats' sense of identification is a separate question, to
which we will return.) Partisan identification is not the sole factor governing
how voters evaluate candidates. Democrats would have liked the avuncular war
hero Dwight D. Eisenhower better if in 1952 he had turned out to be a Democrat, but they still held him in high esteem, and it was Eisenhower's stature and
popularity that enabled him to defeat Adlai Stevenson. Many scholars have assumed that partisans "defect" from their party on account of their weak party
attachments, but defections could just as well be ascribed to the lopsided way in

Table 2.3. Ideological Self-Categorization and Partisan Self-Categorization

	Percentage of Democrats Who Call Themselves Conservatives	Percentage of Republicans Who Call Themselves Conservatives	Percentage of Conservatives Who Call Themselves Democrats	Percentage of Conservatives Who Call Themselves Republicans
1972	18	43	27	41
1974	17	47	25	41
1976	16	48	24	44
1978	18	54	26	41
1980	17	51	25	41
1982	16	51	25	46
1984	16	52	20	49
1986	18	52	24	44
1988	19	55	21	48
1990	16	47	25	44
1992	17	55	20	46
1994	16	64	15	53
1996	16	66	18	54

Source: American National Election Studies, 1972–96.

which the public evaluates certain candidates. When a Republican candidate is popular, Republicans inevitably look more loyal and Democrats less so. It would be a mistake to interpret every landslide election as a sign that partisanship is waning or voters are changing parties.[2]

These distinctions may seem like splitting hairs, but a number of important empirical insights grow out of them. As we will point out in the pages ahead, party identification tends to be correlated with vote choices among individuals at a given point in time, but this relationship is far from exact. Party attachments are more than mere summaries of momentary vote intentions. Moreover, voting and partisanship look very different when traced over time. Votes can swing markedly from one election to the next without changing the distribution of partisan attachments. Much the same may be said for a variety of other attitudes, such as presidential approval or assessments of the parties' competence. They are correlated with partisanship at a given time but are much more prone to change over time.

Before turning our attention to the contrast between party identification and other attitudes and behaviors, let us first examine more closely the meaning and measurement of party identification itself. We have called attention to partisan identities, as distinct from partisan attitudes more generally. How do we know that party identification is more than a figment of social scientists' imagination? How do we know that party identification is a distinct and enduring psychological orientation and not simply a by-product or summary of other attitudes, beliefs, and behaviors? In answering these basic conceptual issues, we will lay the groundwork for a more detailed discussion of partisan stability and susceptibility to short-term influences.

WHAT DO PARTISAN
SELF-CATEGORIZATIONS MEAN?

Why should we believe that citizens harbor genuine, long-lasting attachments to partisan groups? Seven types of evidence speak to this issue. We now consider each in turn.

I. *Partisan attachments are professed repeatedly during the course of a survey interview, even when these attachments are at variance with vote choice.* The strategy behind conventional measures of party attachment is straightforward: Determine whether people identify with partisan groups by asking them directly. In one form or another, these queries ask respondents, "Do you think of yourself as a Democrat, Republican, or Independent?" Although this approach seems sensible enough, it could be the case that respondents are simply guessing or supplying meaningless, random answers. To placate an insistent interviewer, perhaps respondents *call* themselves Democrats and Republicans, but they do not really *feel* like Democrats and Republicans.

Survey researchers have long been concerned with the possibility of vacuous survey responses, sometimes termed "nonattitudes" or "doorstep opinions." Such responses are either outright fabrications or reflect sentiments that flickered at the moment the question was answered but disappeared shortly thereafter. More sophisticated survey analysts have warned against reading too much into the response options that people choose, particularly when respondents are not offered a chance to duck the question entirely. On the other hand, if opinions are real, people should express them again and again, even when they are presented with different response options.

Because the standard partisanship measure has been widely assumed to be both valid and reliable, few surveys have tried to gauge party identification in different ways during the course of a single interview. One important exception is the 1973 National Opinion Research Center (NORC) Amalgam Survey.[3] In the NORC survey, a national sample of 1,489 adults were randomly assigned to three subgroups and interviewed in person. All three groups were initially asked the standard Survey Research Center (SRC) party identification question:

> Generally speaking, do you usually think of yourself as a Republican, a Democrat, an Independent, or what?

Later in the questionnaire, each subgroup was presented with *one* of the following questions about self-definition:

> On this card is a scale with strong Democrats on one end and strong Republicans on the other, and with Independents in the middle. Where would you place yourself on this scale?

> Generally speaking, do you usually think of yourself as a Democrat or a Republican?

> No matter how you voted in the last couple of national elections or how you think you might vote in next November's national election—do you basically think of yourself as a Republican, a Democrat, an Independent, or what?

Toward the end of the lengthy interview, all respondents were asked the Gallup party identification question, which asks about one's *current* sense of self:

> In politics, as of today, do you consider yourself a Republican, a Democrat, an Independent, or what?

Responses to these questions paint a similar picture of party affiliations, notwithstanding variations in wording. As shown in Table 2.4, 87% of the respondents who called themselves Democrats in reply to the SRC question also dubbed themselves Democrats when asked to describe their basic partisan tendencies, holding voting choices in abeyance. The same holds for 79% of self-described Republicans. In general, the correlation between responses to any pair of party identification measures is 0.85 or higher, suggesting that answers to partisanship questions are anything but ephemeral.

To be sure, the distribution of answers varies somewhat, depending on how the question is phrased and which response options are offered to respondents. The seven-point self-placement scale dubs 23% of the sample "Independents," and just 19% of the sample volunteer "Independent" when asked to describe themselves as either Democrats or Republicans. By contrast, 33% of the sample label themselves "Independents" when asked about their affiliations "in politics

Table 2.4. How the Survey Research Center Measure of Partisanship Relates to Alternative Measures

	Democrat (%)	Independent (%)	Republican (%)
Basic self-regard			
Democrat	87	12	4
Independent	7	75	9
Republican	1	5	79
Other (volunteered)	0	1	2
Don't know/refused	5	7	6
N	215	140	107
Forced pair			
Democrat	93	25	4
Independent (volunteered)	2	52	0
Republican	2	13	96
Other (volunteered)	0	3	0
Don't know/refused	4	6	0
N	198	157	94
Self-placement scale			
Strong Democrat	35	0	0
Weak Democrat	34	3	2
Leaning Democrat	26	26	2
Independent	4	52	10
Leaning Republican	0	16	31
Weak Republican	1	1	35
Republican	0	0	17
Don't know/refused	1	3	2
N	188	158	121

Source: 1973 National Opinion Research Center Amalgam Survey.

as of today." Not surprisingly, the precise accounting of who is a partisan depends on the yardstick one uses to gauge identification. In Chapter 7, we point out how variations in the wording of questions may frustrate attempts to compare partisanship in different countries.

It should be stressed, however, that each of these survey measures paints a similar picture of the balance of Democratic and Republican identification. When presented with the standard SRC question, 65% of all partisan identifiers were Democrats. The seven-point self-placement scale produced the same rates of Democrats and Republicans. The figure rose to 66% for the Gallup measure, to 67% for the forced pair question, and 69% for the basic self-regard item. Thus, a preamble that draws respondents' attention to "politics as of to-day" produces faintly different answers from one that warns them to disregard past voting decisions. Question wording affects the absolute size of each partisan group, but a similar portrayal of the relative numbers of partisans emerges regardless of variations in wording or response format.

If alternative measures of party identification each tap the same underlying attitude, why would they not be perfectly correlated with one another? Consider, for example, the imperfect correspondence between answers to the SRC question and the basic self-regard item, which are similar in focus and response options. Why do a handful of respondents initially label themselves Democrats but later call themselves Republicans? Why do some respondents variously claim to be partisans and Independents? One possibility is that attitudes are changing during the course of the interview. This explanation seems unlikely, given the evidence presented below suggesting that partisanship changes so gradually that shifts in party attachment are detectable only over a period of years. A more likely explanation (discussed at length in Chapter 3) is that respondents and interviewers make errors when moving quickly through a lengthy interview schedule. Interviewers may misread questions or inaccurately record answers. Respondents, for their part, may misunderstand the questions or response options. At a more basic level, respondents may have difficulty expressing their opinions in rigid and unfamiliar response categories. Even those accustomed to survey research may find it difficult to summarize and distill the myriad of feelings and thoughts that come to mind at the mention of partisan groups. Add to this the fact that respondents must answer a long series of such questions, and it becomes easier to understand the sloppy manner in which survey responses are supplied.

For these reasons, one should expect variation in survey responses, even when underlying opinions remain intact. Respondents may from time to time portray themselves as more Democratic or Republican than they really are. The survey analyst who wishes to take these measurement errors into account therefore uses multiple readings of the same underlying attitude, anticipating that respondents will, on average, give an accurate account of their feelings of attachment. This principle of redundant measurement undergirds well-known tests of scholastic aptitude, personality, and other psychological traits. A single math problem may give an unreliable indication of quantitative reasoning skills because some students may or may not be prepared for any particular math puzzle. But a lengthy math test will effectively differentiate those with high and low levels of mathematical acumen.

A statistical method used to assess the degree of measurement error and differentiate measurement-related fluctuation from true change is called *confirmatory factor analysis.* Applying confirmatory factor analysis to the various partisanship questions asked on this survey (Green and Schickler 1993), we estimate that the standard three-category SRC measure of party identification has a reliability of approximately 0.86, indicating that about 14% of the observed variance in partisanship is meaningless noise. (See Chapter 3 for more on how we ascertain the reliability of a measure.) As we point out in the next chapter, this figure can be expected to vary somewhat across time and demographic groups because different populations have different amounts of dispersion in their partisan orientations. Younger voters, for example, are less likely to have partisan ties. Thus, a greater proportion of the observed variance in their expressed party affiliations stems from measurement error, which means that the reliability is lower for younger samples. Nevertheless, the finding that 86% of the variance in the three-point SRC party identification item is genuine is corroborated by no fewer than eight other surveys in which party identification was measured repeatedly over time (Green and Palmquist 1994). As a practical matter, this finding means that correlations between any two measures of party identification will seldom be much greater than 0.86, even if underlying partisanship were perfectly stable.

Another indication that multiple measures of partisanship ferret out measurement error is that scales built from multiple questions have greater predictive power than measures based on a single survey question. Consider, for example, the correlation between party attachment and preferences for possible presidential nominees. The 1973 NORC sample was confronted with a series of hypothetical "ballot tests" pitting Democrats against Republicans; adding all of these vote preferences together, we created a scale of support for potential Republican nominees. Taken by itself, the SRC party identification item bears a correlation of 0.62 with this vote index ($N = 341$). When we augment the SRC item by adding to it responses to the "regardless of vote intentions" version of the party identification measure, we obtain a correlation of 0.65 with the vote index.[4]

This small increase illustrates how supplementary measures of party identification help to expunge random response error in what is otherwise a fairly reliable measure. We are left with a purer assessment of respondents' party attachments—and a clearer sense that such attachments are genuine.

2. *People who use partisan labels to describe themselves also indicate their "identification with" and "identification as" members of these partisan groups.* Three in-

novative studies (Greene 1999, 2000; Weisberg and Hasecke 1999) have augmented the standard SRC party identification item with a series of questions designed to tap "social identification" with partisan groups. Using survey measures adapted from Mael and Tetrick's (1992) Identification with a Psychological Group scale, Greene (2000) presented a sample of Franklin County, Ohio, residents with a series of statements with which they could agree or disagree. These statements included "When someone criticizes this group, it feels like a personal insult" and "When I talk about this group, I usually say 'we' rather than 'they.'" Weisberg and Hasecke used a similar scale in their statewide probability survey of Ohio.

This measurement approach is somewhat different from that of the 1973 NORC study, wherein respondents simply repeated the self-labeling exercise using three similar types of questions. Here, respondents were asked to describe their feelings of attachment to partisan groups, with special reference to the extent to which these partisan groups elicit a "we-feeling." Unfortunately, none of these studies reports the relationship between the traditional measure of party identification and comparable measures of social identity. To fill this gap, we crafted three questions for the October 1999 Roper Starch survey, which conducted face-to-face interviews with a national sample of 1,638 respondents. Half of the sample was randomly assigned a battery of social identity questions concerning Democrats; the other half, Republicans. These questions read as follows:

> People have different feelings about [Democrats/Republicans]. I'm going to read three short statements, and for each one, please tell me whether you strongly agree, somewhat agree, somewhat disagree, or strongly disagree . . .
>> When I talk about [Democrats/Republicans], I usually say "we" rather than "they."
>> When someone criticizes [Democrats/Republicans], it feels like a personal insult.
>> I don't have much in common with most [Democrats/Republicans].

For ease of presentation, these three four-category responses were combined into a single ten-point index by adding the first two responses and subtracting the third.

When indices of Democratic or Republican identification are compared with a traditional self-labeling measure, the two prove to be highly correlated.[5] As shown in Table 2.5, 45.5% of all self-described Democrats scored in the top four categories of the Democratic social identity index, compared with 5.1% of all self-described Republicans. Conversely, just 2.1% of all Democrats strongly rejected all Democratic affinities, compared with 25.6% of Republicans. A sim-

Table 2.5. Party Identification by Measures of Social Identification
with Democrats or Republicans

	Democrats (%)	Independents/ Don't Know (%)	Republicans (%)
Strong Democratic identity	12.6	0.4	0.0
	5.3	1.1	0.5
	8.8	2.9	0.5
	18.8	4.0	4.1
	16.1	8.6	6.2
	15.5	15.8	8.2
	11.7	35.6	20.5
	4.1	10.4	17.4
	5.0	14.4	16.9
Weak Democratic identity	2.1	6.8	25.6
N	341	278	195
Strong Republican identity	0.3	0.4	14.0
	0.0	0.4	3.1
	0.3	0.7	10.9
	3.4	4.7	19.2
	6.5	5.4	18.7
	8.8	12.9	13.0
	21.0	24.5	14.5
	12.2	13.7	2.1
	18.1	18.3	3.6
Weak Republican identity	29.5	19.1	1.0
N	353	278	193

Source: Roper Starch National Survey, October 1999.

ilar correspondence between self-label and social identity appears when the
questions concern Republicans. Fully 29.5% of all Democrats strongly repudiated any suggestion of Republican we-feeling, a response pattern characteristic
of just 1% of the Republicans. The sharp separation between Democrats and
Republicans on questions of social identity lends credence to the view that self-
categorization and group identification are empirically quite similar phenomena.

Self-described partisans vary somewhat in the extent to which they feel a
common bond with members of their partisan group, but that is to be expected
based on what we know about the imprecise way in which respondents are classified by both traditional measures of partisanship and the brief three-item so-

cial identity index created here. By the same token, we detect some partisan sentiment among self-described Independents. Keith et al. (1992) have demonstrated that some of the people who categorize themselves as Independents are closet partisans, who think and act as though they harbor partisan attachments but refuse to describe themselves in partisan terms. In our sample, 17% of the Independents scored in the top five categories of Democratic identification and 12% scored in the top five categories of Republican identification. The three-category designation of Democrats, Independents, and Republicans masks a certain amount of heterogeneity within categories. Still, alternative measures of partisan identification reaffirm the idea that the canonical SRC question elicits genuine self-conceptions.

3. *People offer the same descriptions of their partisan attachments over long stretches of time, even when the political context has changed.* We have seen that people offer similar responses when asked to describe their party attachments repeatedly during the course of a single interview. What happens when people are reinterviewed years later? In Chapter 1, we discussed a survey that tracked parents of high school students from 1965 through 1982. This study not only showed that party attachments in 1965 were strong predictors of the vote in 1980 but also attested to the staying power of party attachments among adults. Of the 855 parents interviewed in both 1965 and 1982, 633 (or 74%) gave the same response when asked whether they think of themselves as Democrats, Republicans, or Independents. Of the 644 respondents who in 1965 called themselves Democrats or Republicans, just 37 (5.7%) switched parties seventeen years later. Interestingly, Democrats were as likely to become Republicans as the reverse, but because there were more Democrats to begin with, the total sample drifted slightly toward the Republican Party. This rate of interparty conversion exceeds what could be expected from response error alone. Yet when one reflects on the remarkable political changes that occurred between these two surveys, the degree of stability in party identification is truly impressive.

The same picture emerges when we look at a narrower slice of time. As noted in Chapter 1 (see Table 1.1), the Watergate scandal that drove Richard Nixon from office and led to a rout of the Republican Party in the 1974 elections did not bring about wholesale desertion from the ranks of Republican identifiers. The NES, which fortuitously conducted a panel study spanning the years 1972 to 1976, recorded only modest movement in the Democratic direction during this period. For example, when we look at identification from the Nixon landslide of 1972 to Jimmy Carter's victorious campaign against Gerald Ford, we find that 76% of the 343 Republicans interviewed in 1972 were still Republicans in 1976. This rate of retention is only slightly greater among Democrats; 79% of the 495 Democrats interviewed in 1972 still called themselves Democrats four years later. Just 3.4% of all Democrats and 5.5% of all Republicans switched parties during this period.

Lest one think that the results from the mid-1970s reflect the special political tumult and partisan disarray of the times, the same pattern of persistence over time holds for other panel studies that span changes in party control of the presidency. For example, when partisan affiliations are traced from Eisenhower's landslide victory of 1956 to the aftermath of John F. Kennedy's win in 1960, we find relatively little movement. Of the 989 respondents interviewed at both times, 761 (77%) reported the same partisan label. Only 42 of the 747 partisan identifiers (5.6%) switched party; the bulk of the movement was in and out of the intermediate category of Independent. Similarly, when partisanship is tracked from the Bush administration of 1992 through Clinton's reelection in 1996, we find modest rates of interparty conversion. Of the 500 respondents interviewed at both times, 351 (70.2%) gave consistent answers, and just 14 of the 312 partisan identifiers (4.5%) switched parties.

We defer to the next chapter a more statistically rigorous treatment of the over-time stability of individuals' party attachments, which distinguishes between real partisan change and transitory fluctuations in survey responses. For now, the point is that simple cross-tabulation of opinion over time reveals a high degree of persistence, even when partisan orientations are measured in very different political climates.

4. *The distribution of partisan identification changes slowly over time.* Much of this book relies on the analysis of panel surveys, which track a set of individuals over time. These data enable us to examine change at the individual level— we can detect partisan change even when the overall proportions of Democrats and Republicans remain constant over time. The drawback to panel data is that they are often in short supply. Panel surveys are expensive, difficult to execute, and therefore rare. Those who wish to chart partisanship over long periods eventually must compare cross-sectional surveys conducted at different points in time. Because each cross section contains a different set of respondents, we cannot distinguish between individual-level change and change in the composition of the electorate over time. Nevertheless, in conjunction with panel data, these surveys convey useful information about the pace and direction of partisan change.

By far the most carefully executed survey of this kind is the American National Election Study, which has gauged party identification every other year since 1952. Recall from Chapter 1 that the proportions of Democrats, Republicans, and Independents have changed gradually during the past half century. In the early 1950s, partisans accounted for more than three-quarters of the adult population. Large numbers of new voters born after World War II caused the ranks of the Independents to swell during the mid-1960s. From 1972 on, approximately 35% of the public labeled themselves Independents. Another trend concerns the balance between Democrats and Republicans. In 1952, Democrats outnumbered Republicans by a ratio of 1.7 to 1. Apart from a brief upward spike in 1964, this ratio was more or less constant until 1984, when it dropped to 1.4 to 1, where it has since remained. In subsequent chapters, we will take a closer look at both the pace of change and the extent to which it was concentrated in the South during the early 1980s. For the time being, we wish only to underscore the basic point that party affiliation changes gradually over time. If pollsters in 1976 had gazed twenty years into the future of American politics, witnessing Carter's demise, Reagan's ascendancy, the end of the Cold War, and the like, would they have guessed that the party identification numbers of 1976 could forecast all subsequent NES surveys within an error of plus or minus seven percentage points?

5. *The proportion of the public identifying with any party tends to be relatively unaffected by whether the survey takes place during an election campaign.* Party identification is properly categorized as an attitude, an enduring predisposition to respond to a class of stimulus objects. People harbor a sense of who they are and how they fit in relation to partisan groups. When asked about this self-conception, partisans will respond in consistent ways over time, allowing for the vagaries of survey measurement. The alternative view holds that party identification is situational. It lies dormant or fades away during periods between elections, only to reemerge when awakened by party competition. Fueling this concern is the fact that NES surveys typically are conducted during election years, prompting speculation about the character of partisanship between elections.

Do party identities wane during interelection hiatuses? The answer seems to be "no." Major surveys occasionally interview respondents during off years, and these surveys show no evidence that party identities wane or wander during these years. The parents in the 1973–82 panel were rock solid in their identification over this period. By the same token, the 1993 wave of the 1992–96 panel shows no signs of distinctiveness. And panel studies that have tracked partisanship over the course of an eventful campaign (for example, the four-wave 1980 NES panel study) do not show special signs of volatility. In sum, the over-time correlations in individual-level data do not support the claim that the character of partisanship changes amid the campaign season.

These individual-level findings leave open the question of aggregate shifts toward or away from partisan identities. Do more people identify with political parties during national election years, particularly presidential election years? To make the strongest possible case for this argument, we compiled 677 Gallup Polls that were conducted in person between 1953 and 1996. These polls were conducted at various times of year, with increasing coverage during election years. Because these polls asked respondents to reflect on their partisanship "in politics, as of today," they arguably offer a more volatile rendering of partisan attachments than other polls, which direct respondents' attention to "politics in general" (see Abramson and Ostrom 1992, 1994; for dissenting views, see Bishop, Tuchfarber, and Smith 1994; MacKuen, Erikson, and Stimson 1992). Thus, these surveys provide an upper bound on the degree to which partisan ranks swell during a campaign cycle.

The dependent variable in this model is the percentage of respondents in each poll who label themselves Independents. Our statistical model uses dummy variables to mark each quarter of a presidential and midterm election year. Each of these markers enables us to compare the proportion of Independents in each election quarter with the proportion of Independents in off years. For completeness, we present the regression results with and without controls for linear and quadratic time trends in the proportion of Independents. Such trends improve the fit of the model but do not alter the results concerning election years. Thanks to the large number of polls at our disposal, we are able to estimate the effects of election years with a high degree of precision.

From Table 2.6, we see that presidential and midterm elections are associated with a statistically discernible but small decrease in the number of Independents. National elections lead to a drop of about one percentage point in the percentage of self-identified Independents, regardless of whether we take time trends into account. The maximum seasonal gap is between an off-year election and the third quarter of an election year. Although this contrast is statistically significant, the magnitude is puny: less than two percentage points. Thus, for example, one might expect to see the proportion of Independents climb from thirty in the wake of the 1984 elections to thirty-two in 1987. At best, these findings lend minimal support to Clarke and Stewart's (1998: 365–69) assertion that the proportion of the public claiming a party identification rises during election years as campaigns "mobilize" partisan sensibilities in the electorate.

Table 2.6. How Independent Partisanship Varies with the Election Cycle

Independent Variable	Regression Estimate	Standard Error	Regression Estimate	Standard Error
Constant	28.01	0.24	19.65	0.34
Presidential election year				
First quarter	−0.37	0.75	−0.18	0.48
Second quarter	−1.11	0.73	−1.04	0.48
Third quarter	−1.53	0.72	−1.52	0.46
Fourth quarter	−1.07	0.81	−1.19	0.52
Midterm election year				
First quarter	−0.66	0.72	−0.27	0.47
Second quarter	−0.57	0.69	−0.73	0.46
Third quarter	−1.76	0.69	−1.68	0.45
Fourth quarter	−0.60	0.78	−0.50	0.50
Years since 1953			0.68	0.04
Years since 1953, squared			−0.01	0.001
R^2	0.02		0.59	
N	677		677	

Source: Gallup Polls conducted face-to-face, 1953–95.
Note: The dependent variable is the percentage of respondents calling themselves Independents.

Indeed, the Gallup results may even overstate the effects of election campaigns if apolitical respondents are especially prone to decline an interview during an election season. The weak effects we detect are reduced further as we shift our attention to surveys such as the General Social Surveys (GSS), which use the "politics in general" wording, engage in more rigorous sampling of respondents, and do not embed the partisanship question within a survey focused largely on current political events. Unlike the NES, the GSS routinely takes place during nonelection years as well as election years. Looking at the proportions of party identifiers during the period 1972–98 (Table 2.7), we see absolutely no evidence that party identification surges during presidential or midterm election years. (Analyzing these data with a regression model that allows for either linear or nonlinear time trends does nothing to bolster the argument that elections foster or resuscitate partisan identities.) Party identification does not seem to depend on the partisan atmosphere of electoral campaigns. Even if the true influence of campaigns lies somewhere between the GSS and Gallup results, it seems clear that party attachments endure even during lulls in party competition.

Table 2.7. How Independent Partisanship
Varies between Election Years and Off Years

	Percentage Identifying as Independent	N
1972	26.1	1,607
1973	31.9	1,493
1974	31.3	1,461
1975	36.6	1,485
1976	37.0	1,495
1977	33.3	1,518
1978	36.3	1,527
1980	38.4	1,465
1982	33.5	1,851
1983	34.6	1,593
1984	36.0	1,465
1985	30.2	1,529
1986	33.7	1,467
1987	30.8	1,809
1988	34.2	1,481
1989	29.0	1,532
1990	31.5	1,368
1991	32.3	1,511
1993	34.6	1,597
1994	33.7	2,943
1996	37.0	2,898
1998	37.9	2,823

Source: General Social Surveys.

6. *Despite the marked differences between state and national voting patterns, the distribution of American partisanship does not change appreciably when attention is focused on state rather than national political parties.* During the 1980s, impressed by the success of Republican presidential candidates and Democratic congressional and statehouse candidates, scholars began to wonder whether voters had different "levels" of party identification. Southern voters in particular were suspected of harboring attachments to their state-level Democratic parties that did not extend to their national-level counterparts. The underlying assumption was that partisans were able to make peace with their inconsistent voting patterns by distancing themselves from the national Democratic Party while embracing the local one.

This contrast, however, fails to materialize in surveys of the general public. When respondents are asked to report their partisan affiliations with regard to different levels of government, the discrepancy between "state" and "national" party identification proves to be slight, even though the sequencing of the questions invites respondents to express contrasting affiliations at the two levels. Results from a 1987 NES survey show that people seldom give different answers to state- and national-level questions. In this survey, just under 1% (2 of 237) switched parties when asked about state-level identification. (As we saw earlier, simply due to response error, approximately 1% of major party identifiers can be expected to "switch parties.") The marginal distributions of the state-level and national-level responses are also very similar, with a slight tendency toward more Independents at the state level, and the correlation between state and national party identification (excluding those with no preference) is 0.89—close to the upper bound that one could expect from any pair of imprecise measures.

Why, then, the scholarly emphasis on "multiple levels of party identification," which supposedly "contaminate" traditional national measures of partisanship (Niemi, Wright, and Powell 1987: 1,094)? Explanations abound. First is the extraordinary appetite for supposed problems with the traditional measure of party identification. It is no exaggeration to say that every word in the conventional SRC question has sparked scholarly controversy. Here, the phrase "In general, when it comes to politics" is the culprit. Politics obviously takes place on many different levels, and it is natural to wonder whether individuals attend to these different levels when forming attachments. Second, scholars have been led astray by ignoring the problems of response error. Niemi, Wright, and Powell (1987) define a "multiple identifier" as anyone who jumps from one of the three-point partisan categories to another. Thus, weak partisans who variously call themselves Democrats and Independents are said to have "multiple identities." Our earlier results suggest that this pattern is more likely to be the result of coarse response categories and careless responses than of multiple identities. Third, leading published work on multiple identification in the United States relies on surveys of campaign contributors rather than of the general public (Niemi, Wright, and Powell 1987; Bruce and Clark 1998). Given the political sophistication of these respondents and the close contact that they have probably had with the parties as organizations, it is not hard to understand how some of them might harbor different orientations toward state and local partisans. Even here, it should be stressed that very few of these contributors simultaneously identify with different political parties at the state and national levels.

Finally, some of the emphasis on multiple identities in the United States has drawn inspiration from surveys in other countries, where multiple levels of identification seem more apparent. Clarke and Stewart (1987) and Stewart and Clarke (1998) contend that Canadians frequently identify with one party at the federal level and another party at the provincial level. For example, Clarke and Stewart report that in 1974, 1979, and 1980, between 17% and 25% of Canadians identified with different parties at the federal and provincial levels (p. 391). To some extent, this kind of switching reflects the lack of an "independent" or "none of these" option in the party identification question posed to Canadians (Johnston 1992). An unknown number of nonpartisan respondents are forced into one partisan category at one point, only to bounce randomly to another in a subsequent question. We do not wish to rule out the possibility of multiple identities, but as we note in Chapter 7, surveys that are explicitly designed to uncover them often fail to do so.

7. *Partisans find politics more engaging than Independents.* One indication that partisans harbor real attachments to social groups is that they take an interest in the continual competition between parties. Although the level of political engagement varies within and between partisan groups, partisans differ on average from Independents in terms of the way that they look at campaigns. Partisans are more likely to take an interest in electoral competition, to care which candidate prevails, and to participate in elections (Campbell et al. 1960: chap. 5).

The 1992–94–96 NES panel survey illustrates the persistent differences between partisans and Independents. Before the 1992 and 1996 elections, this group of respondents were asked, "Generally speaking, would you say that you personally care a good deal who wins the presidential election this year, or that you don't care very much who wins?" Since both elections featured a prominent third-party candidate, Ross Perot, Independents might have been expected to find these elections unusually engaging. It turns out, however, that 58% of those who labeled themselves Independents in 1992 ($N = 234$) claimed to "care a good deal" about both elections, compared with 76% of Democrats ($N = 187$) and 77% of Republicans ($N = 159$). A similar pattern emerges when we examine responses to the question "Would you say that you were very much interested, somewhat interested, or not much interested in following the political campaigns this year?" This question was asked four times between 1992 and 1996. Fully 40% of Independents never once report being "very much interested," as opposed to 27% of Democrats and Republicans.

In some ways, these figures understate the contrasts between partisans and

Independents. How people describe their own level of interest may fail to convey the sense of engagement they feel when presented with partisan competition. The best example of how partisan sensibilities express themselves is the election dispute surrounding the 2000 presidential election. The national outcome depended on the vote count in Florida, whose electoral votes were sufficient to make either Albert Gore Jr. or George W. Bush the winner. When the votes were first machine-tallied, Bush held a slender margin, and the Gore campaign demanded that certain counties recount their ballots by hand. Exactly how to recount half-punched or unpunched ballot cards immediately became a point of contention, and Republicans charged that subjective standards would allow the Democrats to steal the election. Meanwhile, Democrats alleged that irregularities caused large numbers of Democratic votes to go uncounted, because voters either were turned away at the polls or had voted in ways that disqualified their ballots. The controversy surrounding the disputed election outcome drew far more public attention than the campaign leading up to Election Day.

Partisan sentiment immediately suffused opinions about election procedures. Republicans discovered new virtues in the way that machines count ballots, and Democrats came to appreciate the advantages of hand-counting. When asked by ABC/ *Washington Post* pollsters ten days before the end of the election crisis "Do you think there should or should not be hand-counts of all the votes in Florida?" a national sample of Democrats favored hand-counts by a margin of 67% to 29% (with a small number of undecideds), whereas Republicans thought otherwise by a margin of 18% to 81%. Independents were predictably divided, with 46% favoring and 52% opposing. In the immediate aftermath of the Supreme Court's decision that effectively declared Bush the winner, *Los Angeles Times* pollsters asked a national sample "Do you personally feel that George W. Bush won the election legitimately or not?" Independents gave Bush the benefit of the doubt by a margin of 53% to 37%, with 11% saying that they did not know. Republicans and Democrats were more certain. Republicans felt that Bush won legitimately by a margin of 91% to 4%, with 5% expressing no opinion. Just 23% of Democrats thought Bush won legitimately, 71% did not, and 6% were unsure.

One may argue that lying beneath the surface of partisanship is a desire to elect an administration that will do one's ideological bidding. By this interpretation, Republicans and Democrats tug in opposite directions because of their policy differences, not their team attachments. The aftermath of the 2000 election shows this interpretation to be insufficient. On every question about the election dispute, the gap between self-described liberals and conservatives is much smaller than the gap between Democrats and Republicans. For example, when asked "If the U.S. Supreme Court had allowed all the disputed ballots in Florida to be counted, who do you think would have ended up with the most votes, Al Gore or George W. Bush?" Republicans with an opinion came down six to one in favor of Bush, Democrats came down six to one in favor of Gore, and Independents were split evenly. By comparison, conservatives sided with Bush by a four-to-three margin, and liberals sided with Gore by a three-to-two margin.

The presidential election crisis of 2000 also illustrates the role of emotions among those who identify with a party. Although the election crisis captivated the entire country, it elicited especially heartfelt reactions among partisans. Table 2.8 presents responses to a Gallup Poll conducted a few days after the resolution of the crisis. Respondents were presented with a series of adjectives and asked whether the word described their "reaction to the fact that George W. Bush has been declared the winner of the presidency." Compared with Democrats, Republicans were vastly more likely to describe themselves as "thrilled," "pleased," and "relieved." Democrats, by contrast, were from six to fifteen times more likely to describe themselves as "angry," "cheated," and "bitter" than Republicans. In every instance, Independents were in the middle, seldom expressing the extreme feelings of anger or thrill. Unlike Democrats, whose primary emotional reaction was a sense of having been cheated, those without a party attachment primarily expressed a sense of relief that the dispute had been brought to a close.

To characterize party identification as an emotional attachment perhaps goes too far in downplaying the role that cognition plays in shaping self-categorization. As we will see in subsequent chapters, citizens do seem to respond to information that changes the way that they perceive the social character of the parties. At the same time, however, the data in Table 2.8 remind us of the emotions that arise from group attachments. Those who root for and empathize with a partisan group feel the emotions of someone who is personally locked in competition with a long-standing and often ungracious rival.

Finally, a less dramatic but more politically significant indication of partisan engagement is voter participation. Table 2.9 tallies rates of self-reported partisan turnout for the 1992, 1994, and 1996 November elections.[6] In each election we see a significant relationship between turnout and party identification ($p <$ .01, one-tailed test). Republicans turned out to vote at higher rates than Democrats, and both partisan groups voted at higher rates than Independents. In

Table 2.8. Emotional Reactions to the Resolution of the 2000 Presidential Election Crisis

	Republican	Independent	Democrat
Angry	5	15	33
Cheated	4	29	60
Bitter	3	12	31
Thrilled	59	16	6
Pleased	91	46	16
Relieved	90	60	40
N (weighted)	276	401	334

Source: CNN/USA Today/Gallup Poll Election, December 15–17, 2000.

Note: Entries are the percentage of each partisan group feeling a given emotion. Don't know/refused responses are in each case less than 3%.

1992 and 1996, for example, Independents accounted for more than half of all nonvoters but approximately one-third of all voters. The relationship between voter turnout and political partisanship is among the most robust findings in social science, extending across a wide range of elections. Given that no single vote is likely to alter the election outcome, voting is an expression of support.

Table 2.9. Voter Turnout by Party Identification, 1992, 1994, and 1996

	Party Identification in 1992		
	Democrat ($N = 191$)	Independent ($N = 216$)	Republican ($N = 149$)
Voted in 1992	72%	65%	81%
Did not vote	28%	35%	19%
	100%	100%	100%
Voted in 1994	85%	74%	91%
Did not vote	15%	26%	9%
	100%	100%	100%
Voted in 1996	85%	74%	91%
Did not vote	15%	26%	9%
	100%	100%	100%

Source: American National Election Studies, 1992–94–96 panel survey.

Note: Voter turnout is self-reported turnout in the November general elections.

Those who identify with a political party are more likely to have something to express.

The link between partisanship and political engagement suggests that partisan feelings grow out of group attachments. Although for many people, partisans included, politics is a remote and uninteresting activity, those who identify with partisan groups are more likely to be engaged spectators if not active participants.

SUMMARY

Party identification is anything but an ephemeral "doorstep opinion." When, like attorneys cross-examining an equivocating witness, we quiz people about their partisanship repeatedly within the same interview, we develop an increasingly precise sense of their party affiliations. When we cross-validate these responses with measures designed to tap social identification, it seems clear that self-described partisans harbor genuine attachments to partisan groups. When respondents are reinterviewed many years later, their partisan attachments remain largely intact. Partisan identities seem unusually resistant to context effects, for the ranks of partisans remain relatively constant amid the ebb and flow of campaign activity. We shall see in subsequent chapters that the same may be said of the ratio of Democrats to Republicans; the changing political fortunes of the parties for the most part leave little imprint on party identification.

Our emphasis on the continuing significance of party attachments runs counter to the torrent of scholarship suggesting that genuine partisanship is a thing of the past. To be sure, the proportion of self-labeled partisans declined after the 1950s, not only in the United States but in many other countries as well. Dalton, McAllister, and Wattenberg (2000: Table 2.1) charted eighteen democracies over time and found a statistically significant decline in the number of partisan identifiers in nine of these countries. These trends mean that fewer citizens are impelled by their partisan attachments to go to the polls and to support their party's candidates. That said, it is important for one to maintain a sense of proportion when interpreting this trend. First, in countries such as the United States, the level of partisan identification has rebounded considerably from its nadir in the 1970s. As the U.S. population has aged and as the stereotypes of partisan groups have changed in the eyes of certain regional or social groups, party attachment has grown. News of declining partisanship is out-of-date here and may become so elsewhere. Second, the decline in party attachment has by no means driven partisans to extinction. In surveys conducted since the mid-1980s, approximately two out of three American adults describe themselves as Democrats or Republicans, and when pressed further in subsequent questioning, some of the remaining Independents reveal partisan inclinations, a point demonstrated forcefully by Keith et al. (1992). This is hardly a case of "parties without partisans," as Dalton and Wattenberg (2000) would suggest. Last, as we saw in the previous chapter, partisanship packs the same wallop as it did a generation ago. In terms of candidate preference in presidential races, the gap between Democrats and Republicans remains as large as ever. Although political scientists sometimes wax nostalgic about the days when partisanship really meant something, the fact is that the elections of 1912, 1920, 1924, 1928, 1948, and 1952 all featured large numbers of partisans voting against their party's nominee. Partisanship is alive and well, and as far as we can tell, it is as influential for us as it was for our parents and grandparents.

Chapter 3 A Closer Look
at Partisan Stability

The previous chapter sought to establish that partisan identification is sufficiently meaningful and enduring to warrant the detailed quantitative examination that we will now give it. Here, we elaborate on our discussion of the stability of party attachments, as contrasted with other political attitudes and social identities. Our central hypothesis is that partisan self-conceptions much more closely resemble ethnic or religious self-conceptions than they do evaluations of political leaders, opinions about party platforms, or vote intentions. In the wake of scandal, economic downturn, or military setback, self-conceptions tend to persist, whereas political evaluations often change dramatically.

In principle, chronicling the stability of partisan identities is a fairly straightforward descriptive task. Chart these attachments over time using panel surveys; compare the observed rates of change with corresponding rates for other types of political attitudes or social identities; evaluate whether in this regard partisan affiliations more closely resemble evaluations or identities.

In practice, the task is fraught with methodological difficulties, most of which stem from the fact that surveys do not gauge attitudes precisely. Survey respondents are asked a small number of questions (usually just one) about a given topic; the response categories are coarse; and the respondent may be less than careful when choosing among them. Subtle variations in the ways that these questions are read, interpreted, and recorded may contribute to misleading response variability. And even when the questions and response alternatives are fully understood, respondents may still be uncertain about which response best reflects their own thoughts and feelings. As we saw in the previous chapter, answers occasionally change when respondents are quizzed repeatedly about their partisanship within the course of a single interview.

Comparison across different attitudes and different measures presents additional problems. Party identification is sometimes measured using three response categories (Democrat, Independent, Republican), but five- and seven-category scales are also used (see below). Attitudes toward the presidential candidates are sometimes gauged by 101-category "thermometer" ratings; sometimes, by three- or five-category scales that relate whether respondents reported anything that they liked or disliked about the candidates. The more variegated the scale, the less likely it is that respondents will give the exact same response over time. So if our measure of stability is the percentage of respondents who give consistent responses, scales with different numbers of response options may produce different conclusions. By contrast, survey items that lump respondents crudely into a small number of response categories tend to have lower test-retest correlations. By virtue of how this statistic is calculated, the correlation between answers given at successive points in time will tend to be smaller. So if correlations are our yardstick, our conclusions may again be thrown off by variations in the ways that attitudes are measured. Before we may compare the stability of partisanship with the stability of other attitudes, we must devise a way to assess stability that does not depend on the accuracy with which attitudes are measured.

Thus, this chapter begins with a methodological discussion of the meaning and assessment of stability. We propose two conceptions of stability, one that focuses on the location of individuals relative to other people in the population and another that examines how an individual's location at any point in time compares with that person's long-term average. We then propose a statistical estimator for each of these conceptions that gauges stability in ways that are fairly robust to problems of mismeasurement. The rest of the chapter examines a series of panel surveys and finds strong support for the generalization that partisan attachments, and core social identifications more generally, are unusually persistent over time.

WHAT IS STABILITY?

When we speak of stable attachments, are we talking about the stability of individuals in relation to one another or in relation to some fixed point? This concern arises because most analysts of panel data use correlation coefficients to gauge attitude stability. Correlation coefficients have the advantage of lending themselves to easy interpretation. A correlation of zero implies that knowing where a person ranks in terms of party attachment at one time provides no clues about a person's ranking at a subsequent time. A correlation of 1.0, on the other hand, implies that those with the strongest affinity for Republicans at one time will have the strongest Republican attachments later. Correlations of 1.0, however, do not rule out the possibility of attitude change. Suppose that partisanship were measured along a continuum ranging from one to seven, in proportion to increasing Republicanism. Three respondents, respectively, score {1, 3, 5} at one time and {2, 4, 6} the next. The over-time correlation would be 1.0, yet each respondent became more Republican in orientation. The computation of the correlation coefficient is blind to this upward drift in the distribution.

Correlation coefficients therefore describe the extent to which respondents maintain their *relative positions* as the distribution of partisanship evolves over time. We will observe high correlations if those with the stronger-than-average Democratic attachments remain so at some future time, regardless of whether that average changes. This information about the relative spacing of individuals is informative but is not the complete story. To gauge whether an individual's attachments remain stable in relation to some fixed point, we need to augment the analysis of correlations with other statistics. One statistic is the sample mean. If the average respondent has remained in place, we need not worry that correlations mask partisan drift of the sort illustrated above. Another statistic of interest is the variance, which gauges the degree of dispersion in the sample. Suppose our three respondents had gone from {2, 3, 4} to {1, 3, 5}. Again, the correlation would be 1.0. Although the mean remained constant over time, the first and third respondents changed their attitudes. Inspecting the data to ensure that both the mean and the variance remain constant over time ensures that the correlation coefficient conveys meaningful information about attitude stability.

In addition to examining the stability of the partisan distribution and individuals' relative positions within it, we wish to investigate also whether individuals tend to return to their long-term attachments and, if so, how quickly. This analysis takes us beyond descriptive statistics such as correlations and means. To appreciate the manner in which partisanship unfolds over time, we must posit some type of a time-series model that traces individuals (subscripted with an i) over a series of time periods (subscripted with a t). The model most frequently used to characterize partisan change treats party identification ($y_{t,i}$) as a manifestation of partisanship yesterday ($y_{t-1,i}$), plus changes due to political evaluations ($X_{t,i}$), plus unobserved perturbations ($u_{t,i}$).[1]

$$y_{t,i} = \alpha_i + \beta_i y_{t-1,i} + \gamma_i X_{t,i} + u_{t,i} \qquad (3.1)$$

Here, α_i and β_i represent each individual's intercept and autoregressive parameter, respectively. The parameter γ_i denotes the effect of political evaluations, construed broadly to encompass ideological proximity to the parties, performance evaluations, and candidate assessments. When γ_i is zero, one's partisanship does not change in response to current political conditions. Large values of γ_i, on the other hand, mean that party identities change markedly in the wake of current evaluations.

The parameter β_i determines the speed with which partisans return home to their long-term average after a short-term perturbation. If $\beta_i = 1$, none of the short-term movement disappears from one period to the next. In this case, an individual's partisanship follows a "random walk"—a path that over time shows no tendency to return to some equilibrium value. Substantively, this random walk means that partisans do not tend to return to the party ties they once held. If one is a Republican today, one can be expected to be a Republican tomorrow, regardless of whether one used to be an ardent Democrat. By contrast, when $\beta_i = 0$, an individual's partisanship immediately reverts to its equilibrium level as soon as the perturbation causing the individual to depart from this central tendency disappears. If a lifelong Democrat wakes up one morning feeling Republican, chances are that this feeling will pass by supper time. Between these two extremes, intermediate values of β_i determine whether the process of reequilibration takes weeks or years. For example, when $\beta_i = 0.5$, a short-term change in partisanship loses half of its influence during the next period of time.

To illustrate how the parameter β_i affects the way in which an individual's partisanship evolves over time, Table 3.1 presents a hypothetical example of three voters with β_i parameters $\{1, 0, 0.5\}$ who are surveyed over the course of twenty consecutive one-month periods. For simplicity, we will assume that $\alpha_i = \gamma_i = 0$ for each person and that party identification is measured (without error) on a seven-point scale ranging from -3 to $+3$. To simulate disturbances,

Table 3.1. Illustration of How Individual-Level
Dynamics Affect Patterns of Partisan Change

Period	β			Disturbance
	1	0	0.5	
1	0	0	0.000	0
2	1	1	1.000	1
3	1	0	0.500	0
4	1	0	0.250	0
5	1	0	0.125	0
6	2	1	1.063	1
7	1	−1	−0.469	−1
8	1	0	−0.234	0
⋮	⋮	⋮	⋮	⋮
20	3	0	1.150	0

we roll a die and treat $\{1, 2 = -1; 3, 4 = 0; 5, 6 = 1\}$. Thus, our disturbances are, on average, zero.

In the first month, each of three respondents is at his or her equilibrium of zero. In the second period, a pro-Republican disturbance of $+1$ propels each of the respondents to a score of one, which denotes "leaning Republican." During the next three periods, no new disturbances alter partisan attachments ($u_{t,i} = 0$). Notice how the three hypothetical voters behave during this period of quiescence. The voter with $\beta_i = 1$ has no equilibrium and remains unchanged. By contrast, the voter with $\beta_i = 0$ returns immediately to his or her equilibrium partisanship of zero. Halfway between is the person whose autoregressive parameter is 0.5, gravitating slowly back to an equilibrium of zero. Note that over the twenty months, the voter with $\beta_i = 0$ never strays more than one scale point away from the equilibrium. By contrast, the voter following a random walk generated by $\beta_i = 1$ has moved from pure Independent to strong Republican by period twenty, with no tendency to return to Independence.

Which one of these voters best exemplifies stable partisanship? The most steadfast partisan is the voter with $\beta_i = 0$. This voter is on a short tether, never straying far from some equilibrium value, unless the disturbances continually favor one party. Even then, once the political environment returns to normal (that is, the disturbance for that period is zero), long-standing attachments reassert themselves. By contrast, the least stable partisans are those for whom $\beta_i = 1$. For these voters, each disturbance leaves a permanent imprint. Partisanship becomes a "running tally" of evaluations, to borrow Fiorina's (1981) memorable phrase. At any time, party identification is simply a sum of the disturbances to date.

With this hypothetical example in mind, we have a better idea about what to expect from a statistical analysis designed to estimate β_i. If the typical citizen is a "tethered partisan," analysis of survey data should suggest that β_i is close to zero. On the other hand, if partisanship represents a running tally, we should find that β_i is close to one. Some blend of the two ideas would be suggested by midrange values of β_i. Thus, the stage is set for an empirical test that speaks to the question of how partisan attachments develop over time.

A MORE VARIEGATED SCALE OF PARTY IDENTIFICATION

Before delving into estimation, we must first come to grips with problems of measurement. The foregoing discussion presupposes that party identification is an interval scale. In this idealized model, people fall at points along a continuum ranging from Democrat to Republican, and this continuum has regular gradations so that it behaves as though it were a thermometer or bathroom scale. Clearly, a three-point classification of partisanship fails to satisfy this assumption. As we saw in Table 2.5, self-described Democrats vary in their degree of identification, and there is no guarantee that Democrats are as "far" from Independents as Independents are from Republicans. If we are to make use of these statistical models, we need to create measures that are more suitable for analysis.[2]

To make partisanship more conducive to linear statistical models, the three-point measure is commonly expanded into a seven-point scale. For decades, the NES and surveys patterned after it have asked a follow-up question after the "stem" party identification measure. Respondents who call themselves Democrats or Republicans are asked

> Would you call yourself a strong [Republican/Democrat] or not very strong [Republican/Democrat]?

The idea behind this question is to allow analysts to differentiate between strong and weak partisan loyalties. From the standpoint of measurement validity, however, the follow-up question may be problematic. "Strong Democrats" are not immediately recognizable as a social group. Accordingly, some scholars have complained that it may invite respondents to describe the degree of party loyalty that they have exhibited in past elections (Miller 1991). Of even more questionable validity is the follow-up question directed at those respondents who initially call themselves Independents:

> Do you think of yourself as closer to the Republican Party or to the Democratic Party?

Unlike the stem question, this question focuses attention on parties rather than on partisans. And although the question uses the phrase "think of yourself," the ensuing phrase "closer to" may invite respondents to evaluate their ideological proximity to the parties. By expanding the basic three-category measure in this way, one risks contaminating the central conception of party identification with other partisan attitudes.

Nevertheless, the common practice among analysts of survey data is to combine answers to the stem and branch questions, thereby creating a seven-point scale. At the ends of the scale are "Strong" Democrats and "Strong" Republicans. Next to them are "Weak" Democrats and Republicans. Independents who "lean" to the parties occupy the third and fifth places in the continuum. Finally, "Pure" Independents fall in the middle. Typically, these categories are assigned metric scores ranging from one (Strong Democrat) to seven (Strong Republican). It is important to bear these gradations in mind when evaluating evidence of partisan change. Scholars who track the changes that occur from one year to the next often concern themselves with movements between adjacent categories in the seven-point continuum. Changing from a Strong Democrat to a Weak Democrat is a subtle alteration of one's social identity, quite different from changing one's self-conception to Republican (in much the same way that changing one's self-conception from an Orthodox Jew to a Conservative Jew is very different from changing from Jew to Protestant). One must be careful not to exaggerate the significance of small changes at the individual level.

Although we are critical of the face validity of the branching questions that give rise to this scale, the seven- and three-point variants of the partisanship measure generally produce similar results once one takes account of the fact that the latter categorizes people more crudely. And although the 1–7 metric seems rather arbitrary, it does not seem to create statistical distortions. Scoring the partisanship scale in some other fashion or treating the scale points as merely a series of ordered categories using more complex statistical procedures (compare Green and Palmquist 1994) does not greatly affect the results. Although we would prefer to work with a highly nuanced index created from a long series of redundant rather than branched partisanship questions, existing measures seem adequate for our purposes.

ESTIMATING INDIVIDUAL-LEVEL DYNAMICS
USING MEAN-CORRECTED PANEL ANALYSIS

Working now with a continuous measure of party identification, we return to our dynamic model of individual-level partisanship. Although equation 3.1 has heuristic value, it is statistically intractable given the panel data at our disposal. The panels interview respondents too few times to enable us to track each individual's time series. As a practical matter, we cannot expect to estimate both the intercept and slope for each individual. To make this individual time-series approach feasible, we allow intercepts to vary across individuals but assume that all individuals share a common dynamic parameter, β. Also, for the moment, we will focus only on the autoregressive component of party identification. Thus, the model becomes

$$y_{t,i} = \alpha_i + \beta y_{t-1,i} + u_{t,i} + \varepsilon_t \qquad (3.2)$$

As before, each individual has a distinct intercept α_i, so that when $\beta < 1.0$, each person gravitates toward his or her own long-term equilibrium. These so-called fixed effects capture enduring unobserved differences among individuals. The variable ε_t represents time effects, for example, shifts in the mean attributable to swings in political fortunes. Whether one chooses to include these time shocks does not change the results, but we will revisit the issue of time shocks in subsequent chapters because they are central to our understanding of the link between individual-level and aggregate-level partisanship. We will show that at the individual level, voters return quickly to their long-term attachments. However, voters tend to respond in the same way to short-term events, which may cause the overall distribution of party identification to lurch in one direction before returning to its long-term equilibrium. For the moment, our main objective is to estimate β leaving aside for now the question of whether it makes sense to assume that all individuals share the same β value. Values close to one imply that individuals return to their equilibria slowly, if at all; values close to zero imply that people quickly return to their long-term attachments.

Estimating β presents special statistical problems because we observe partisanship at only a few points in time, and our observations are clouded by a certain degree of response error. Standard regression analysis will fail under these conditions. To estimate β in a consistent fashion, we use the instrumental variables estimator proposed by Anderson and Hsiao (1982) and refined by Arellano (1989).[3] Because this method has not been applied to survey data in political science, we conducted a series of Monte Carlo experiments to ensure that this estimator works well even when continuous data are observed in integer form, as is the case with the seven-point party identification scale. Simulated partisanship data were generated with means, variances, and covariances characteristic of NES data. Attesting to the robustness of the method, the instrumental variables regressions successfully recover the β parameters used to generate the data even when partisanship is assumed to be misreported and crudely categorized.[4] Indeed, one of the virtues of the instrumental variables method is its ability to correct problems arising from mismeasurement.

Table 3.2 reports the instrumental variables estimates for the five American panel studies in which party identification was measured at roughly similar intervals. The first survey is the 1956–60 NES panel, which tracked respondents from Eisenhower's landslide reelection through Kennedy's victory. The second survey is the four-wave 1980 Major Panel Study, which charted Jimmy Carter's remarkable decline in popularity amid mounting economic and international problems. The third is a five-wave study, in which residents of Los Angeles and Erie, Pennsylvania, were interviewed at approximately six-week intervals (Patterson 1982). This study traced the campaign across the divisive Republican primary and general election campaign of 1976 that led to Democratic control of Congress and the presidency. The 1990–91–92 NES tracked opinion from the 1990 campaign through the aftermath of the Gulf War and into George Bush's extraordinary drop in popularity in 1992. The 1992–94–96 NES also spanned an eventful period that encompassed Bill Clinton's first election victory, the Republican takeover of Congress, and Clinton's reelection.

Analyzing five different data sets serves a number of purposes. Each data set helps to corroborate the others. The fact that different amounts of time elapsed between the interviews in each survey permits further testing of the notion that individual-level party identification is autoregressive. If the Patterson study were to reveal that $\beta = 0.85$ for six-week intervals, the 1990–91–92 NES should show $\beta = 0.85^{(52/6)} = 0.24$ for fifty-two-week intervals because the autoregressive parameters decline geometrically with time. More important, the wide array of time periods these surveys cover enables us to study the conditions under which party identification is responsive to short-term forces.

Although the time lags between surveys vary from one study to the next,

Table 3.2. Individual Mean-Corrected Time-Series Analysis of Individual-Level Dynamics in Party Identification

	1956–58–60 NES Panel	1980 NES Major Panel	Erie/Los Angeles Panel, 1976	1990–91–92 NES Panel	1992–94–96 NES Panel
Model with Time Shocks					
Dynamic parameter (β)	0.144	0.011	−0.067	0.310†	0.250
Standard error of β	0.120	0.098	0.089	0.157	0.182
Time shock: waves 2–3	0.084	−0.055	−0.023	−0.163*	−0.212*
Time shock: waves 3–4			0.024		
Time shock: waves 4–5			0.035		
Number of respondents (N)	1,045	591	413	940	544
Number of waves (t)	3	4	5	3	3
Approximate time between panel surveys	2 years	3 months*	6 weeks	1 year	2 years

Note: The first wave of the 1980 panel preceded the second by five months. Estimates were obtained using the instrumental variables method described in Anderson and Hsiao (1982) and Arellano (1989). Estimates obtained using generalized method of moments were identical for three-wave analyses and very similar for panels with more than three waves.

*$p < .05$, two-tailed test; †$p < .05$, one-tailed test.

three of the five surveys paint a similar picture of individual-level dynamics. As shown in Table 3.2, three of the point estimates are substantively small and statistically indistinguishable from zero. The estimate from 1992–94–96 is somewhat larger, at 0.25. The largest estimate, 0.31, comes from the 1990–91–92 NES. Perhaps the Gulf War in 1991, which made members of the Republican administration into triumphant patriots and the Democratic opposition in Congress into unsympathetic naysayers, left an unusual imprint on party attachments. It may be that when the Democrats made their comeback in 1992, the advent of a strong third-party candidacy in the form of Ross Perot prevented some wayward Democrats from returning to the fold. Although statistically significant, this estimate is still fairly weak, indicating that two-thirds of each perturbation dissipates after a year's time and that essentially nothing remains after two years.

Although the results vary from survey to survey, even the largest dynamic parameter estimates are fairly small. The fact that β is typically close to zero implies that individual partisanship hovers around each person's fixed intercept, or equilibrium. Over the span of a few months or years, one's recorded party identification is essentially a draw from a population with mean α_i. These individual-level time series evidently have little or no memory for perturbations: The citizen who is above his or her expected level of partisanship at one point has an expected partisanship of α_i at the next period. In other words, individual-level time series may be approximated by the equation

$$y_{t,i} = \alpha_i + u_{t,i} + \varepsilon_t \qquad (3.3)$$

In effect, people gravitate toward their personal means (α_i) although they are buffeted occasionally by idiosyncratic shocks $(u_{t,i})$ and changes in the political environment that shift the distribution of partisanship in one direction or another (ε_t).

Before drawing out additional implications of this characterization, we must first address two important objections to this finding, both of which insist that we expand and refine our models and estimation procedures. The first objection is that individuals may follow different dynamic paths. Although samples analyzed as a whole may indicate that the dynamics are weak on average, it is possible that some individuals have very strong β parameters. One way to test this hypothesis is to hunt for subgroups that have distinctive dynamic coefficients. As Box-Steffensmeier and Smith (1997) point out, conjectures about individual heterogeneity are suggested by two prominent theories about public opinion change. The first is Converse's (1976) hypothesis that as citizens become exposed to politics, they form more stable partisan attachments. This claim suggests a potential interaction between age and individual dynamics, on the grounds that older citizens should be less susceptible to change. Expressed in terms of equation 3.1, the β_i values tend to be smaller among older citizens, who revert to their long-term equilibrium more quickly than do younger citizens. The second hypothesis derives from Zaller's (1992) model of persuasion, in which citizens with different levels of exposure to new information and prior opinionation are differentially susceptible to change. Those with more information have firmer attitudes, but they are also more likely to receive news that would disrupt their opinions. Citizens with less information have more labile opinions, but their inattentiveness insulates them from opinion change. Again in terms of equation 3.1, we should see higher average β_i values among less-informed citizens, for whom the new information that is received has a more long-lasting effect.

Neither hypothesis derives support from the individual mean-corrected time-series analyses. We divided each of the samples from the two larger surveys into three age categories (thirty and younger, thirty-one to sixty, and sixty-one and older). *None* of the age subgroups in any of the surveys shows any statistically meaningful evidence of variation in β parameters. (Admittedly, because of restrictions of sample size, these age categories do not isolate very young respondents.) Similarly, when we stratify the sample by interest in politics, we find no meaningful variation in the estimates. Again, all indications suggest that β does not vary detectably from zero across different strata of political interest.[5] Across an array of different subgroups, the following generalization appears to hold: Partisan attachments waver around an individual's long-term mean.

The other objection is that our model neglects observed sources of partisan change. Rather than lumping all of the short-term forces into the disturbance term, we should introduce predictors that are thought to shape party attachments: presidential approval, vote intentions, candidate evaluations, and issue proximity. This objection returns us to equation 3.1, which included measures of short-term forces. The limiting factor here is the availability of suitable data. Very few surveys have queried respondents about their partisan affiliations four times.[6] Of the small group of studies that meet this requirement, some do not furnish four waves of information about potential independent variables. The best study for this purpose is the five-wave panel survey conducted during the 1976 campaign, which repeatedly asked about both party identification and presidential approval, an independent variable that arguably encompasses both policy and performance evaluations. Other studies, such as the four-wave 1980 NES and the three-wave 1990–91–92 and 1992–94–96 NES surveys furnish only three waves of presidential approval data, and we must therefore be more tentative about the inferences we draw from them.

The model used for analyzing these data is a direct extension of the autoregressive models described above. The principal difference is that one of the predictors is now a contemporaneous measure of presidential approval (scored from 1 = Strongly Approve to 5 = Strongly Disapprove). Thus, current party identification is treated as a function of both lagged partisanship and current presidential approval.

$$y_{t,i} = \alpha_i + \beta y_{t-1,i} + \gamma X_{t,i} + u_{t,i} + \varepsilon_t \qquad (3.4)$$

In contrast to equation 3.2, which lumps all unobserved sources of partisan change into the disturbance term $(u_{t,i})$, equation 3.4 makes explicit the components of partisan change.

The estimation of this model is also a direct extension of the Anderson-Hsiao-Arellano method. The list of instrumental variables is augmented to include past approval, so that the estimator corrects for measurement error in both approval and lagged partisanship. It also has the virtue of correcting for two-way causation between party identification and approval. Thus, we need not make the strong assumption that approval causes partisanship and not vice versa. In short, instrumental variables regression allows us to be agnostic about the adequacy of the measures and the direction of causality.

On balance, the results presented in Table 3.3 suggest that presidential approval shapes party identification in the short run but that the effects dissipate quickly. The five-wave panel survey spanning the 1976 campaign shows no evidence that approval influences party identification. The estimate of γ is trivial in size and statistically indistinguishable from zero. But data from the 1980 NES suggest that Jimmy Carter's plummeting approval ratings during the election year nudged voters slightly in the Republican direction. The γ coefficient of 0.187 implies that respondents who strongly approved of Carter in January but strongly disapproved of him in June experienced a shift of 0.748 along the seven-point party identification scale. On the other hand, the fact that β is just 0.076 means that partisanship snapped back to its long-term equilibrium when an individual's approval of the president returned to its mean. Notice that as far as partisan dynamics are concerned, expanding the model to include presidential approval does not alter our earlier results: Individuals quickly return to their equilibria in the wake of short-term perturbations.

Table 3.3. Individual Mean-Corrected Time-Series Analysis of Individual-Level Dynamics in Party Identification, Allowing for Effects of Presidential Approval

	Erie/Los Angeles Panel, 1976	1980 NES Major Panel	1990–91–92 NES Panel	1992–94–96 NES Panel
Model with Time Shocks				
Dynamic parameter (β)	−0.069	0.076	0.400[†]	0.257
Standard error of β	0.091	0.212	0.182	0.188
Effect of approval (γ)	0.006	0.187[†]	−0.164[†]	0.049
Standard error of γ	0.073	0.094	0.098	0.101
Time shock: waves 2–3	−0.023	−0.046	0.041	−0.194*
Time shock: waves 3–4	0.024			
Time shock: waves 4–5	0.035			
Number of respondents (N)	413	591	940	544
Number of waves (t)	5	3	3	3
Approximate time between panel surveys	6 weeks	3 months	1 year	2 years

Note: In all surveys, approval was measured from 1 = Strongly Approve to 5 = Strongly Disapprove. The instrumental variables used in this analysis were differenced approval and differenced party identification.
*$p < .05$, two-tailed test; [†] $p < .05$, one-tailed test.

To varying degrees, the same pattern emerges from other surveys. The 1990–91–92 NES produces almost the same γ estimate as the 1980 NES. Here, moving the full length of the presidential approval scale from Strongly Approve to Strongly Disapprove (four scale points) produces a shift of 0.66 in the Democratic direction. The autoregressive parameter of 0.40 implies that less than half of this partisan change persists after one year and that it is all but forgotten four years later. The 1992–94–96 panel produces statistically insignificant estimates of γ (0.049, SE = 0.101) and β (0.257, SE = 0.188). Taking all four sets of estimates into account, we would conclude that dramatic shifts in presidential approval lead to faint, transitory changes in partisanship.

As we will see in the next chapter, this pattern also emerges from aggregate data. The balance of Democrats and Republicans changes as political events unfold, but these changes tend to be small and develop gradually over time. The reason is that party identification is for the most part unresponsive to changes in the environment, and these environmental factors tend to evolve slowly over time. The economy undulates through periods of recession and prosperity; scandals and international events grab headlines and then fade from public memory. Seldom does the political environment change with both force and permanence. The preceding analysis of individual time series helps us understand the connection between microlevel and macrolevel phenomena. Individual time series do respond to political conditions, but the response is so transitory that aggregate movements of the type that could be dubbed a "realignment" are extremely rare.

PARTISAN DISTRIBUTIONS OVER TIME:
EVIDENCE FROM POOLED PANEL ANALYSIS

Another way to assess partisan stability is to examine individuals in relation to one another. If individuals were arrayed along a continuum ranging from Democrat to Republican, to what extent would the distance between any two individuals remain constant over time? This question returns us to the problem of interpreting correlations. We need to devise a method by which to assess the correlation between individuals' actual (as opposed to measured) partisanship at different times.

Fortunately, fairly well-established techniques exist for separating trait from measurement error in these situations. The algebra underlying these techniques is outlined in the appendix, but the intuition behind these statistical procedures can be stated quite simply: Attitude change and random measurement fluctuation generate very different sorts of correlation matrices. When partisanship changes over time and is measured without error, the correlation between partisanship in waves one and three (denoted r_{13}) is the product of r_{12} and r_{23}. A quite different pattern emerges when partisanship is stable but measured with error: r_{13} far exceeds $r_{12}\, r_{23}$. Indeed, if underlying partisan attachments were entirely stable but measured with error, r_{13} would equal r_{12}. *What matters is not the size of the observed correlation between any two successive measures but the rate at which this correlation declines over time.*

Suppose, for example, that respondents were interviewed each year for three successive years. Imagine that the correlation between party identification as measured in waves one and two is 0.5. From this number alone, one could not tell whether partisanship had changed or whether it was mismeasured at one or both times. The inference we make will depend on how the party identification in the third wave correlates with party identification in the two preceding waves. If r_{13} and r_{23} were found to be 0.5, we would conclude that underlying partisanship is perfectly stable: No matter how much time elapses between measurements, the correlation remains the same. On the other hand, if $r_{23} = 0.5$ but $r_{13} = 0.25$, the conclusion would be very different: Party identification changes rapidly over time but is measured perfectly.

Table 3.4 presents the correlation matrices for the American panel studies that contain at least four waves of interviews during which party identification was assessed. A cursory look at these matrices reveals that the correlations do not decline geometrically over time. Instead, the correlations decline gradually. Between 1956 and 1958, partisanship correlates at 0.850. Between 1956 and the postelection survey of 1960, this correlation remains 0.804, whereas a pattern of decline consistent with attitude change would have generated a correlation of 0.850·0.842 = 0.716. The same pattern holds for each of the panel studies. Attitude change does occur, but the imperfect correlation between the survey measures is primarily due to response error.

This point can be established more rigorously by calculating the disattenuated correlations between partisanship in waves two and three. The 1980 NES and 1976 Erie/Los Angeles panel, which interviewed respondents every few months, naturally show the highest correlations. Table 3.5 reports that these correlations are near 0.99, which is to say that true partisan change during these presidential campaigns was minimal.[7] The one-year span between 1993 and 1994—a tumultuous period of defeat and disarray for the Democratic Party—also featured a high degree of stability. Net of measurement error, the correlation is 0.977. Finally, the surveys conducted in 1958 and 1960 show little parti-

Table 3.4. Descriptive Statistics for Party Identification,
Measured at Four Successive Points in Time

| | Wave | | | | | |
	1	2	3	4	Mean	SD
1956–58–60 NES ($N = 989$)						
1956	1.00				3.678	2.230
1958	0.850	1.00			3.468	2.263
1960 (preelection)	0.834	0.879	1.00		3.545	2.258
1960 (postelection)	0.804	0.842	0.890	1.00	3.593	2.421
1976 Erie/Los Angeles ($N = 494$)						
January/February	1.00				3.348	2.092
April/May	0.874	1.00			3.251	2.113
June/July	0.868	0.905	1.00		3.241	2.161
August/September	0.853	0.889	0.896	1.00	3.255	2.165
September/October	0.841	0.887	0.903	0.900	3.243	2.208
1980 NES ($N = 713$)						
January	1.00				3.623	1.990
June	0.853	1.00			3.690	2.043
September	0.862	0.878	1.00		3.642	2.044
November	0.831	0.863	0.887	1.00	3.693	2.103
1992–93–94–96 NES ($N = 500$)						
1992	1.00				2.934	2.041
1993	0.838	1.00			2.950	2.058
1994	0.824	0.889	1.00		3.032	2.175
1996	0.779	0.843	0.867	1.00	2.856	2.152

Table 3.5. Observed and Disattenuated Correlations between Party Identification
at Successive Points in Time

	Observed Correlation	Disattenuated Correlation	N	χ^2 (degrees of freedom)	p
1958–60 NES	0.879	0.965	989	0.42 (1)	.52
1976 Erie/Los Angeles, April–July	0.905	0.989	494	3.76 (3)	.29
1976 Erie/Los Angeles, July–September	0.896	0.989	494		
1980 NES, June–September	0.878	0.987	713	2.96 (1)	.09
1993–94 NES	0.889	0.977	500	0.04 (1)	.85

san change, with a correlation of 0.965. If we extend the pooled panel analysis to studies that interview respondents three times, we find similar results, albeit with somewhat more restrictive statistical assumptions.[8] From 1974 to 1976, the disattenuated correlation is 0.984. Among parents in the Youth-Parent Socialization Study, partisanship in 1973 bears a 0.981 correlation with partisanship in 1982; among their children, this correlation is 0.728 (Green and Palmquist 1994: Table 1). It seems apparent that the relative positions of individuals within the distribution of partisanship change slowly over time and that the observed (uncorrected) correlations between measured party identification greatly overstate the degree of change.

Bringing together the various perspectives on partisan stability, we may now take a fresh look at the patterns of partisan change that emerge in the most extensive assessment of party identification, the five-wave Erie/Los Angeles panel study of 1976. We infer from our mean-corrected panel analysis that partisanship evolves over time with almost no memory: At each point in time, one's party identification is simply a long-term mean plus some transitory disturbance. We also know from our pooled panel analysis that individuals maintain their relative positions within the partisan distribution. People tend to move in unison, if they move at all.

What light do these results shed on alternative ways of assessing partisan stability? Table 3.6 confirms that it makes little difference whether we treat the seven-point measure of partisanship as continuous or ordinal. Similarly, an ordinal three-point measure behaves almost identically to an ordinal seven-point scale. More revealing is the contrast between these analyses and more naïve measures of partisan change, such as the proportion of respondents who switch from one partisan category to another. If one gauges stability simply by counting the number of people who change their answers from one interview to the next, partisan change seems to run rampant, particularly for the seven-point measure. Between February and April, 37% of the respondents changed their scores on the seven-point scale, and 20% changed their scores on the three-point measure. The fact that these rates vary markedly between the two measures of partisanship underscores our concern about the arbitrariness of this common way of gauging partisan stability.

Another concern is that these rates grossly overstate true attitude change. Notice that in Table 3.6 the frequency with which switching occurs climbs slowly over time, which is consistent with the view that most of the *apparent* change is due to random response variability rather than real changes in identity. Even when partisanship is measured repeatedly during the same interview,

Table 3.6. Alternative Measures of Partisan Stability, 1976

Relationship between Responses Given in February and . . .	Interparty Conversions	Switching Categories (3-Point)	Switching Categories (7-Point)	Correlation, 3-Point Scales	Correlation, 7-Point Scales	Disattenuated Correlation, 3-Point[a] Scales	Disattenuated Correlation, 7-Point[b] Scales	Disattenuated Correlation, 7-Point[c] Scales
April/May	11	99	183	0.81	0.87	0.96	0.96	0.96
June/July	12	94	188	0.82	0.87	0.96	0.96	0.95
August/September	13	100	199	0.80	0.85	0.95	0.95	0.94
September/October	16	111	203	0.78	0.84	0.96	0.95	0.94

Note: N = 494. Disattenuated correlations assume that measurement reliability is the same for the February and April/May surveys.

[a] Adjusted for measurement error. The three-point scale was analyzed as a series of ordered categories.

[b] Adjusted for measurement error. The seven-point scale was analyzed as a series of ordered categories.

[c] Adjusted for measurement error. The seven-point scale was treated as a continuous metric scale.

one can expect scores to change. Beneath the surface, party attachments evolve very slowly over time.

It should be emphasized, however, that small changes in underlying party attachments do tend to add up over time. Although they are scarcely noticeable during the course of a campaign, these changes can produce substantial change over several decades. A two-year correlation of 0.95 implies a thirty-two-year correlation of 0.44. Although a correlation of 0.44 is still considerable, it does mean that many partisans will change their identities over the course of their adult lives. Our view is not that partisan identities are immutable but rather that they change gradually and often for reasons that are not directly connected to political events. Presidential evaluations, for example, seem not to produce sizable and lasting change in party attachments. Instead, partisan change often seems to spring from changes in a person's immediate environment—where they live and with whom they interact. Unfortunately, from a research standpoint, these social influences typically go unmeasured in political surveys.

IS PARTISAN STABILITY SPURIOUS?

A second objection to the latent variable model presented above is that the correlation between successive measures of partisanship may stem from persistent political evaluations, such as approval of the incumbent president. Franklin and Jackson (1983), for example, explain persistent party attachments as an outgrowth of stable ideological assessments of the party platforms. In essence, people maintain their attachments because the ideological evaluations on which they rest do not change. Although this argument is more difficult to maintain for more rapidly evolving opinions, such as presidential approval or vote intention, this criticism deserves special attention.

In previous work, we demonstrated in detail that an individual's position within a distribution of partisanship is weakly affected by short-term evaluations (Green and Palmquist 1990). Survey data collected during the 1980 presidential campaign, which saw Jimmy Carter's approval ratings drop sharply between January and June, enabled us to study whether hostility toward the president pushed people in the Republican direction. Using pooled regression analysis, we discovered that feelings about Carter, evaluations of his performance in office, and agreement with him on leading issues of the day seemed to have little relation to party identification. That is, when we regressed current party identification on lagged party identification and current evaluations, we found that these evaluations exert small and statistically insignificant effects.

This finding contradicted the findings of scholars such as Brody and Rothen-berg (1988) who had studied the 1980 election but whose statistical analysis ig-nored the special estimation problems that arise in this sort of analysis. Specif-ically, their regressions failed to allow for the possibility that the independent variables are measured with error and that short-term evaluations are both causes and consequences of party attachments. Using instrumental variables regression to correct these problems, we discovered that the relative spacing of individuals within the distribution of partisanship is weakly affected by these short-term evaluations. Moreover, the same conclusion holds when we return to the 1956–60 and 1972–76 NES panel surveys, both of which have been used to demonstrate how party identification changes with voters' ideological affin-ity for the parties (Franklin and Jackson 1983). Upon reanalysis of these data, however, we find little convincing evidence that party identification shifts in an enduring way when people change their views about the party platforms. Peo-ple may move temporarily, as suggested by the mean-corrected panel analysis above, but they eventually return to their long-term equilibria. Thus, when we examine these data using pooled regression techniques, which focus on the rel-ative spacing of individuals, we find short-term forces to have small effects (Schickler and Green 1995).

The same point can be established using more recent survey data. The 1992–93–94–96 NES panel provides a wealth of measures, including party evalua-tions that blend ideological and performance assessments. For example, re-spondents in each wave of this survey were asked which party would do a bet-ter job of handling "the nation's economy," its "foreign affairs," and the task of "making health care more affordable." Because these items are tied directly to perceptions of the parties, respondents often claim that their party is most ef-fective on all fronts. As pointed out in Chapter 1, however, the correlation is far from perfect. As a detached observer might expect, the Democratic Party gets relatively good marks on health care, and the Republicans tend to prevail on foreign affairs. The prospective performance evaluations of the parties, in other words, are strongly correlated with, yet distinct from, party identification.

To investigate whether prospective evaluations of the parties are the glue that holds party identification together over time, we revisit our pooled regression model. Now, the model includes prospective evaluations, as described in the appendix.[9] Again, our aim is to estimate the disattenuated correlation between party identification in 1993 and 1994, but this time the model explicitly allows for the possibility that evaluations of the parties determine party identification and that these evaluations may be correlated over time. In keeping with previous findings based on the 1980 NES, we find that controlling for short-term factors makes little difference. Before prospective evaluations are taken into account, the correlation between party identification in 1993 and 1994 is 0.98.[10] After short-term evaluations are taken into account, the correlation remains 0.98. In sum, we find no support for the view that other political evaluations account for the over-time persistence of party identification.

STABLE COMPARED WITH WHAT?

Amid all this talk of partisan stability, it is easy to lose sight of the contrast between party identification and other facets of public opinion. Lest one think that techniques for handling measurement error inevitably show that political attitudes are stable, consider what happens as we move from party identification to evaluations of the political parties and incumbent presidents. These party evaluations are gauged by the "feeling thermometer" measures for the two parties. The measure used here is the difference between the thermometer rating for the Democratic and Republican parties. Presidential approval is based on a single branched question that places respondents on a continuum from Strongly Approve to Strongly Disapprove. Unfortunately, only one panel study furnishes four waves of evaluations data from which to compute error-corrected correlations; when analyzing the other surveys, we are forced to estimate these correlations on the basis of three waves of interviews. This constraint forces us to assume that errors of measurement have constant variance over time. For purposes of comparison, we recompute the over-time correlations for party identification and other opinions using the same statistical model.

Table 3.7 compares the stability of party identification with the stability of party affect and the stability of presidential approval after correcting for measurement error. The comparison with party affect is particularly telling in light of the debate between running-tally and social identity models of partisanship. From a rational choice perspective, in which party identification is merely an information-saving device, there is no reason to expect party identification to be more stable than party affect. One likes the party that provides the greatest benefits, however defined. But from a social identity perspective, there is a critical difference between party identification and feelings of warmth toward the parties: The former is linked to the voter's self-concept and thus should be resistant to change. The latter, though affected by the voter's party identification,

Table 3.7. Stability of Party Identification, Party Ratings, and Presidential Approval

	Disattenuated Correlations		
	Party Identification	Party Thermometers	Presidential Approval
1972–74	0.96	0.81	
1974–76	0.97	0.97	
1976, waves 1–2	0.96		0.82
1976, waves 2–3	0.99		0.95
1976, waves 3–4	0.99		0.89
1976, waves 4–5	1.00		0.94
1980, waves 1–2	1.00	0.91	0.81
1980, waves 2–3	1.00	0.97	0.99
1990–91	1.00	0.99	0.94
1991–92	0.93	0.89	0.77
1992–93	0.93	0.91	
1993–94	0.98	0.96	0.88
1994–96	0.95	0.93	0.87

Note: Estimates were obtained by maximum likelihood estimation using covariance matrices as input. For details on the methods used for calculating disattenuated correlations from panel surveys, see Green and Palmquist (1990) and Palmquist and Green (1992).

is much more likely to be subject to the vicissitudes of everyday politics. In other words, a scandal-plagued Democratic administration may well lead Democrats to feel less warmly toward their party, but it should have a much less noticeable effect on Democrats' self-concept.

The expectations of this interpretation are borne out by a comparison of the stability of party identification and party affect. In eight of nine instances, the estimated correlation for party identification is higher than the corresponding correlation for party affect. In the remaining case, the estimates are the same. Party identification is even more distinct from presidential approval, for in every instance, party identification is more strongly correlated over time. The contrast is particularly marked during periods when presidents came under fire. During the early stages of the 1980 and 1992 presidential campaigns, large segments of the electorate changed their opinions of Carter and Bush. Some erstwhile supporters turned against them, whereas others remained supportive; individuals thus changed their relative positions. These events did less to disrupt party identification. The correlations are higher, suggesting that fewer partisans exchanged positions within the distribution of partisanship.

PARTY IDENTIFICATION AND OTHER
SOCIAL IDENTITIES

In terms of persistence over time, party identification finds a much closer parallel to other social identities, namely, religion, ethnicity, and social class. Like party identification, these constructs are measured in surveys by asking respondents to categorize themselves as part of a social group. In the 1992–96 NES panel, ethnic identification was gauged by asking respondents, "In addition to being an American, what do you consider your main ethnic or nationality group?" to which respondents could supply up to two answers. Social class was measured with a branched question that began with a filter: "There's been some talk these days about different social classes. Most people say they belong either to the middle class or the working class. Do you ever think of yourself as belonging to one of these classes?" Roughly three-quarters of a national sample tended to respond affirmatively, whereupon they were asked "Which one?" The remainder were invited to answer anyway: "Well, if you had to make a choice, would you call yourself middle class or working class?" Religious affiliation was measured somewhat differently. Those who reported that they regularly attended religious services were asked the denomination of their place of worship, and others were asked whether they ever "think of [themselves] as part of a particular church or denomination" and, if so, whether they "consider themselves Protestant, Catholic, Jewish, or what." Protestants were then queried further to describe their religious denomination. It is unfortunate that religious identification is assessed by reference to religious practice, although it seems unlikely that worshipers identify with a religion other than the one whose services they attend.

Assessing stability over time is complicated by the fact that panel surveys tend not to repeat "demographic" or "background" questions. These constructs are generally presumed to be both stable and well-measured—an assumption that we think plausible but would nonetheless like to demonstrate empirically. Most of the studies that try to measure change in religious affiliation do so by means of retrospective surveys in which respondents are asked to recall their former religion (for example, Newport 1979; Witt, Crockett, and Babchuk 1988), a technique that is less reliable than tracking a group of individuals over time. In the rare cases in which questions are repeated, they tend to be administered only twice, which makes it impossible to differentiate attitude change from response error. This limitation constrains interpretation of the 1992–94–96 and 1972–74–76 NES panel surveys, which, with one exception, asked these questions only twice. More useful is the Youth-Parent Socialization Panel

Study, which asked parents about their religious and class affiliations in 1965, 1973, and 1982. We will glean what we can from each of these studies in an effort to compare the stability of various forms of social identity.

We begin with the most recent data, those from the 1992–94–96 NES. Table 3.8 charts survey responses between 1992 and 1996, with the exception of social class, which was measured only in 1992 and 1994. To facilitate comparison, we have constructed a dichotomous representation of each form of social identification (for example, Republican, non-Republican; Protestant, non-Protestant) and computed the change in log-odds that occurs as one compares those who identified with this group in 1992 and those who did not.[11] This statistical device enables us to compare variables that have very different distributions. Some, such as Italian ethnic identification, are very skewed, and others, such as social class, are more balanced. The log-odds transformation puts them on more or less equal footing. Stability is gauged by the rate at which these log-odds scores decline over time.

It is apparent from Table 3.8 that certain social identities are extremely durable. Ethnic identification among blacks, Hispanics, and Italians scarcely changes over time. Other forms of identification, such as Protestant, Irish, German, and Republican affiliation, are more prone to change but nonetheless highly stable. The least stable identities in our list are more diffuse ethnic identities, such as English/British, a result that is confirmed when we replicate our analysis using three measurements of ethnic identity taken in the 1972–74–76 NES panel survey. These data produce similar results: Among European ethnic groups, Italian identification is the strongest; English/British, the weakest. (This pattern persists even after allowance is made for measurement error, using the fact that ethnic identification is asked at three points in time.) A more extensive investigation of these ethnic identities lies beyond the scope of this book, but it does seem that the most salient and meaningful ethnic identities in the United States are the ones that prove to be the most stable.

Social class is a somewhat more complicated story. Although most respondents reported that they associated themselves with a particular social class, responses to this question were quite unstable; more than half of those who said "no" in 1992 said "yes" in 1994. In addition, the self-categorization into working and middle classes changed frequently, at least by comparison with these other types of social identification. These comparisons, however, are clouded by uncertainties of measurement. It could be that social class is stable but poorly measured. We therefore turn to the parent sample of the Youth-Parent Socialization Panel Study, which asked about religious and class affiliation on three

Table 3.8. Persistence in Ethnic, Religious, Class, and Party Identification, 1992–94–96

	German Ethnic Identification in 1992		Italian Ethnic Identification in 1992		Irish Ethnic Identification in 1992		Black/African American Identification in 1992	
	No	Yes	No	Yes	No	Yes	No	Yes
In 1996?								
No	467	23	572	4	512	22	520	5
Yes	33	74	3	18	29	34	22	50
Log-odds	3.82		6.75		3.31		5.47	

	English/British Ethnic Identification in 1992		Hispanic Ethnic Identification in 1992		Protestant Identification in 1992		Republican Identification in 1992	
	No	Yes	No	Yes	No	Yes	No	Yes
In 1996?								
No	497	28	550	3	181	27	378	33
Yes	43	29	3	37	37	242	49	125
Log-odds	2.48		6.88		3.78		3.37	

	Social Class Identification in 1992		Social Class Identification in 1992	
	No	Yes	Middle Class	Working Class
In 1996?				
No	72	64		
Yes	79	361		
Log-odds	1.64			
In 1994?				
Middle Class			228	75
Working Class			60	194
Log-odds			2.29	

Note: Ethnicity was coded "yes" if the respondent mentioned this type of ethnic background when furnishing an open-ended response to the question "In addition to being American, what do you consider your main ethnic group or nationality group?"

occasions. Recall that if mismeasurement were the sole source of opinion change, we should obtain the same log-odds statistic regardless of how much time elapsed between interviews.

That is in fact what we observe in Table 3.9 for both measures of social class. The log-odds ratios for whether a person ever thinks of himself or herself as "being in one of the classes" is abysmally low but largely invariant as to time frame (0.67 for 1965–73 and 0.74 for 1965–82). Stronger but unchanging log-odds ratios hold for whether one identifies oneself as working or middle class: 2.10 for 1965–73 and 2.18 for 1965–82. Murky though respondents' answers seem to be, the underlying sense of identification seems to be highly stable over time. The fact that these measures of association decline slowly over time suggests that one's sense of social class is quite stable, once we take into account the difficulty of measuring this identity using survey questions. These findings make sense in light of other research that suggests the American public's reluctance to use class labels while underscoring its attentiveness to markers of social class (Jackman and Jackman 1983).

Note that this pattern of stability emerges also as we turn our attention to religious and party identification. Transition between Protestant and non-Protestant categories is rare, and the rate at which it occurs climbs slowly over time. The log-odds ratios are 6.87 for 1965–73 and 6.55 for 1965–82. Republican identification follows a similar pattern. For the period 1965–73, the log-odds ratio is 3.60, compared with 3.55 for the full 1965–82 period.

We have therefore come full circle to the theme with which this chapter started: Identification with a political party is analogous to identification with religious, class, or ethnic groups. To be sure, these broad categories encompass identifications that vary in depth and persistence. Identification as Italian American seems to run more deeply than identification as English American, and presumably the same holds for certain intradenominational distinctions as well. Party identification falls somewhere in the middle of this spectrum. At the same time, all of these affiliations tend to be quite different from evaluations of political parties and leaders. How one feels about figures in the political environment changes much more rapidly than how one classifies oneself in terms of broad social categories.

INTERGENERATIONAL TRANSMISSION

Consistent with the notion that people harbor party attachments that endure over time is the remarkable persistence of geographic patterns of party cleav-

Table 3.9. Persistence in Religious, Class, and Party Identification, 1965–73–82

	Protestant Identification in 1965		Ever Think of Being in a Social Class, 1965		Social Class Identification, 1965		Republican Identification, 1965	
	No	Yes	No	Yes	Middle Class	Working Class	No	Yes
In 1973?								
No	229	19	72	113	288	128	564	45
Yes	8	639	158	484	76	276	67	196
Log-odds	6.87		0.67		2.10		3.60	
In 1982?								
No	229	23	81	127	298	123	556	52
Yes	9	631	133	435	84	307	58	189
Log-odds	6.55		0.74		2.18		3.55	

age. Authors such as Key (1949) and Sundquist (1973) have demonstrated how states as similar ethnically and economically as New Hampshire and Vermont can acquire and retain very different party complexions. It seems clear that coalitions formed in one era may shape party attachments many years later, even after the coalitions and the politicians who forged them have passed away. Because these geographic patterns sometimes last longer than an individual's political lifetime, it is natural to suppose that party attachments are handed down from one generation to the next.

Tracing political attachments across generations is exceedingly difficult, and only one panel survey enables us to compare the party identities of children with those of one of their parents.[12] As noted above, both parents and children were first interviewed in 1965. The children in this initial survey were seventeen years old, and their parents were typically in their mid-forties. The children were most recently interviewed in 1997 at age forty-nine. Thus, in the 1997 survey, the children were approximately the same age as their parents had been during the mid-1960s.

Table 3.10 presents the correspondence between the social identities of parents and children. The parents' partisan identities in 1965 are compared with those of their children in 1973, 1982, and 1997. In young adulthood, the attachments of parents and children correspond closely. In 1973, for example, the offspring of Republican parents were 4.4 times more likely to call themselves Republicans than the offspring of Democratic parents. But the correspondence diminishes with time. By 1997, the children of Republican parents are just 1.6 times more likely to become Republicans themselves, a pattern that does not change appreciably when we exclude respondents from the South or correct for measurement error. This relationship is not trivial, but neither is it overwhelming.

Nor is this relationship impressive when compared with another social identity, religious affiliation. Table 3.11 shows the association between parents' religion as measured in 1965 and their children's religion as measured in 1997. We see that 87% of the children of Protestant parents later called themselves Protestant, and 71% of the children of Catholic parents later identified as Catholic. Reminiscent of the role of political Independents as a middle ground is the category of people who harbor no religious affiliation. Protestants are more likely to have children who later identify with no religion than call themselves Catholic. Similarly, the offspring of Catholics are more likely to identify with no religion than to become Protestant. But compared with partisanship, religious affiliations tend not to drift across generations, and even the "no religion" category attracts just a small fraction of those whose parents affiliated with a religion.

Table 3.10. Parent-to-Child Transmission of Party Identification

Offspring's Party Identification	Parent's Party Identification in 1965		
	Democrat	Independent	Republican
1973			
Democrat	52%	32%	17%
Independent	42%	51%	51%
Republican	7%	17%	31%
	101%	100%	99%
1982			
Democrat	45%	27%	12%
Independent	42%	54%	47%
Republican	13%	19%	41%
	100%	100%	100%
1997			
Democrat	41%	28%	17%
Independent	31%	48%	39%
Republican	28%	24%	45%
	100%	100%	101%
N	268	144	179

Note: Column percentages may not sum to 100% because of rounding error.

Table 3.11. Parent-to-Child Transmission of Religious Affiliation

Offspring's Religious Affiliation	Parent's Religious Affiliation in 1965				
	Protestant	Catholic	Jewish	Other	None
1997					
Protestant	87%	8%	8%	21%	50%
Catholic	3%	71%	0%	5%	10%
Jewish	0%	0%	83%	0%	0%
Other	2%	5%	0%	58%	20%
None	7%	16%	8%	16%	30%
	99%	100%	99%	100%	100%
N	383	121	24	19	10

Note: Column percentages may not sum to 100% because of rounding error. The "Other" category comprises Orthodox, nontraditional Christians, Muslims, and non-Western religions.

These findings place important limits on what one can claim on behalf of party attachments. Although teenagers are strongly influenced by their parents' party affinities, this imprint fades over time as young adults are exposed to other influences and develop their own views. No more than one-third of the variance among middle-age individuals can be predicted by one of their parents' party identities; indeed, of the 189 offspring who called themselves Republican in 1997, 74 were raised by Democratic parents and 80 by Republican parents. Authors such as Sears et al. (1980) may go too far in characterizing party identification as a "symbolic" attachment that is acquired through pre-adult socialization and therefore without an instrumental basis. To be sure, party identities reflect socialization experiences, but not to the same extent as religious identities, which are often instilled through a formal process of indoctrination and continually reinforced through religious worship. The party attachments of teenagers are much more informal and tenuous, and a much greater proportion of teenagers reach voting age without a sense of party affiliation. As Jennings and Niemi (1981) pointed out in their early analysis of these data, the parent-to-child transmission of party identification is most likely in households that actively discuss politics. But many households do not discuss politics in any sustained way.

Given that exposure to politics tends to begin later and occurs with less frequency than exposure to religion, it should not be surprising that party attachments undergo more change as people enter adulthood. This period is also one of rapid change, during which people are exposed to new social environments and ideas. For many, this is the first time that they have given any thought to the parties and their platforms or sorted out which groups are associated with which parties. As much as we would resist the claim that party identities change in the short run in response to campaigns, scandals, and recessions, we do not want to portray party identification as a fixed characteristic that is established early in life. As we will argue in Chapter 5, partisans remain open to new information, and one reason that generations develop different party attachments is that they arrive at different impressions of which groups comprise and typify Democrats and Republicans.

SUMMARY

Those who set out to study social identities in a quantitative fashion quickly discover that data are in short supply. Although social scientists and humanists display a special fascination for the topic of social identity, survey researchers have seldom tracked these identities over time. As a result, we lack the luxury of examining a broad range of social identities. Social class, ethnicity, religion, and party exhaust the list of social categories about which we have adequate longitudinal data. To our knowledge, multiwave panel studies have never tracked identities such as environmentalist, Southerner, feminist, Chicago Bears fan, and so forth. (Such questions are rare even among cross-sectional surveys.) For this reason, any attempt to situate partisan stability in relation to the stability of other social identities involves a certain amount of speculation.

Two broad propositions seem consistent with the available data. First, party identification and most other social identities are highly stable over time. There are of course exceptions. We have seen that certain ethnic groups represent very weak objects of identification, and the same is undoubtedly true of groups such as yuppies or the underclass, which exist solely as abstract social categories, have no internal structure as groups, and lack the wherewithal to mobilize their members. Partisan groups are quite different, because partisans comprise teams that compete against one another in an effort to control the state. Although not as organized as religious groups or as embedded in daily life as class groups, partisan groups nonetheless represent vivid points of social orientation for the electorate. Even people who do not identify with partisan groups know enough about them to recognize that they do not view them as objects of attachment.

Second, social identifications such as party attachment are more enduring than evaluations of organizations or people. Politics generates a steady stream of news about the behavior of politicians and parties, but rarely does this news influence the voter's sense of self. Again, there are important exceptions. The decision of a Democratic president to go to war against the Kaiser in 1917 seems thereafter to have put a Republican stamp on German-American voters. Disappointment with Jimmy Carter, anger over abortion policies and federal opposition to tax breaks for religious schooling, and Republican overtures to religious leaders drew evangelical Christians to the Republican Party under Ronald Reagan (Nesmith 1994). Proposition 187, the Republican-endorsed ballot measure in California that sought to curtail social services for immigrants, pushed Latinos in the Democratic direction. Rarely, however, does a catchall party in the American mold move dramatically in ways that symbolize its hostility to a particular social group.

The typical ebb and flow of political fortunes associated with scandal, war, and economic performance tend to have little enduring influence on the partisan identities of voters. And when these events do move partisans away from their long-term attachments, they tend to reequilibrate rapidly once the short-term tide has subsided. Nevertheless, short-term forces can have important repercussions for the partisan balance in the electorate. The political climate leaves an enduring imprint on new cohorts of voters who enter the electorate with weak party ties. Moreover, as we shall see in the next chapter, political fortunes favoring one party often persist for months or even years. Thus, the forces that pull partisans away from their long-term equilibria may produce subtle but sustained shifts in the partisan distribution. In the next chapter, we examine the aggregate consequences of individual-level change and cohort replacement.

Chapter 4 Partisan Stability:
Evidence from Aggregate Data

Because partisan attachments predict how individuals vote, the distribution of these attachments in the electorate has important consequences for election outcomes. Although the outcome of each election reflects the idiosyncrasies of personality, campaign events, and policy stances, it remains the case that candidates tend to fare better at the polls when their fellow partisans constitute a larger share of the electorate. We are surprised when Kansas elects a Democratic member of Congress, or West Virginia a Republican. And when the distribution of party identification changes over time in a region, we see profound changes in election outcomes.

This point is illustrated vividly by the partisan politics of the South. In the 1950s, the overwhelming majority of Southern voters called themselves Democrats, and Republican candidates seldom won seats in the U.S. House. Indeed, recognizing their slim chances of victory in these Democratic strongholds, few Republicans bothered to run at all. A half century later, the situation is reversed, and Democrats struggle to field viable candidates in Republican enclaves from South Carolina to Texas.

Table 4.1. How the Distribution of Party Identification Affected Presidential Voting, 1960 and 2000

	Percentage Voting for Kennedy in 1960	Percentage Voting for Gore in 2000	Percentage Voting for Gore if Party Identification Were Distributed as in 1960
Democrats	80.8	91.5	91.5
N	640	400	500[a]
Independents	45.6	41.8	41.8
N	298	380	233[a]
Republicans	6.8	7.7	7.7
N	459	312	359[a]
All voters	49.0	50.3	53.3[b]
N	1,397	1,092	

Note: Table presents results only from those who reported voting. Data are weighted by sample weights.
[a]Simulated Ns values.
[b]Simulated vote outcome.

The influence of partisanship on presidential election outcomes can be illustrated by a counterfactual exercise. The election of 2000 produced a dead heat between George W. Bush and Al Gore. Gore received 48.4% of the vote, to Bush's 47.9%, only to lose narrowly in the Electoral College. In this election, according to the NES survey, Gore received 92% of the vote from Democrats, 42% from Independents, and 8% from Republicans.[1] As shown in Table 4.1, these numbers resemble voting patterns in 1960, another close presidential contest between a sitting vice president, Richard Nixon, and a challenger, John F. Kennedy. Gore, although more successful in garnering votes from Democrats than Kennedy, labored under a disadvantage. Democrats comprised 37% of the voting electorate in 2000 compared with 46% in 1960. If the electorate of 2000 had the same balance of Democrats, Republicans, and Independents as the electorate of 1960, Gore would have won an additional 3% of the vote.

Although the forgoing example artificially assumes that nothing about the contestants would have changed in a different partisan environment, the basic point remains: The relative proportions of Democrats and Republicans can be quite important politically. The significance of the partisan balance, which MacKuen, Erikson, and Stimson (1989) have termed *macropartisanship,* is reflected in the intense scholarly interest in an array of interrelated research questions. How stable is the partisan balance, and to what extent does it change in the wake of economic downturns or political scandal? Are the misfortunes of the political parties inscribed in the allegiances of voters, and if so, for how long? If the aggregate distribution of partisanship varies over time, what does that suggest about the nature of individuals' party attachments?

In this chapter, we take a closer look at the behavior of partisanship in the aggregate. Using summary statistics on the ratio of Democrats to Republicans, we show that the distribution of partisanship evolves slowly over time, both during and between election campaigns. When times are good, the partisan balance tips gradually in favor of the party that controls the White House; when scandal or economic downturn erodes presidential popularity, the out-party draws more adherents. Aggregate time-series analysis, in other words, allows us to better understand the "time shocks" that we posited in our investigation of individual-level panel data. The microlevel and macrolevel processes fit together in a coherent fashion.

Described in this way, macropartisan movement conjures images of a public rationally choosing its partisan allegiances on the basis of expectations about party competence, but one must bear in mind the sluggish pace with which this process unfolds over time. In the last chapter, we saw that time shocks of appreciable size rarely turn up in panel data. The present chapter underscores this point, showing that the aggregate distribution of partisanship seldom shifts abruptly. Instead, change tends to occur gradually, so that only dramatic changes in party fortunes sustained over long stretches of time are sufficient to produce politically significant swings in the balance of Democrats and Republicans. Even so, we find changes in economic performance and presidential popularity alone to be insufficient explanations for what are generally termed realignments. Although both factors played an important role in the transformation of Northern party loyalties during the New Deal and Southern party loyalties during the 1980s, the partisan movement that occurred went beyond what can be explained by reference to short-term political conditions. To explain the magnitude of these changes, one must take into account the transformation of the social stereotypes of the parties, a theme to which we will return in Chapter 6.

This chapter begins with a discussion of how the partisan balance may be analyzed over time, both during and between elections. After touching upon a wide array of issues surrounding the measurement of aggregate partisanship, we examine whether it is linked statistically to changes in consumer sentiment and presidential approval. Our findings suggest that although partisanship does drift with political and economic circumstances, the extent and pace of partisan change are considerably smaller and slower than previous scholarship has suggested. Moreover, although economic and political evaluations are often credited with the growth in Republican identification during the 1980s, short-term evaluations explain a relatively small portion of this change in partisanship while incorrectly predicting large Democratic gains during the Clinton presidency. Taken together, the evidence suggests both the remarkable resilience of the partisan balance and the limited explanatory power of short-run evaluations. To account for large-scale transformations of party systems, one must look beyond economic performance and presidential approval to circumstances that fundamentally reshape the social imagery of the parties.

DATA AND MEASURES

The nature of macropartisan change is a subject of lively debate in which methodological questions often take center stage. The quality of the data and the way that they should be analyzed have been the subject of vigorous disagreement. In light of these debates, the natural starting point for any investigation of aggregate partisanship is a review of some of the issues surrounding definition, measurement, and statistical inference.

Macropartisanship, as conceived by MacKuen, Erikson, and Stimson (1989), is the percentage of Democrats divided by the percentage of Democrats and Republicans. Thus, if Democrats accounted for 30% of the adult population and Republicans 20%, macropartisanship would be calculated as 30/(30 + 20) = 60%. This operationalization has two noteworthy features. First, this formula omits self-defined Independents. This fact is often jarring to students of public opinion, in light of the extensive scholarship devoted to political independence. Although it is customary to view the mid-1960s as a high water mark for the Democrats, the computation of macropartisanship makes the mid- to late-1970s look even more propitious. Even though the latter period witnessed a decline in Democratic identification and growing ranks of Independents, the ratio of Democrats to Republicans reached its apogee during the 1970s. It turns out, however, that alternative definitions of macropartisanship (for example, the proportion of Democrats or the mean of a three-point scale) produce similar statistical results. Although reasonable people may disagree about whether macropartisan conditions were more favorable to the Democrats in the 1960s than the 1970s, more or less any definition of macropartisanship leads to similar conclusions about the pace of partisan change and the extent to which it relates to political conditions. Second, the operationalization proposed by

MacKuen, Erikson, and Stimson is the ratio of two percentages, and as such, it tends to amplify small changes in survey results. In the previous example, had the results been 32% Democrat and 18% Republican, the macropartisanship score would have jumped four percentage points to 64%. This arithmetic subtlety is important to bear in mind, for as we will see, even three- and four-point changes in macropartisanship rarely occur over short periods of time.

Another set of issues concerns the source of macropartisanship data. One impetus to the study of macropartisanship was the accumulation and accessibility of privately conducted national surveys. Organizations such as Gallup, Louis Harris & Associates, CBS, and Roper had for decades conducted surveys in which respondents were asked about their party attachments. For many years, these polls were disregarded by academics, who relied on the American National Election Studies, which had much higher response rates and, arguably, more scientifically defensible sampling procedures. But as pressure mounted for researchers to study partisanship between elections as well as during campaigns, they became increasingly interested in private polls. Although the sampling methods of these polls have remained a cause for concern, the polls nonetheless provide an opportunity for studying change over time, on the grounds that sampling biases remain more or less constant.

The seminal work of MacKuen, Erikson, and Stimson (1989) used data gathered by the Gallup Organization, whose polls have regularly assessed party identification since the 1940s. The findings of this study, however, were immediately challenged by Abramson and Ostrom (1991), who pointed out that Gallup used a distinctively worded question to measure party identification. Rather than prefacing the party identification query with the phrase "Generally speaking, do you usually think of yourself . . . ," the Gallup question asked, "In politics, as of today, do you consider yourself . . . ." Abramson and Ostrom contend that the short-term focus of the Gallup question biases the results in favor of findings that show instability and responsiveness to political conditions. This dispute generated a wave of subsequent studies examining the consequences of question wording. Of particular interest is the macropartisanship series based on surveys conducted by CBS/New York Times, which relied on the traditional "generally speaking" wording. Compared with the Gallup Polls, CBS polls proved to be somewhat less responsive to changes in presidential approval. So in keeping with previous research, we will rely primarily on the Gallup measures but use CBS/New York Times polls for the purposes of corroboration.

The macropartisanship time series tends to be constructed using quarterly time units. The reason is that neither Gallup nor CBS polls are conducted at regular monthly intervals; in fact, many months have no polls at all. This limitation also applies to measures of consumer sentiment, which have been conducted monthly going back only to the 1970s. One advantage of aggregating the data into quarterly units is that it reduces random sampling fluctuation by lumping together thousands of surveys conducted during each quarterly interval. A disadvantage is that aggregation muddies the timing of the causal interplay between short-term events and macropartisanship. It turns out, however, that more sophisticated statistical methods designed to grapple with sampling error and unevenly spaced data (see Green, Gerber, and De Boef 1999) yield substantively similar results. Thus, although it is possible to increase the statistical complexity with which these data are analyzed, we are convinced that relatively simple methods convey much the same story.

Finally, the analysis of long time series of opinion data is hampered by changes in survey methodology over time. One of the most significant changes has been the replacement of face-to-face interviewing with surveys conducted over the telephone. Although some surveys, such as the CBS/New York Times survey, have been conducted by phone throughout their history, the Gallup survey switched from face-to-face interviewing to predominantly phone interviewing during the mid-1980s. Thus, to construct a time series that links the period of face-to-face interviewing to phone interviewing, one must take into account the fact that Gallup's phone surveys consistently portray the public as more Republican than Gallup's face-to-face surveys conducted at approximately the same time. After analyzing periods during which Gallup used both kinds of surveys, we estimate this bias to be approximately three points, and the macropartisanship series we present has been adjusted to reflect the change in survey methodology.

The quarterly Gallup macropartisanship series is graphed in Figure 4.1 for the period covering the first quarter of 1953 through the fourth quarter of 1999.[2] Figure 4.1 encapsulates much of American political history for the second half of the twentieth century. The series begins with the sweeping Republican victory of 1952. Late in Eisenhower's term, the partisan balance began to tip in the Democratic direction. Democratic gains continued until 1966, when the Republicans regained lost ground. After Nixon's reelection in 1972, party identification became more Democratic, only to reverse sharply after Carter took office in 1977. The Democratic edge receded until Republican advances were finally halted in 1985 at the same high water mark achieved under Eisen-

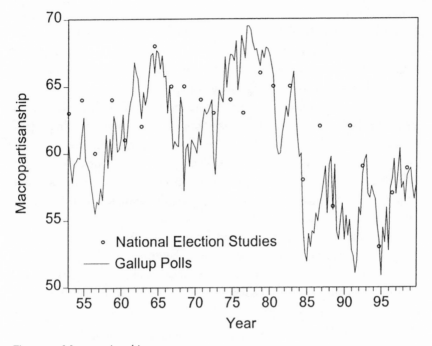

Figure 4.1. Macropartisanship, 1953–99.

hower in 1956. From that point, partisanship remained more or less stationary, with the Democrats holding a slight edge.

For purposes of comparison, Figure 4.1 also shows the macropartisanship scores derived from the biennial NES surveys. It is interesting to note that for those quarters in which both Gallup and NES data are available, the NES data are much less variable over time even though the NES surveys have fewer respondents and should therefore be more prone to sampling variability. Between 1952 and 1998, macropartisanship scores derived from biennial NES surveys have a standard deviation of 3.5, as opposed to 4.3 for Gallup surveys conducted during the corresponding quarters ($N = 24$). Again, without denying that partisanship changes over time, we would point out that the Gallup series tends to amplify the magnitude of these changes.

What do the changes charted in Figure 4.1 tell us about the persistence of partisan attachments? It is important to bear in mind certain inherent ambiguities that arise in the interpretation of aggregate time series. Unlike surveys that reinterview a certain group of people over time, aggregate studies look at a series of surveys, each of which interviews different people. Thus, aggregate data cannot tell us whether individuals have changed their minds or whether the composition of the population has changed because of immigration and generational replacement. To the extent that aggregate changes do reflect individual opinion change, the magnitude of opinion change remains unclear. From Figure 4.1 alone, we cannot tell whether all voters changed their opinions slightly or just a few voters changed dramatically.

Given the uncertainties of interpretation, the study of macropartisanship is best viewed as a supplement to the analysis of panel data presented. In the previous chapter, we saw that microlevel time series have very little "memory." Although individuals are occasionally buffeted by political events, they tend to snap back to their long-term partisan proclivities over the course of a few months. If so, why does the graph of macropartisanship occasionally wander away from its long-term mean?

Part of the answer may be generational replacement, for as Table 4.2 indicates, young voters entered the electorate in the 1980s with more Republican zeal than the typical respondent who was interviewed in the 1960s or 1970s. This pattern continued into the 1990s; indeed, the age cohort born during the

Table 4.2. Macropartisanship by Birth Cohort, American National Election Studies

	Decade of Survey				
Birth Year	1952–58	1960–68	1970–78	1980–88	1990–98
1900–1909	0.588	0.649	0.625	0.589	0.570
	(740)	(922)	(929)	(401)	(123)
1910–19	0.686	0.660	0.620	0.642	0.627
	(977)	(1,128)	(1,233)	(784)	(497)
1920–29	0.667	0.669	0.664	0.632	0.643
	(910)	(1,205)	(1,285)	(866)	(754)
1930–39	0.716	0.670	0.608	0.617	0.612
	(313)	(960)	(1,067)	(809)	(689)
1940–49		0.685	0.669	0.627	0.586
		(321)	(1,464)	(1,116)	(886)
1950–59			0.700	0.575	0.577
			(824)	(1,354)	(1,286)
1960–69				0.562	0.531
				(653)	(1,152)
1970–79					0.517
					(442)

Note: The number of partisans on which the macropartisanship score was computed is shown in parentheses.

1970–79 period was the most Republican of any age group tracked over five decades of NES surveys. Meanwhile, those born between 1910 and 1939 scarcely moved at all on a decade-by-decade basis between 1970 and 1998. Even so, generational replacement can go only so far as an explanation. When age cohorts are tracked over time, one sees short-term movement in their party attachments, particularly when the groups are broken down by region (see Chapter 6). Although the pattern is uneven in Figure 4.1, there appears to be a tendency toward increasing Republican identification after 1980. Thus, macropartisan change seems to be a blend of opinion change and cohort replacement.

To link partisan change at the microlevel and macrolevel in the short run (which for our purposes refers to spans of two years or less—the length of time between national elections), we hypothesize that the causes of microlevel change themselves tend to linger over time. Although economic performance, for example, exerts transitory effects, its influence is felt quarter after quarter, as economic recessions and recoveries gradually unfold. The Zeitgeist of the moment shapes the partisan proclivities of young voters, who have yet to acquire a firm partisan attachment, while at the same time drawing older voters away from their long-term equilibrium, albeit only slightly. The net result of these processes is that the partisan balance strays from its historical average. To assess this characterization, we must take a closer look at the process of partisan adjustment. To what extent do short-term forces such as presidential approval and consumer sentiment shape the partisan complexion of the electorate?

SOURCES OF MACROPARTISAN CHANGE

The central hypothesis of the macropartisanship literature is that presidential popularity, as well as the favorable economic conditions that contribute to it, bring new adherents to the president's party. This conjecture grows out of several theoretical perspectives on the sources of partisan change. Those who regard partisan attachments as retrospective "running tallies" (Fiorina 1981) would naturally expect the economic and political climate to alter party loyalties, as voters reward or punish officeholders on the basis of past performance. Similarly, if party identification is taken to be an expression of which party the public expects to perform best in the future (Achen 1992), past performance serves as an important guide to future expectations. Finally, those who contend that party identification summarizes an individual's ideological proximity to the parties might plausibly expect shifts in presidential approval to induce partisan change, on the grounds that the public rates the president on the basis of what he stands for programmatically. Thus, although we would predict that macropartisanship will change little in the wake of changing political and economic conditions—except insofar as the social images of the parties change concomitantly—critics of the traditional view contend that partisanship is responsive to short-term forces.

The independent variables conventionally used to explain macropartisan change are consumer sentiment and presidential approval, measures that date back several decades. Because theories about party evaluations hinge on voters' subjective understanding of the state of the economy, previous analysts have tended to shy away from hard economic indicators, such as inflation, unemployment, or real disposable income. Instead, they use the University of Michigan's Consumer Sentiment Index, which dates back to 1953. This scale ranges from zero to 200. When compiled quarterly from 1953 through 1999, its mean is 87.9, and its standard deviation, 11.4. The fact that measures of macropartisanship and consumer sentiment are drawn from different polling houses bolsters the analysis because the sampling errors of one time series are unlikely to be repeated in the other. The same cannot be said of analyses that examine how macropartisanship changes with presidential approval; the measure of the latter is also derived from Gallup Polls. As we point out below, there is some indication that this fact may itself inflate the correlation between macropartisanship and approval (Green, Palmquist, and Schickler 1998).[3]

When attention is drawn to the twists and turns in the macropartisanship series by itself, as in Figure 4.1, it is easy to lose sight of the fact that it is one of the most stable aggregate time series in American politics. Turning to Figure 4.2, we see that macropartisanship looks quite placid compared with the percentage of the public that approves of the president's performance in office. Presidential approval has a standard deviation of 11.6 and occasionally swings by more than thirty percentage points in the span of a year. By contrast, macropartisanship has a standard deviation of 4.5, and two-thirds of the observations during the past half century have fallen within the range of 55% to 65%. The sole exception to the generalization that macropartisanship seldom moves very fast or very far occurs during the first Reagan administration, when macropartisanship fell from 66% during the end of the 1982–83 recession to 52% immediately after Reagan's reelection. As we point out in the next chapter, during this period the South experienced its long-awaited transformation into a two-party system. Were we to restrict attention to areas other than the South, partisan change would be less dramatic.

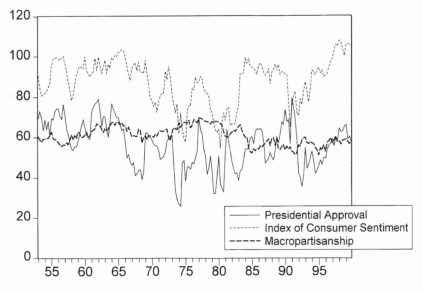

Figure 4.2. Macropartisanship, presidential approval, and consumer sentiment, 1953–99.

From Figure 4.2, we see that the ups and downs of the economy and presidential popularity bear some relationship to the undulation of the macropartisanship series. As we examine both interadministration and intra-administration changes in presidential approval ratings, we find that the more popular a sitting president, the more attractive his party as an object of identification. Reagan's travails during the early years of his administration propped up Democratic partisanship, and his rebound after 1983 rekindled its long-term decline. Lyndon Johnson's declining popularity from 1964 to 1968 coincided with a gradual erosion of the Democratic edge in partisanship. The link between presidential approval and partisanship is by no means exact, however. Nixon's steep drop in popularity during his second administration appears to have had little effect, as does the transition from a disgraced Nixon in 1974 to a more popular Gerald Ford or Carter's fall from public favor in 1977–78.

Because consumer sentiment and presidential popularity track so closely, it is difficult to disentangle their effects visually, but it seems that the party in power benefits from an atmosphere of economic optimism. The erosion of consumer confidence under Johnson, Ford, and Carter seemed to drive voters away from their respective parties. The recoveries of the early 1950s, 1970s, and 1980s, by contrast, coincided with growing ranks of Republican identifiers, and the strong economy of the early 1960s seemed to help the Democrats. Fig-

ure 4.2, in sum, suggests a link between consumer outlook and party affiliation.

To gauge more systematically whether changes in political and economic
evaluations lead to change in macropartisanship, we start with a simple time-
series regression model linking consumer sentiment to macropartisanship.
Later, we will introduce presidential popularity as well, but for the purposes of
exposition, let us keep the initial model as simple as possible:

$$\text{Macropart}_t = a + b(\text{Macropart}_{t-1}) + c(\text{Consumer Sentiment}_t \\ \times \text{Party}_t) + d(\text{Party}_t) + u_t \qquad (4.1)$$

In this equation, time is indexed by the quarterly subscript t. Macropartisanship is a function of three observable factors: its past values, consumer sentiment, and the party of the incumbent president. To accommodate the fact that
prosperity increases or decreases Democratic partisanship depending on which
party holds the presidency, we multiply consumer sentiment by party, which is
scored -1 for Republican and 1 for Democrat. Transformed in this way, rising
consumer confidence would be expected to bolster macropartisanship, regardless of which party controls the White House. At the end of the equation is the
disturbance term (u_t), which encompasses all sources of partisan change other
than consumer sentiment and past partisanship (for example, generational replacement, immigration, noneconomic evaluations, and the like).

The parameter b determines the rate at which a perturbation to the macropartisanship series dissipates over time. When $b = 1$, disturbances never decay.
Imagine, for example, that macropartisanship stands at 50%. One day, a group
of Republican immigrants is naturalized, causing the macropartisan balance to
drop to 49%. If $b = 1$, this new group should permanently alter macropartisanship; absent any further disturbances, macropartisanship will remain at
49%. On the other hand, if $b = 0$, macropartisanship immediately reequili-
brates to its preexisting state after a perturbation. To continue the previous example, one could imagine the Democratic Party making special overtures to
immigrants so that the next round of naturalization restores the equilibrium of
50%.

Intuitively, the scenario in which $b = 1$ seems more plausible. Newly minted
Democrats and Republicans are likely to remain so, and parties can only do so
much to restore a preexisting equilibrium. By contrast, it seems unlikely that b
should be exactly one, for there would be no tendency to return to equilibrium.
If macropartisanship follows such a "random walk," the distribution of partisanship at some point would become very lopsided, implying that a minority

party does nothing to rehabilitate its deteriorating image. The very fact that macropartisanship has for decades fallen within a narrow range of Democratic advantage is inconsistent with the frequently discussed hypothesis that $b = 1$. (Random walks with as much short-term movement as macropartisanship rarely hover between 50% and 70% for so long.) Thus, before estimating b using regression analysis, our expectation is that this parameter is close to but somewhat less than one. Notice that this expectation is the opposite of what we found from our individual-level panel analysis in Chapter 3. At the individual level, β is approximately zero because each individual tends to return quickly to his or her personal baseline. But aggregate dynamics are altogether different because they reflect changes in the composition of the electorate and aggregate short-term forces that temporarily push the distribution of partisanship in one direction before slowly reequilibrating.

Regression also enables us to estimate c, the immediate effect of observed economic evaluations. When c is different from zero, the model implies that macropartisanship changes in response to short-term shifts in economic conditions. Any change to macropartisanship at one point in time affects future values of macropartisanship, so a one-unit shift in economic conditions changes macropartisanship by cb^k during the kth quarter after the shift occurred. The higher the value of b, the more long-lasting the effects of changing economic evaluations. Because effects persist, care must be taken when interpreting the regression results. If an economic downturn lasts several quarters, the cumulative influence of eroding consumer sentiment begins to add up. A convenient formula for calculating the cumulative effect of a *permanent* one-unit shift in consumer sentiment is $c/(1 - b)$. When $b = 0$, the cumulative effect is simply c. When $b = 1$, the cumulative effects become infinite. For intermediate ranges of b, this formula provides a handy upper bound on the magnitude of the effect of consumer sentiment on the macropartisan distribution.

Table 4.3 presents the results of this regression model. The estimated autoregressive parameter (b) is 0.92, which means that 8% of any perturbation to macropartisanship dissipates after one quarter. Macropartisanship gradually returns to its long-term equilibrium in the wake of a short-term event. Over the course of a four-year presidential term, however, just $0.92^{16} = 26\%$ of a disturbance remains. Disturbances are all but forgotten over an eight-year span, as just 7% of the original effect persists. This pattern of slow equilibration contrasts with the rapid equilibration that we saw at the individual level in Chapter 3. Individual voters return rapidly to their own long-term means in the wake of a disturbance. Aggregate dynamics reflect also the replacement of indi-

Table 4.3. Effects of Consumer Sentiment
on Macropartisanship, 1953–99

	Estimate
Macropartisanship, lagged on quarter	0.92
	(0.03)
Party (-1 = Republican, 1 = Democrat)	-2.36
	(1.08)
Michigan Consumer Sentiment Index $\times$ party	0.027
	(0.012)
Constant	4.94
	(1.83)
Adjusted R^2	0.84

Note: N = 188, based on quarterly data from the first quarter of 1953 through the fourth quarter of 1999. Macropartisanship is measured using Gallup Polls. Entries are coefficients, with standard errors in parentheses.

viduals within the population and the minting of new partisans, particularly among young citizens.

The short-term influence of consumer sentiment (c) is estimated to be 0.027. This estimate is statistically significant but small. A swing of two standard deviations in consumer sentiment (22.8 index points) produces a change of just three-fifths of a percentage point in macropartisanship during that quarter. Only very large economic shocks sustained over a long time are sufficient to alter the partisan balance. For example, suppose consumer sentiment drops 22.8 points below its mean and remains there for two years. Macropartisanship would be expected to shift by 3.7 points. After ten years of this economic misery, the macropartisan balance would tip by 7.4 points. Although a macropartisan shift of this magnitude is not trivial, neither is it immense.

Actual economic cycles, thankfully, seldom take the form of economic catastrophe. More typical economic swings are too short-lived to exert their maximal effects on public opinion. The deep recession and strong recovery that occurred during Reagan's first term, for example, saw consumer sentiment drop to 66 at the end of 1981. In 1983, the economy suddenly rebounded, and consumer sentiment surged upward by approximately 28 points and remained in the 90s until fall of 1990. According to the estimates in Table 4.3, the well-below-average performance of the economy in Reagan's early years caused macropartisanship to shift in a Democratic direction from 57 to 61, whereas the slightly above-average economy after the recovery brought macropartisanship back down to 58. Notice that these predicted changes fail to correspond to the extraordinary change that actually occurred. Between the first quarter of 1983 and the first quarter of 1985, macropartisanship dove from 65 to 52. Although this abrupt change in the partisan complexion of the electorate is often attributed to the economic conditions of the time, the regression estimates of Table 4.3 suggest that only a fraction of this change can be attributed to economic recovery.

Economic conditions, of course, are just one sort of short-term influence contributing to partisan change. A more inclusive accounting of political fortunes may be made using presidential approval, which has been shown to reflect not only the economy but also the state of foreign affairs, scandal, and personal esteem in which the president is held. Following MacKuen, Erikson, and Stimson (1989), our regression model grows to

$$\text{Macropart}_t = a + b(\text{Macropart}_{t-1}) + c(\text{Consumer Sentiment}_t \times \text{Party}_t) + g(\text{Approval}_t \times \text{Party}_t) + d(\text{Party}_t) + u_t \qquad (4.2)$$

In this expanded model, g represents the immediate influence of presidential approval, net of consumer sentiment and past macropartisanship.

Table 4.4 shows that when presidential approval is added to the model, the effects of economic conditions vanish. Economic conditions matter because

Table 4.4. Effects of Consumer Sentiment and Presidential Approval on Macropartisanship, 1953–99

	Model 1	Model 2
Macropartisanship, lagged one quarter	0.88	0.87
	(0.03)	(0.03)
Party (-1 = Republican, 1 = Democrat)	-2.57	-2.41
	(0.66)	(1.06)
Michigan Consumer Sentiment Index × party		-0.003
		(0.015)
Presidential approval × party	0.047	0.049
	(0.012)	(0.015)
Constant	7.56	4.75
	(1.88)	(1.58)
Adjusted R^2	0.85	0.85

Note: $N = 188$, based on quarterly data from the first quarter of 1953 through the fourth quarter of 1999. Macropartisanship is measured using Gallup Polls. Entries are coefficients, with standard errors in parentheses.

they influence presidential popularity; they have no direct effect of their own. This point is important to bear in mind when extrapolating to other time periods, such as the Great Depression, for we may calculate the effects of short-term conditions by reference to either consumer sentiment or the popularity of the president. By encompassing both economic and other short-term forces, presidential approval represents a more proximal cause of partisan change.

Looking more closely at the effects of presidential approval, we find them to be statistically significant and moderate in size. The slope estimate is 0.049, which implies that a change in approval of two standard deviations (23.2 percentage points) translates into an immediate 1.1 percentage-point change in macropartisanship. Again, it is apparent that appreciable movement in macropartisanship requires the political climate to change dramatically over long stretches of time. Were a surge in approval of 23.2 percentage points to be sustained over two years, macropartisanship would shift by 5.9 points. After ten years, macropartisanship would move by 8.7 points—important, but not overwhelming.

These estimated effects become even weaker when we make allowances for the fact that the presidential approval measure is also drawn from the same Gallup Polls. If these polls draw unusually Democratic samples during a given quarter, approval too will be biased in a Democratic direction. One way to correct this problem is to use an alternative measure of macropartisanship, gathered by a different survey organization. As noted above, CBS polls have the advantage of using the "generally speaking" wording of the partisanship question; the drawback is that they date back only to 1976 rather than 1953. Reestimating equation 4.2 for the period 1976–99 using both Gallup and CBS macropartisanship data, we find dramatic differences in the apparent influence of presidential approval (Table 4.5). For example, whereas the Gallup macropartisanship measure generates an estimate of 0.054 for presidential approval, CBS produces a coefficient of just 0.020. Apparently, the practice of using Gallup surveys to measure both the independent and dependent variables gives an exaggerated account of the short-term fluidity of partisan attachments.

Another important reason to suspect that the estimates of Tables 4.3 and 4.4 overstate the effects of short-term forces goes beyond issues of question wording, sampling artifacts, and model choice. Since MacKuen, Erikson, and Stimson (1989) brought these trends to the attention of the discipline, scholars have returned to them again and again, continually reanalyzing the same period. This is a common problem in the statistical analysis of time series and often causes analysts to overfit the idiosyncrasies of a particular set of data—that is, analysts mold regression models to follow the twists and turns observed over a

Table 4.5. Effects of Short-Term Forces on Gallup and CBS Measures of Macropartisanship, 1976–99

	CBS Polls	Gallup Polls
Macropartisanship, lagged one quarter	0.96	0.92
	(0.02)	(0.04)
Party (-1 = Republican, 1 = Democrat)	-1.07	-1.98
	(0.86)	(1.20)
Michigan Consumer Sentiment Index $\times$ party	0.001	-0.010
	(0.012)	(0.017)
Presidential approval $\times$ party	0.020	0.054
	(0.015)	(0.020)
Constant	2.39	4.59
	(1.44)	(2.20)
One-period moving average	-0.62	-0.19
	(0.09)	(0.11)
Adjusted R^2	0.80	0.88

Note: $N = 96$, based on quarterly data from the first quarter of 1976 through the fourth quarter of 1999. Entries are coefficients, with standard errors in parentheses. The moving average specifications correct for the possibility of sampling error in the measurement of macropartisanship.

stretch of time, forgetting that the purpose of time-series regression is to estimate the parameters *a, b,* and *c.* The most common symptom of overfitting is that models developed to analyze a particular time period perform badly when applied to new data points. Put somewhat differently, there is little surprise in finding a statistically significant correlation between economic conditions and macropartisanship in the 188 quarterly observations covering the period 1953–99. After all, the first 140 observations in our data set inspired the initial report by MacKuen, Erikson, and Stimson, and the first 176 observations were analyzed by Erikson, MacKuen, and Stimson (1998) and Green, Palmquist, and Schickler (1998). To gauge the validity of these studies, we must examine how well they forecast observations that come in after the ink has dried.

In many ways, the period after 1989 makes for a telling test of the hypothesis that partisanship is shaped by "fundamental" economic and political conditions (Erikson, MacKuen, and Stimson 1998). George Bush's popularity soared and plummeted, and the economy went in and out of recession. For the first time in decades, a Democratic president presided over a period of sustained economic growth. According to the estimates in Table 4.4, Democratic partisanship as registered in Gallup surveys should have soared to levels reminiscent

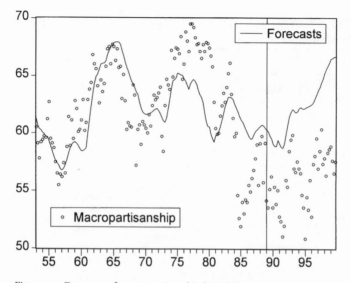

Figure 4.3. Forecasts of macropartisanship based on consumer sentiment and presidential approval, using data from 1953 to 1988.

of the 1960s. As Figure 4.3 illustrates, forecasts generated by model 2 in Table 4.4 based on data for the period 1953–88 suggest that in 1999:4 Gallup macropartisanship was expected to be 67. Economic fundamentals were as good as they had ever been, and Clinton had presided over good times for many years. Add to this the fact that the waning years of the Bush administration saw a fair amount of anxiety about the economy, and the result is a predicted eight-point shift in the Democratic direction between 1990 and 1999. In fact, the Democrats picked up fewer than three points during this period. At the close of 1999, Gallup macropartisanship stood at 57.5, which is scarcely different from the 56.9 recorded at the beginning of Clinton's second term. Contrary to the model's predictions, Democratic partisanship has failed to rise with strong economic growth and a long string of solid presidential approval scores. The farther one strays from the data that first inspired the macropartisanship literature, the more inaccurate the out-of-sample forecasts become.[4]

Flawed out-of-sample forecasts suggest that the link between macropartisanship and political conditions may be more muted than originally thought. Although it is no doubt true that it is easier to attract adherents to the Democratic Party when it presides over good times, what is remarkable is the *limited* extent to which party identification responds to the political environment. By way of comparison, the median change in presidential approval over the course of one quarter was 3.3 percentage points during the period 1953–99. (Remember that presidential approval is scored as "percentage approving," which makes it less susceptible to movement than macropartisanship, which is percentage of *partisans* who call themselves Democrats.) The median quarterly change in the Gallup macropartisanship measure was 1.2 points, of which at most 0.3 points is explained by change in consumer sentiment and presidential approval using the coefficients in Tables 4.3 and 4.4. One can well understand why party identification is often characterized as the ballast of the electoral system.

REALIGNMENTS AND MACROPARTISAN ADJUSTMENTS ARE DIFFERENT IN KIND

These aggregate time-series results fit well with many of the themes developed in previous chapters. Consistent with our findings using individual-level survey data, aggregate data indicate that "time shocks" occasionally occur as the result of abrupt changes in presidential approval. At the same time, we find sizable time shocks to be rare. The Clinton presidency is an interesting case in point. In the 1990s, it was finally the Democrats' turn to reap the benefits of economic prosperity and a reasonably popular incumbent president, whose centrist policies after 1994 seemed ideally suited to win new party adherents. As it turned out, the balance of party attachments changed modestly during Clinton's second term in office, when the public maintained a consistently favorable view of both the economy and president. Without denying that macropartisanship is affected at the margins by short-term forces, we would underscore the fact that this relationship is less powerful than one would gather from much that is written on the topic.

THE NATURE OF REALIGNMENTS

Before MacKuen, Erikson, and Stimson's (1989) work on macropartisanship, students of electoral politics frequently used the term *realignment* to describe large shifts in party attachments. These shifts might occur within the electorate as a whole or among a restricted set of social groups; either way, realignment was regarded as a sea change in party affiliation, not merely an ebb and flow of small adjustments (Burnham 1970). MacKuen and his colleagues introduced a conception of party realignment as a continuous process. Every day, citizens update their attachments on the basis of current conditions. The implication is that big realignments and small realignments differ in degree, not in kind. What distinguishes them are the political and economic circumstances necessary to bring about fundamentally reorganized party attachments.

Our statistical results call into question the isomorphism of big and small realignments. Consider, for example, the realignment of party loyalties during the New Deal. As far as scholars can tell from the fragmentary evidence of voting patterns, the transformation of party identification seems to have occurred between 1926 and 1936, with the decisive Republican edge under Calvin Coolidge giving way to the decisive Democratic edge under Roosevelt. The stock market crash of 1929 and the ensuing depression undercut Herbert Hoover's popularity, which in turn weakened the standing of the Republican Party.[5] After Roosevelt's victory in 1932, his popularity continued to draw people into the ranks of the Democratic Party. By 1937, when some of the earliest surveys show a decisive Democratic advantage in party identification, the partisan balance had come to rest near the 60–65% mark, where it would remain for the next forty years. If we imagine that under Coolidge, 60–65% of the partisans were Republicans, this shift in partisan attachments amounts to something on the order of twenty to thirty points. What would it take to produce a macropartisan change of this magnitude?

To answer this question, we return to the estimates reported in Table 4.4, which give a maximal account of how much partisanship responds to short-term forces. Using these estimates, we can simulate how partisanship would have changed in response to Hoover's sliding popularity and Roosevelt's triumphant first term in office. Our scenario begins with Republicans as the predominant party. The system under Coolidge is presumed to be in equilibrium, with Coolidge's approval rating holding steady at 60%. By painting such a placid picture, we deliberately ignore any aspects of the Roaring Twenties that would have built up special goodwill toward the Republicans, in the spirit of trying to confect a Democratic realignment after the stock market crash. Hoover is assumed to enjoy the same 60% rating until the fourth quarter of 1929, when economic disarray erodes his popularity at a rate of 2.5 points per quarter, eventually bringing him to his nadir of 27.5% (just slightly above Nixon before his resignation). In 1933, Roosevelt takes office and maintains a steady stream of 80% approval ratings throughout his first term. Note that this stylized rendering of the New Deal realignment makes every effort to describe conditions in ways that would foster realignment. In fact, no president has ever recorded

80% for any year since Gallup Polls introduced modern sampling methods in the early 1950s. By the same token, the ratings posited for Hoover may be too low to account for the fact that he received more than 40% of the major party vote in the presidential election of 1932.

Nevertheless, it seems clear from Figure 4.4 that the realignment of the 1930s cannot be explained solely by reference to changes in presidential popularity. Using the estimates in Table 4.4, we find that this dramatic swing in political fortunes accounted for at most a twelve-point swing in macropartisanship, which is roughly half of what apparently occurred. This figure is reduced further when we draw parameter estimates from Table 4.5 based on our analysis of CBS data. The CBS estimates suggest a more gradual transition and one that never goes beyond a ten-point swing to the Democrats. Unless we are mistaken about the magnitude of the New Deal realignment, disapproval of Hoover, or enthusiasm for Roosevelt, it appears that the macropartisanship model can explain at most half of the apparent change. The transformation of partisan at-

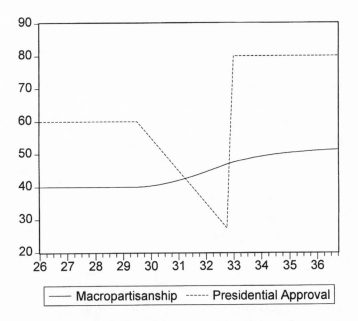

Figure 4.4. Simulated effects of changing presidential approval, 1926–36.

tachments during this period was more than a matter of voters rejecting a failed Republican president and embracing his Democratic successor.

Why, then, the profound shift in party loyalties? The social stereotypes associated with Democrats and Republicans as partisan groups seem to have changed fundamentally during this period. The partisan symbolism of the New Deal was more than mere rhetoric. Although Roosevelt ran for president in 1932 on a platform that emphasized fiscal responsibility and budget balancing, by 1936 he had launched programs that would altogether change the size and scope of the federal government. These programs would both reflect and galvanize the emergent Democratic coalition of Southerners, labor unions, minorities, and urban centers. As the party increasingly gave voice to these groups, Democrats came to regard themselves as forward-looking reformers whose governmental programs and regulations had the interests of ordinary citizens at heart. Although the New York wing of the Democratic Party had made considerable inroads during the 1920s, it was still the Republican Party that was home to progressives, Italians, Slavs, blacks, and many urban dwellers. By the end of the 1930s, however, the liberal wing of the Democratic Party had become its dominant image in the (Northern) public's mind. This new image did not take root overnight, and indeed the authors of *The American Voter* note with some amusement that as late as the 1950s, some of their respondents continued to revere the Republican Party as the party of Abraham Lincoln. Some states, such as Minnesota, did not experience a wholesale transformation in party loyalties until the 1940s, and some cities, such as Philadelphia, did not switch to the Democratic Party until the 1950s. Although local political conditions expedited or delayed the transformation of voter attachments, the older stereotypes of the parties' supporters eventually gave way.

Changing social images of the parties, of course, are not the only force that could produce this type of polarization. One could argue that people choose their parties on the basis of ideological affinity. Applied to the New Deal, this argument runs as follows: The economic dislocation of the early 1930s convinced the public that the welfare state and federal regulatory power must be expanded to an unprecedented degree. This program was championed by the Democratic Party but rejected by the Republicans, thereby drawing liberal voters into the Democratic fold. Meanwhile, the expansion of federal power drove away Western Democrats, who resented the meddlesome behavior of the federal government in local and regional affairs and lacked the race-based one-party system that maintained Democratic hegemony in the South.

Although we are in general skeptical of ideology-based explanations of party identification, the New Deal represents an instance in which such explanations work. Here was an unusually clear ideological divide between the parties, dramatized again and again as the Republicans denounced relief programs enacted by the Democratic executive and legislature. In the formative moment when the new party system emerged, and issues such as the scope of government replaced the tariff, it is quite possible that ideological affinity shaped party attachments to an unusual extent.

One sees this pattern in the aftermath of the collapse of the Italian political system during the early 1990s. When the Socialist and Christian Democratic parties dissolved and split, their identifiers gravitated to new parties that were similarly situated ideologically. Thus, when we asked party identifiers in 1997 to recall which party they had formerly belonged to in the old party system, we found that three-quarters of those who identified with the centrist parties (Christian Democratic Center [CCD], Christian Democratic Union [CDU], Italian Renewal [RI], Italian Popular Party [PPI], and Patto Segni) had formerly identified as Christian Democrats. By contrast, only a small proportion of identifiers with noncentrist parties (Communist Refoundation [RC], Democratic Party of the Left [PDS], Verdi [the Green Party], Lega Nord, and Fiamma Tricolore [MSFT]) were formerly Christian Democrats.

Ideological appeal and social identification are in many ways overlapping sources of party identification. As Brady and Sniderman (1985) argue, social groups and ideological labels may become fused in the public mind so that what looks like ideologically motivated reasoning is in fact achieved by reacting favorably or unfavorably to reference groups. During the late 1930s, Western Democrats may have drifted in the Republican direction because they neither agreed nor identified with the liberal Northeast wing of their party. Perhaps Westerners did not identify with Roosevelt Democrats because they were liberal. Perhaps Westerners did not agree with the liberals because they were composed of untrustworthy immigrant stock. Or perhaps it is the special combination of both ideological and social aversion that causes people to change their partisan identification, as opposed to remaining a marginalized faction within their long-standing party. Unfortunately, the fact that the New Deal antedates modern survey research prevents us from providing firm answers.

SUMMARY

Party identification reflects the political tenor of the times. The influences of the political environment are most noticeable among new voters, whose partisan attachments often bear the stamp of the political Zeitgeist that prevailed when they reached voting age or became naturalized citizens. But a president's popularity also shapes the attractiveness of his party in the eyes of older citizens. The triumphal Johnson of 1964 or Reagan of 1984 recruited partisan identifiers, whereas the Nixon of 1974 or Carter of 1980 repelled them. There can be no doubt that parties are well-advised to install popular leaders who preside over economic growth.

That said, the partisan attachments of the electorate are less fickle than is often assumed. Even presidents who are markedly more or less popular than the norm produce no more than gradual change in party attachments—unless something about their presidency fundamentally alters the social imagery associated with the parties. A classic instance of this sort of change is the passage of the Voting Rights Act of 1965. By reenfranchising Southern blacks and drawing them into the Democratic Party, the Voting Rights Act set in motion a transformation of social imagery. Southern white voters entering the electorate after 1965 were far less likely to think of themselves as Democrats than those entering the electorate before 1965. The answer to the question "What sort of person is a Democrat?" was up for grabs after 1965, and over the next thirty years, an increasing proportion of Southern whites would conclude "not me."

By contrast, Clinton did little to alter the social stereotypes of the parties. As prosperous as the United States was under the Clinton administration and notwithstanding his hollow declaration that the era of big government had ended, the social imagery of the Democratic Party was much the same at the end of his presidency as when he took office. Its ongoing slide in the South reached the point at which there were relatively few conservative white Democrats left to lose. The macropartisan balance returned to equilibrium, which is why the dramatic swings in political fortunes—Clinton's defeat on health care, the Republican juggernaut of 1994, the repeated shutdown of the federal government, Clinton's decisive reelection victory, his impeachment and acquittal—had little effect on party allegiances. Each of these developments, to be sure, affected the standing of one party or the other, but none led ordinary citizens to rethink the question, "What sorts of people are Democrats or Republicans?"

Chapter 5 Partisan Stability and Voter Learning

Our characterization of partisanship emphasizes the role of social identification. Based on their understanding of which groups support each party and their own affinity for these groups, many citizens come to see themselves as members of partisan groups in much the same way that certain people incorporate religious, regional, or ethnic groups into their self-conceptions. Partisan identities in adults typically persist because group stereotypes persist, and the location of the self amid various social groups persists.

Although persistence is the rule, partisan attachments may change as people acquire new information. Just what kinds of information are sufficient to produce partisan change is the subject of vigorous disagreement, one that turns on fundamental differences in the way that partisanship and voter psychology are understood. Our perspective stresses the importance of social group imagery and the ways that people attach themselves to groups, themes we will develop further in Chapters 6 and 7. To clear the way for this argument, we must first come to grips with two competing perspectives, both of which focus on the manner in which voters process new information about politics.

The first takes issue with the premise that party identification is a form of social identity, arguing instead that party identification reflects assessments about what the political parties are likely to deliver when in power. Voters who call themselves Republicans, by this account, are simply indicating their belief that the Republican Party is the party best suited to run the country to their satisfaction. If someday the Republican Party were to falter in ways that made some other party's stewardship more attractive, they would cease to be Republicans. By this account, party identification has little to do with social identities; stable party attachments must come from stable perceptions of what the parties will do in office. For ease of exposition, we will refer to this argument as the *revisionist interpretation.*

A second challenge derives from the work of those who first advanced the concept of party identification. These scholars frequently asserted that the stability of partisanship reflects a defensive psychological reaction whereby partisans resist political information that paints their group in a negative light. Party attachment, it is argued, functions as a "perceptual screen" filtering out news that would disrupt the social bond that links citizens to partisan groups. Thus, it is not simply that people have found a match between their group stereotypes and their self-images; in addition, people avoid or ignore information that fails to correspond to their preconceptions. Let us call this argument the *biased learning hypothesis.*

Both of these arguments draw attention to the manner in which voters assimilate new information about the parties. Whether party identification is a perceptual screen or shorthand for prospective evaluations of the parties' performance in office, the stability of party attachments follows from the premise that voters maintain their assessments of the parties over time. In this chapter, we examine how voters' party evaluations and party identifications evolve. We begin by explicating the revisionist argument and embedding it within a more general model of voter learning. This model suggests a number of testable propositions, and the middle section of this chapter shows the revisionist interpretation to be inconsistent with the way that voters in fact update their assessments of the parties.

Next, we turn our attention to the perceptual bias argument, which makes predictions that are at odds with our learning model. Reviewing the experimental and survey evidence, we find no support for the claim that partisans are unswayed by discordant information. This empirical claim bolsters Key's (1965) criticism of *The American Voter.* Arguing that Campbell et al. (1960) exaggerated the electorate's inattentiveness to public affairs, Key tried to show that the public was not so beholden to long-term attachments as to be unable to shift opinion in light of new facts. Whether one prefers to dub the public's capacity to update its opinions "responsible" (Key 1965), "reasonable" (Popkin 1991), or "rational" (Page and Shapiro 1992), the point remains that partisan ties do not prevent voters from learning.

Although this contention is at variance with the early conceptualization of party identification, excising the theory of biased learning in some ways bolsters the view that party identification is a true form of social identity. Partisans neither shed their attachments when their party performs poorly nor maintain their attachments by shutting out bad news. On the contrary, the public does take notice of political events, and news tends to affect Democrats and Republicans in similar ways. Seldom, however, does the political or economic environment change in ways that would impel Democrats and Republicans to relabel themselves. That partisans typically maintain their self-conceptions in the face of unflattering news suggests that these self-conceptions run deep.

REVISIONIST INTERPRETATIONS OF PARTY IDENTIFICATION

Scholarship on party identification has been greatly influenced by two works: *An Economic Theory of Democracy,* by Anthony Downs (1957), and *Retrospective Voting in American National Elections,* by Morris P. Fiorina (1981). Downs and Fiorina contend that identification with political parties grows out of voters' assessments of the parties' aims and abilities. Downs envisions voters as consumers who seek to maximize government's production of what they regard as attractive political outcomes at minimum cost to themselves. These thrifty citizens tend to invest a minimal amount of time and energy gathering political information. After all, voters seldom have the opportunity to determine single-handedly the outcome of an election or government decision, so it makes no sense for them to keep abreast of current affairs unless they happen to find politics entertaining. Party identification serves as a decision shortcut. Rather than continually assessing the merits of each party's candidates and policy stances, cognitive misers make a guess about which party better serves their interests and reassess this estimate when new information becomes readily available. In effect, party attachments stand in for a more thorough assessment of what kinds of benefits each party's policies and candidates are likely to provide.

Party identification, from this vantage point, is rooted in political perceptions, albeit ones that may be naïve or uninformed. Citizens care first and foremost about what the parties are likely to do in office and "identify" with the party that they perceive to be most congenial to their programmatic tastes. Identification, in this sense, has little to do with affinity for fellow partisans. Instead, "thinking of oneself as a Democrat" is interpreted to mean that one sides with Democrats ideologically.

Fiorina advances a related argument about the development of party attachments. Voters have little time or inclination to study politics closely and rely instead on their intuitive assessment of how public affairs are being managed, assessments that are based on readily available information about recessions or scandals. Partisanship represents a "running tally" of how each voter assesses the parties' performance in office. When citizens first encounter politics, they may inherit the partisan identities of their family and friends, but as they accumulate experience, their attachments come to reflect their assessments of how the parties have performed in office. Party identification, according to this characterization, is more analogous to presidential approval than to religious affiliation. Continually updated in light of current information, partisanship may undergo considerable change as events alter public confidence in each party or as changes in party leadership alter perceptions of the parties' policy stances and skill at managing public affairs.

Downs and Fiorina have profoundly shaped the way that scholars look at party identification, and their influence has grown in recent years. Tracing successive editions of leading texts such as the *Change and Continuity* series (Abramson, Aldrich, and Rohde 1982: 161; 1995: 247) or *Controversies in American Voting Behavior* (Neimi and Weisberg 1976: 310; 1993: 268), one finds increasing skepticism toward the traditional view of party identification. Whereas early editions of these texts stressed the affective bond between citizens and parties, more recent editions suggest that voters continually reassess the fit between their goals and what the parties have to offer.

In addition to shaping the conceptualization of partisanship, Downs and Fiorina set in motion a line of empirical research that endeavors to show how party identification moves with changing political and economic conditions. Following Downs, Jackson (1975) and Franklin and Jackson (1983) use individual-level survey data to show that partisanship is molded by ideological proximity to the parties. Fiorina (1981) and Brody and Rothenberg (1988) use panel surveys to argue that partisanship shifts with retrospective evaluations of how the incumbent party has managed national affairs, especially economic affairs.

For methodological reasons, the tide turned against this line of argument. In several previous works (Green and Palmquist 1990; Green 1991; Palmquist and

Green 1992; Schickler and Green 1995, 1997), we showed that the analysis of individual-level survey data is sensitive to various assumptions about measurement error and the flow of causation among the variables in a statistical model. When these assumptions are relaxed, the revisionist conclusions are reversed. Instead of demonstrating how partisanship changes with ideological affinity to the parties or with evaluations of performance in office, survey data attest to the long-term stability of partisanship in the face of changing political conditions. Our assessment of partisan change, as presented in Chapter 3, is that short-term political forces exert a weak and transitory influence on party identification.

Possibly as a consequence of these methodological critiques or simply because of a new fascination with aggregate time-series data, the production of revisionist studies of individual-level partisan change has slowed considerably. A small number of revisionist studies continue to find their way into print, but their analyses of survey data are as susceptible to the same methodological objections as those of their forebears. Looking at the literature as a whole, we are aware of no statistical studies that convincingly demonstrate that individuals' partisan attachments are profoundly influenced by the ebb and flow of political fortune.

The revisionist literature, however, switched course in the 1990s. During the 1970s and 1980s, revisionist scholars sought to predict and explain partisan instability. Deferring to the growing body of evidence attesting to the stability of partisan attachment, scholars have more recently sought to explain *stable* partisanship by reference to utility-maximizing voters. The most important work in this new genre is Christopher Achen's (1992) attempt to situate partisanship within a Bayesian model of voter learning. Characterizing voters as rational actors who efficiently update their party affiliations on the basis of new information, Achen demonstrated formally that a model of party identification could generate, among its empirical implications, stable partisanship among adults. Achen's important essay strengthened the revisionist case, allowing it to sidestep the issue of partisan stability, while at the same time supplying a mechanism for life-cycle effects that had previously been attributed to maturation (Alwin and Krosnick 1991). This rational actor model has been touted for its ability to explain a wide range of known facts about party identification (Achen 1992: 204–6).

The significance of Achen's model for the study of party identification leads us to examine more closely its underlying assumptions and empirical ramifications. After all, if Achen is right, then discussion of partisan stability is largely irrelevant to understanding whether partisanship is a social identity or rather a running tally of evaluations—either characterization could produce the observed level of stability. For this reason, we devote the next section of this chapter to a close critique of Achen's model of partisanship. Recognizing that some readers may wish to skip the technical discussion, we briefly summarize the conclusions as follows: Achen's model supposes that voters learn over time which party will perform best in office. As evidence accumulates, voters become certain about which party will best suit their tastes. Experience gradually teaches them which party to trust. However, the implication that rational voters form stable party attachments on the basis of experience and observation hinges on the assumption that the underlying character of the parties never changes over time. When this assumption is relaxed, Achen's model becomes a special case of a learning model that is more general and, to our mind, more plausible. The upshot of this alternative model is that rational voters no longer develop unchanging partisan attachments. As long as there is some chance that the parties will change over time, new information alters the partisan identities of rational voters. The revisionist model predicts stability only under very special conditions: Either the parties never change, or the amount of new information about party performance is nil. These assumptions, as we will see, are at variance with a welter of public opinion data. Party attachments are stable, but not because the public is blind to changes in the political environment.

RATIONAL LEARNING ABOUT PARTIES

Like Anthony Downs, Achen strives to build a model of political partisanship on the premise that voters are rational and forward-looking. Voters use the laws of probability to update their prior beliefs about the parties, which are based initially on information they infer from their parents' political views, by using the additional political information they receive over their own lifetimes. Voters are rational in the sense that this updating process extracts an optimal amount of information from preexisting beliefs and news about the political environment. Citizens then base their voting decisions on their assessments of which party they expect to provide greater benefits. For Achen, then, party identification is nothing more than the voter's "current estimate of the benefit differential between the parties" (p. 202). Achen does not make explicit what he has in mind by "benefits" but at various points alludes to favorable economic performance and ideologically attractive policies. Self-conceptions, social identities, and the like play no apparent role in this definition.

The key ingredient in Achen's model of voter learning is a "stable two-party system." The benefits that each party can be expected to offer if it holds office are assumed to be set at some unobserved level. This level remains constant over time, which is to say, the parties never change their policy positions, competence in economic management, or skill in managing foreign affairs. Rather, in this static party model the two parties "offer benefits to voters that oscillate over time around a fixed but unknown mean. . . . The benefits vary independently from one term of office to the next around a central tendency. Thus, the parties may oscillate left or right by chance, but they do not drift steadily in any one direction. In effect, the model describes a stable period between realignments" (p. 199).

Citizens form their party identifications by estimating the underlying party benefits differential and siding with the party that offers the greatest utility. The process involves acquiring information about the benefits that each party provides (or promises) each period, which constitutes a noisy measurement of the constant benefit level provided by each party. The voters' inference problem is to update their initial opinion about the parties, making guesses about the true party mean benefit level using a lifetime of observations of the actual benefit levels that the parties provide. Achen's model takes Fiorina's running tally idea and gives it a prospective twist. People do not simply reward or punish the parties on the basis of retrospective performance evaluations. Retrospective judgments are influential only insofar as they inform expectations about how the parties will perform in the future.

From these assumptions, Achen demonstrates that a rational learning model can produce a number of interesting theoretical results about how citizens learn over time. He shows that, for example, as citizens accumulate experience observing the parties, the value of additional information declines. As a result, all things equal, we should observe that older citizens place less weight on recent performance than younger citizens. More important, Achen's model generates results that seem to square with much of what we know about party identification. His model predicts that judgments about the parties become more precise as time passes and citizens acquire information and that, as a result, party identification becomes increasingly stable over a voter's lifetime. These enticing predictions lend plausibility to Achen's characterization of party identification and the way in which voters learn. A closer look at this model, however, uncovers a number of additional predictions that do not square with empirical observation. To draw out these errant predictions, we must retrace Achen's steps in the development of his model. This formal exposition of rational learning has the additional benefit of setting the stage for our subsequent discussion of biased learning.

A Generalized Learning Model

In Achen's account, voters begin life with some ideas about the political parties and some sense of how sure they are about their views. That is, each voter begins with some prior belief about the party "differential," which is the difference between the benefits the voter expects from the Democrats minus the benefits expected from the Republicans. Associated with this prior belief, which is denoted a_0, is a variance P_0, which captures the voter's level of certainty about his or her initial beliefs about the parties. (Readers may find it convenient to refer to Table 5.1, which summarizes the notation used in this model.) The voters observe the behavior of the parties over time and get some additional information about the party differential. Suppose the true party differential at time t is α_t. At time t the voters observe

$$y_t = \alpha_t + \varepsilon_t \tag{5.1}$$

where ε_t is an error term, independently distributed $N(0, h)$, with positive h. Following Achen, we will assume that the voters need only worry about estimating the relative party benefits and that the properties of the error term, such as its distribution and variance, are known.[1] Equation 5.1 says that each period's observation is a noisy reading of the true party differential at the time of the observation. If the true party differential is correlated over time, voters can use in-

Table 5.1. Summary of Notation Used in the Kalman Filter Model

Symbol	Explanation
y_t	Observed benefit differential, period t
α_t	Actual benefit differential, period t
ε_t	Measurement error in observed benefit differential, period t
u_t	Random component of change in actual benefit differential, betweeen period $t - 1$ and period t
h	Variance of ε_t
q	Variance of u_t
a_0	Initial voter beliefs about actual benefit differential
P_0	Variance of voter initial beliefs
a_t	Voter estimate of benefit differential at period t
γ	Autoregressive parameter linking differential from period to period
P_t	Variance of voter estimate of benefit differential at period t

formation from today's performance to make inferences about what the parties will be offering the next period. Suppose the party differential changes over time according to the rule

$$\alpha_t = \gamma \alpha_{t-1} + u_t \tag{5.2}$$

where γ is a positive constant less than or equal to one, and u_t is an error term, independently distributed $N(0, q)$. One special case of equation 5.2, $\gamma = 1$ and $q = 0$, implies that the true party differential stays constant over time. Alternatively, whenever $q > 0$, the ideological positions, relative skill, or attractiveness of the party leaders may vary over time.

Voters combine their prior beliefs and what they observe to estimate the party benefit differential. If voters are rational, they will use the best possible method for combining their prior beliefs and current information. The optimal estimate of α_t, where optimal means minimizing the expected square error, will be denoted by a_t. This estimator is

$$a_t = (1 - K_t)\gamma a_{t-1} + K_t(y_t) = \gamma a_{t-1} + K_t(y_t - \gamma a_{t-1}) \tag{5.3}$$

where $K_t = (\gamma^2 P_{t-1} + q)/(\gamma^2 P_{t-1} + q + h)$
The variance of the estimator a_t is P_t, where

$$P_t = hK_t \tag{5.4}$$

These equations are known as the *Kalman filter algorithm*. A more extensive description of the Kalman filter, along with demonstrations of its properties, can be found in Harvey (1989). Under the assumption of normality of the errors, the Kalman filter model, like Achen's model, can be derived from Bayes's rule (see Meinhold and Singpurwalla 1983), a basic probability axiom. The Kalman filter in fact represents a generalization of Achen's model of Bayesian learning, which now permits us to relax the assumption that party benefits remain constant.

In what sense do voters use the Kalman filter to process information? Although the exact formula used to combine new and old information is somewhat complicated, the properties of the Kalman filter are quite intuitive. The estimate of today's party difference (equation 5.3) is a weighted average of what we had expected the party difference to be and an "error correction" that adjusts our estimates according to how far off today's actual observation (y_t) is from what we expected on the basis of previous observations (γa_{t-1}). After observing y_t, our revised estimate of α_t captures all the information we have and forms the basis for next period's expectation, which is then revised again if there is a further prediction error. The amount of weight placed on this period's observation y varies according to how much information is contained in the new observation. When h is large, the amount of noise contained in each new observation of party performance is large, and so the revision of our beliefs about the parties is relatively small in response to a surprising value of y. When h is small, y is a very good reading of where the parties are, and so voters will put a lot of weight on recent performance.

When q is large, implying that the true underlying party differential moves around a lot, voters will ignore the past and place more value on the current observation. As q becomes very large, all weight is placed on the new information, and nothing can be learned from earlier periods. On the other hand, when q is small, the parties do not move around much. Old observations, which are embedded in last period's forecast, contain useful information about the current party differential. As a result, the amount of weight placed on new information will be small. When q is exactly zero, the parties never change, and after an initial period of learning, new information has no value at all. This is precisely the case that Achen models (see Achen 1992: 202).

An interesting feature of the Kalman filter is that, as of time t, all the useful information from the past is embodied in a_{t-1}, the voter's best estimate of the party differential in period $t-1$. The specific values of y and a_0 that led to this judgment about the party differential can be "forgotten" without any loss. Regardless of whether the party differential is constant over time, preserving a running tally of the parties' qualities is, from the standpoint of the rational voter, as good as memory-based processing, even if there is no cost to storing memories. Thus, this learning model is one of on-line processing (McGraw and Lodge 1996) and, as such, makes few cognitive demands on voters. They need not remember the details of the past; these details have been incorporated into their ongoing assessments of the parties.

How Influential Is New Information?

In the generalized learning model, as voters accumulate experience with the political parties, the weight that they assign to new information (vis-à-vis information they have accumulated in the past) stabilizes at some positive value. Initially, voters are unsure of the parties' relative benefit levels and revise their views relatively quickly when they receive new information about the parties. Since the parties do not remain fixed over time, the amount of useful knowledge that is contained in past observations diminishes as time passes. The rate at which old information loses its value varies with q, which captures how fast party positions and other attributes change. For any particular value of q, there is some point in the past beyond which historical reflection yields very little useful additional information, and so the weight placed on these outdated observations goes toward zero. At this point, the voters' learning rule approaches the "steady-state" updating formula, after which the voters' assessment of the parties becomes a weighted average of the current observation and past observations, with the weight on the current observation equal to K.

If voters are to make the most of the information at hand, how much weight should they place on today's observation versus past observations? The formula for K shows when the weight on the current observation will be highest. The value of K is increasing in q/h, the "signal-to-noise" ratio. As the parties become more changeable, q rises. Old information becomes less useful in figuring out where the parties currently stand. In this situation, voters place more weight on what they see today, which raises K. The optimal use of past performance is also affected by the quality of incoming information. As h increases, today's observation of the party differential is a less and less precise measurement of where the parties actually stand. As a result, voters should place less trust in any single observation because it may be misleading. On the other hand, when h is very low, the voters can (almost) pin down the parties from this period's observation alone. Under these conditions, past information adds little to current information. The past should be disregarded completely when $h = 0$.

What does the static party model say about the use of past versus current information about the parties? In the static party model, $q = 0$, and so the steady-state value of K is zero. Comparing this with the more general model we present, the restricted model predicts that the weight placed on new information will fall as time passes and then stabilize at zero weight placed on new information. This extreme result follows from the assumption that the party differential is fixed. When $q = 0$, as supposed by the Achen model, no old observations are ever discarded as useless, and eventually the voters have the parties completely pinned down. In fact, throughout life voters will place equal weight on all the information they receive, *no matter how old that information is.* Taken literally, the model implies that the voters can learn as much about the current party differentials from last year's observation as from observations taken decades earlier. Because the voters accumulate more information over time, the weight placed on each piece of information must fall until the voters place an arbitrarily small amount of weight on each individual observation. Eventually, experienced citizens cease to learn about the party differential. In Achen's model, rational partisans become rock-solid partisans.

In contrast, when $q > 0$, the past can tell voters only so much about the present; because the parties are changing, recent observations always provide new information about where the parties are today. As a result, the more general model predicts that early in life voters will place a lot of weight on new information but that the weight they place on new information will decline over time and then stabilize at some amount greater than zero. How much greater than zero will depend on how much confidence the voters have in their ability to infer the parties' positions from their current observation and how quickly they think parties move around over time.

Table 5.2 illustrates some different learning patterns assuming diffuse priors ($P_0 = 10$, $h = 1$) and different values of c, the voter's signal-to-noise ratio. One noteworthy feature of the table is the fact that K, the weight assigned to newly observed information, remains sizable even when c is quite small. For example, when the signal-to-noise ratio is just 0.05 and $\gamma = 1$, new information is assigned a weight of 0.2. Thus, *even when the underlying party differential changes very little over time (compared with random fluctuations in observed party perfor-*

Table 5.2. Effect of Recent Experience on Party Evaluations Once the Updating Process Has Reached a Steady State

		Autoregressive Coefficient (γ) Linking Party Differential at Time $t - 1$ to Party Differential at Time t			
		0.10	0.50	0.90	1.00
	1.00	0.501	0.531	0.597	0.618
	0.50	0.335	0.372	0.468	0.500
Signal-to-noise ratio (q/h)	0.25	0.201	0.246	0.347	0.400
	0.05	0.048	0.061	0.141	0.200

Note: Entries are weights (K) given to the most recent period's observation of party performance.

		Autoregressive Coefficient (γ) Linking Party Differential at Time $t - 1$ to Party Differential at Time t			
		0.10	0.50	0.90	1.00
	1.00	1	2	2	2
	0.50	2	2	2	3
Signal-to-noise ratio (q/h)	0.25	2	3	4	4
	0.05	2	4	8	7

Note: Entries are number of periods that must elapse before weights are within 10% of the steady-state value of K.

mance), rational learning nonetheless involves placing considerable weight on contemporaneous information. By the same token, this scenario implies that older observations gradually become uninformative: A prior that is weighted 0.8 in period 1 carries a weight of just 0.11 in period 10. Even in very placid times, therefore, rational citizens continue to update their assessments of their parties. They discard old information and form new impressions on the basis of current events.

Whereas Achen draws a rigid distinction between periods of realignment and periods of stable two-party politics, our model accommodates both situations within a common analytic framework. In effect, our model permits voters to be on the lookout for signs of change in party competence. Even when voters are aware that such changes seldom occur, the *possibility* of change alters the way in which they would optimally update their beliefs about party capabilities. In the static model, citizens eventually reach a point at which they have watched the parties for so long that their current observations cease to be informative. In the Kalman filter model, by contrast, new information is accorded considerable weight by experienced observers, even when the rate of party change is quite gradual.

ASSESSING THE LEARNING MODEL'S
EMPIRICAL IMPLICATIONS

The Kalman filter offers a parsimonious formal model of learning that is more flexible than Achen's static party model. Yet, the model is entirely abstract. When we speak of the passage of time, it is unclear whether we mean minutes or months or millennia. Perhaps voters are rational but *slow* learners. Perhaps they live their lives largely oblivious to current events, in which case it should hardly be surprising that rational learning occurs at a sluggish pace. Or perhaps the ideological gap between the parties changes so imperceptibly that voters have little upon which to base revised assessments (Franklin 1992; see also Campbell et al. 1960: 256, on the slackening of partisan debate). To establish that party identification is, in principle, susceptible to rapid change, we must show that evaluations of the parties change rapidly and markedly over time.

We begin by examining the aggregate distribution of party performance evaluations, as assessed by Gallup Polls during the period 1952–96 (Figures 5.1 and 5.2). For the sake of comparability with the Gallup macropartisanship series presented in Chapter 4, we have rescaled prospective evaluations in a similar manner. That is, we ignore respondents who see no difference between the

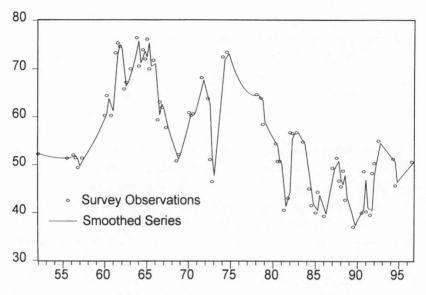

Figure 5.1. Proportion of the public stating that the Democratic Party is better able to manage the economy. To facilitate comparison with the macropartisanship series, these samples were restricted to those who believed one of the parties to be a better economic manager.

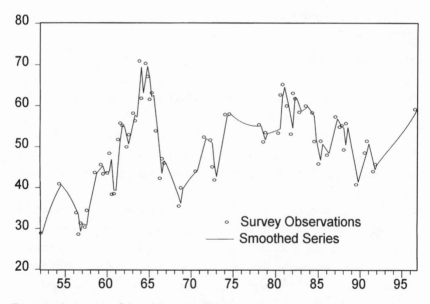

Figure 5.2. Proportion of the public stating that the Democratic Party is better able to maintain peace. To facilitate comparison with the macropartisanship series, these samples were restricted to those who believed one of the parties to be better at preserving peace.

parties and plot the percentage who see the Democrats as likely to do a better job. One performance series asks which party will do a better job of keeping the country prosperous; the other, which party will keep the nation out of war.[2] Although there may be other dimensions along which the parties could be evaluated, their capacity to secure peace and prosperity are undoubtedly the most important.

Figures 5.1 and 5.2 attest to the speed and frequency with which evaluations of the parties have changed.[3] Between 1957 and 1958, the Democratic rating on economic performance shot from 51% to 68%; another surge occurred between 1960 and 1961, when the rating climbed from 60% to 75%. These gains dissipated rapidly a few years later, as the 71% ratings typical of 1965 gave way to ratings of 61% in 1966. Nixon's reelection campaign pushed the Democratic rating from 68% in 1971 to just 47% by the end of 1972. Swings of more than ten points in the span of a year or two occurred periodically from that point on: 1972–74, 1978–80, 1980–81, 1981–82, 1983–84, and 1991–92. No less dramatic swings punctuate the series of prospective evaluations based on the criterion of keeping the country out of war. It seems clear, then, that the public, however inattentive it may be, adjusts its assessments of the parties rapidly in the wake of changing national or international conditions. This finding echoes a theme advanced by Page and Shapiro (1992), whose extensive investigation of public opinion trends demonstrates how the public's policy orientations adjust to changing social and economic conditions.

Party identification, however, moves much more sluggishly than party evaluation. The dramatic improvements in assessments of Democratic competence between the late Eisenhower and early Johnson administrations (which saw economic evaluations shift by twenty-five percentage points and peace and prosperity ratings by forty-five) and sharp declines during the Reagan era (economic ratings dropped from the mid-sixties under Carter to the low forties at the end of 1984) corresponded with much smaller shifts in party identification. The contrast between macropartisanship and similarly scaled evaluations is apparent from the degree of dispersion in each series. When we consider the sixty quarters during which data for all three series are available, the standard deviations for party identification, economic evaluations, and foreign policy ratings are 4.7, 11.4, and 9.5, respectively.

Much the same conclusion comes through when we trace individuals' attitudes over successive waves of a panel study. In the 1990–91–92 NES panel, respondents were asked to rate the parties in terms of economic and foreign policy stewardship. Table 5.3 presents the correlations between responses to these

Table 5.3. Stability of Individual-Level Party Identification and Prospective Performance Evaluations

Polychoric correlations			
Three-point party identification			
1990	1.000		
1991	0.888	1.000	
1992	0.852	0.836	1.000
Which party will better handle the economy?			
1990	1.000		
1991	0.669	1.000	
1992	0.559	0.580	1.000
Which party will better handle foreign affairs?			
1990	1.000		
1991	0.536	1.000	
1992	0.466	0.487	1.000
Attitude stability corrected for measurement error			
	R^2, Wave 2	R^2, Wave 3	Reliability
Party identification	1.000	0.920	0.872
Economic evaluations	0.928	0.698	0.694
Foreign affairs evaluations	0.914	0.755	0.561

Source: Data are from the 1990–91–92 National Election Study Panel. $N = 942$. Disattenuated correlations estimated using weighted least-squares on polychoric correlation matrices.

questions at each point in time. Because the prospective performance evaluations have just three response categories, we report the polychoric correlations (Joreskog and Sorbom 1993), which correct for the ordinal nature of the data. For the sake of comparability, polychoric correlations for the party identification measures were based on the three-point categorization of Democrats, Independents, and Republicans. The correlations between party identification at different points in time are always higher than for performance evaluations. Correcting for measurement error using the techniques described in Chapter 3, we find party identification to be substantially more stable than prospective evaluations of party performance. The disattenuated R-squared when 1991 attitudes are regressed on 1990 is 1.0 for party identification, 0.93 for economic evaluations, and 0.91 for foreign policy evaluations. In the more unstable environment a year later, a gap between partisan attachments and other attitudes also emerges. When 1992 is regressed on 1991, party identification registers a 0.92, compared with 0.70 for economic evaluations and 0.76 for foreign affairs.

The manifest differences between party identification and prospective performance evaluations suggest that the power of rational learning models may vary depending on which facet of partisan attitudes one considers. Achen contends that his model accounts for certain key empirical regularities associated with party *identification,* but those regularities differ from what we find when looking at *prospective performance evaluations,* despite the fact that Achen equates the two conceptually. It cannot be said that people fail to update their opinions of the parties in light of current events. Over short periods of time, evaluations do change, sometimes substantially. Party identification, however, tends to hold steady even as assessments about the parties and their leaders change.

DOES STABLE PARTISANSHIP RESULT
FROM BIASED LEARNING?

What accounts for the placid dynamics of party identification? One possibility is public inattentiveness to politics, but as we have seen, this hypothesis is inconsistent with the way in which the public updates its assessment of the political parties. Another explanation for partisan stability contends that partisans do not update their attitudes in a manner consistent with rational learning. A recurrent theme in *The American Voter,* its precursor *Voting* (Berelson, Lazarsfeld, and McPhee 1954: 223), and its successor *Elections and the Political Order* (Campbell et al. 1966) is that "identification with a party raises a perceptual screen through which the individual tends to see what is favorable to his partisan orientation" (Campbell et al. 1960: 133). Stokes (1966: 127) argues that "for most people the tie between party identification and voting behavior involves subtle processes of perceptual adjustment by which the individual assembles an image of current politics consistent with his partisan allegiance." Perceptual bias looms large in Stokes's explanation of a central generalization about American public opinion, namely, the stability of party attachments and vote intentions: "The capacity of party identification to color perceptions holds the key to understanding why the unfolding of new events, the emergence of new issues, the appearance of new political figures fail to produce wider swings of party fortune. To a remarkable extent these swings are damped by processes of selective perception."

This explanation for partisan stability takes issue with the core assumption of the rational learning model—updating prior views on the basis of new evidence. This challenge raises a number of empirical questions: Do people assimilate new information in an efficient and unbiased manner; that is, do they update their prior beliefs in accordance with Bayes's rule, as in equation 5.3? Or are they selective in the way that they gather and absorb news, thereby failing to assign due weight to new information? A Bayesian public may be ignorant or inattentive, but it is not closed-minded. New information is processed without regard for whether it conforms to preexisting beliefs or partisan attachments. If the economy's vital signs are widely reported to be deteriorating during a Democratic administration, both Democratic and Republican Bayesians will tend to revise downward their assessment of the Democrats' economic stewardship. Democrats might greet the bad economic news with disappointment, but they nonetheless acknowledge its implications when evaluating political leaders. Biased learning, by contrast, means that the weight assigned to new information (K) is a function of whether new information conforms to prior beliefs.

Curiously, given this proposition's long pedigree, the perceptual screen argument has seldom been subjected to a direct empirical test. Reviewing the literature on perceptual bias, Gerber and Green (1999) point out that of the various studies that purport to demonstrate perceptual bias through laboratory experiments or surveys, only a handful actually adduce evidence that contradicts the Bayesian learning model presented above, and these studies are either flawed or contradicted by others that fail to replicate the pattern of biased learning.

Most studies that claim to find evidence of perceptual bias in fact find something quite consonant with the Bayesian model: People whose prior beliefs or tastes differ continue to disagree after receiving new information. For example, the often-cited fact that Democrats and Republicans each tend to declare their party's presidential nominee the more effective debater is not convincing evidence of selective perception because each group of partisans doubtless applies different ideological criteria when evaluating the candidates' ideas. If Republicans like the sound of a cut in the capital gains tax and Democrats do not, they will react differently when the candidates announce their disagreement on this issue. These divergent reactions are not a matter of perceptual bias. Each voter may correctly perceive the candidates' positions on this issue but react differently, depending on his or her views about such a tax cut.

From time to time, political events unfold in ways that please one partisan group and anger another. The Supreme Court's resolution of the crises surrounding the 2000 presidential election is an excellent case in point. More than a month after the election, the Court handed down a decision that overturned the Florida Supreme Court's ruling ordering ballot recounts, requiring it to reformulate its standards for doing so. Because the Court's decision of December

12 insisted that any recounts must be completed before December 13, the decision made further legal maneuvering pointless, and Al Gore conceded defeat
shortly thereafter. The Court was split down ideological lines, with the peculiar
twist that liberal justices argued in favor of the Florida court on the basis of fed-
eralism, whereas conservative justices grounded their decision on the equal
protection clause. Predictably, evaluations of the Court were henceforth col-
ored by partisanship. Between August 29, 2000, and January 10, 2001, Democratic approval of the Supreme Court fell precipitously according to Gallup
Polls. In the fall, 70% of Democrats had approved of the "way the Supreme
Court is handling its job," and 18% disapproved. After the infamous decision,
42% approved and 50% disapproved. On the other hand, Republicans found
new virtues in the Court. Whereas 60% approved and 35% disapproved in the
fall, these numbers had changed to 80% and 15% by January. Clearly, each partisan group was using different standards by which to judge the Court's handi-
work (Simmons 2001).

Partisan groups may also diverge insofar as they use similar terms to express
different views. For example, when asked in 1980 whether the term "knowledgeable" described Jimmy Carter, Democrats and Republicans took sharply
different views. One possibility, consistent with perceptual bias, is that Republicans had conveniently forgotten Carter's background in nuclear engineering
and his copious knowledge of domestic and international affairs. Another possibility is that Republicans hesitated to call Carter knowledgeable because they
found him aloof and out of touch with ordinary people and the government-
induced problems that they confront.

Selective perception must also be distinguished from rational updating based
on divergent prior beliefs. Political scandals, for example, may evoke divergent
reactions from adherents of each party because each group of partisans harbors
different priors about the susceptibility of certain politicians to misbehavior.
Those who believed Nixon to be a scoundrel before Watergate were naturally
more prone to think that he knew of the break-in at Democratic headquarters
by those connected with his reelection campaign. Partisan differences could reflect perceptual bias, but they could just as well reflect the fact that people draw
different conclusions when they start with different initial assumptions.

When perceptual bias is being studied, holding tastes constant is a critical
component of an effective research design. If in a college dormitory half the
students like Mexican cuisine and the other half do not, we would not cite
mixed reviews of the lunch menu when tacos are served as evidence of perceptual bias. The issue of perceptual bias hinges on how evaluations change when

the same dish is prepared by a gourmet chef; presumably, both those who like and dislike Mexican cuisine should like the food better. Similarly, it is often found that those who engage in risky behaviors such as smoking are more likely than other people to dismiss scientific studies purporting to show the adverse health consequences of these activities. This, too, is consistent with the Bayesian learning model, as groups like smokers and nonsmokers harbor different prior beliefs before encountering the data. The decisive question is how the views of smokers and nonsmokers *change* after they encounter the new scientific report. The Bayesian model predicts that both groups will become more concerned about health risks but smokers will remain more skeptical than nonsmokers.

In political science, it has been more or less assumed for decades that partisan attachments color perception in ways that prevent opinion change, even though the evidence supporting this view fails to control for preexisting tastes and beliefs. To gauge the empirical adequacy of the Bayesian learning model and the alternative hypothesis of selective perception, we must take a fresh look at the evidence. Let us briefly examine four important areas in which partisanship might function as a perceptual screen: how the public judges the parties' competence, evaluates the incumbent president, assesses the performance of presidential candidates during televised debates, and assigns blame during presidential scandals.

Evaluations of Party Competence

Our first test of the biased learning model focuses on the way partisan groups evaluate which party does a superior job of managing the economy. If biased learning is at work, we should find supporters of the incumbent president's party unswayed by bad economic news; conversely, an improving economy should do little to make the president's opponents more impressed with his party's ability to manage economic affairs. By focusing on evaluations of the parties' economic acumen as opposed to assessments of the economy itself, we present the Bayesian model with an especially difficult test, for here what Stokes calls "subtle processes of perceptual adjustment" should come to the fore.

The early 1990s was an especially good period for charting economic evaluations. Unlike other periods, during which conservatives might have concerned themselves with inflation while liberals focused on unemployment, this period featured very little inflation. Increasing economic productivity, growth, employment, and international trade were largely "valence issues" during this pe-

Table 5.4. Prospective Economic Evaluations of the Parties, by Party
Identification in the Initial Wave of Each Panel Survey

	Party Identification in 1990		
	Democrat	Independent	Republican
1990–91–92 Panel Study: Economic Evaluations			
1990	39.0	13.2	3.5
1991	37.7	14.4	3.5
1992	63.2	31.2	11.5
N of cases	405	319	261

	Party Identification in 1992		
	Democrat	Independent	Republican
1992–93–94 Panel Study: Economic Evaluations			
1992	64.2	27.9	7.8
1993	44.3	17.2	7.3
1994	29.4	15.5	2.2
N of cases	201	233	179

	Party Identification in 1994		
	Democrat	Independent	Republican
1994–96 Panel Study: Economic Evaluations			
1994	31.9	11.6	1.1
1996	55.6	27.0	10.4
N of cases	232	215	182

Note: Entries are the percentage of each partisan group saying that the Democratic Party does a better job of handling the economy.

riod, that is, issues on which the public harbored similar aims, even if they might have differed on the question of how best to achieve them.

Table 5.4 presents the results from three panel studies that track Democrats, Republicans, and Independents over one and two years. Entries to the table are the percentages of each partisan group who indicate that the Democratic Party does a better job of handling the economy. Not surprisingly, when asked to make this sort of judgment, Democrats expressed much more confidence than Republicans in the Democratic Party's economic stewardship. What is interesting, however, is the extent to which the three partisan groups moved together from one survey wave to the next as the economic fortunes of the parties changed. None of the groups changed their assessments between 1990 and

1991. All became more pro-Democratic from 1991 to 1992 and 1994 to 1996; all became more pro-Republican from 1992 to 1994.

The pace and magnitude of these opinion changes should be underscored. Far from being reluctant to recognize their party's deficiencies, Democrats shifted markedly between 1992 and 1994. Whereas 64% of Democrats in 1992 indicated that the Democratic Party was best able to manage the economy, this figure declined to 44% in 1993 and to 29% in 1994. Republican movements are smaller in terms of percentage points, but one may refine the analysis further by asking whether these three partisan groups are equally affected by information in ways that might be masked by percentage-point movements. Such a test requires us to specify a statistical model, such as a logistic model, that transforms the observed probabilities so as to constrain them between zero and one.[4] When we use this model to test whether partisan groups in each panel move at different rates from one survey wave to the next, as would be expected if one group of partisans were resisting discordant information, we cannot reject the null hypothesis that all three groups move at the same rate ($\chi^2 = -2(L_0 - L_1)$ = 13.38, $df = 10$, $p > .10$). Much as a Bayesian learning model would suggest, perceptual bias seems not to prevent partisans from updating their evaluations in light of new information.

Presidential Approval

At any given time, those who identify with the Republican Party are much more likely than their Democratic counterparts to approve of a Republican president or disapprove of a Democratic one. These divergent evaluations do not in themselves make the case for biased perception, since they may well reflect the different policy orientations of the two groups of partisans. A more telling assessment of perceptual bias tracks presidential approval over time. Do Democrats, Republicans, and Independents interpret events differently, such that approval rises among one partisan group while falling or remaining unchanged among others? This question presents the learning model with an especially demanding test, as divergent policy views could lead Democrats to applaud policy initiatives that Republicans abhor, causing attitude polarization. The extent to which partisan groups move in parallel over time reflects both the unbiased manner with which learning occurs and the ratio of valence to position issues in politics.[5]

Edwards's (1990) compendium of presidential Gallup approval ratings disaggregated by respondents' party provides a readily accessible means for answering this question. Edwards presents annual figures on the percentage of

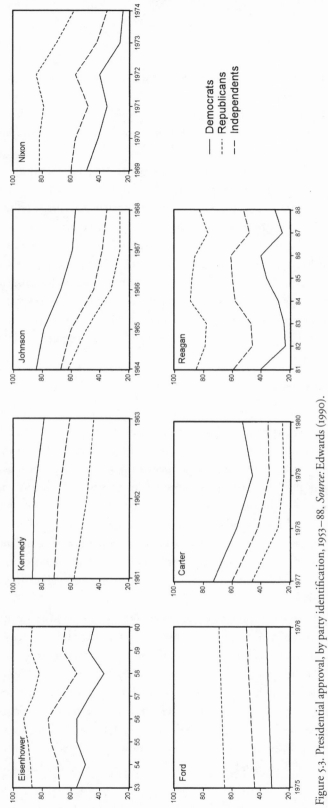

Figure 5.3. Presidential approval, by party identification, 1953–88. *Source:* Edwards (1990).

131

Democrats, Republicans, and Independents who approved of the way the president was handling his job for the period 1952–88. These data are graphed in Figure 5.3. The trajectories of presidential approval track quite closely across the three partisan groups. Indeed, Figure 5.3 is a striking demonstration of unbiased learning.

Looking at annual changes in approval (discarding, necessarily, the first year of each presidency), we find very high correlations between the ways in which the partisan groups update their assessments. Annual percentage-point changes in presidential approval among Democrats and Republicans correlate at 0.77 ($N = 29$); this figure rises to 0.79 when changes are recalculated in terms of shifts in log-odds. A more rigorous analysis of these data reveals that the changes in presidential approval (scaled in terms of log-odds) across the three partisan groups cannot be differentiated statistically. If selective perception is at work, it cannot be detected from the way that partisans evaluate the president, which is arguably the most important and widely studied public opinion series in American politics.

Presidential Debates

Political scientists studying debates have often concluded that they function to reinforce existing partisan propensities. Partisans are predisposed to like their party's nominee and agree with what he or she has to say; debates simply provide a forum for reaffirming these preexisting sentiments. When evaluating who "won" the debate, partisans disproportionately back their party's nominee. Again, however, this pattern does not speak unambiguously to the issue of perceptual bias. If liberals and conservatives resonate to different policy proposals, their divergent impressions of who won may simply reflect their different ideological tastes. A more compelling test looks at how assessments change across successive debates, a design that holds constant the ideological appeal of the two candidates.

One of the few surveys to examine how viewers respond to a sequence of debates is a pair of CBS/New York Times polls conducted during October 1984. These debates are especially interesting because the candidates acquitted themselves differently in their two confrontations. In their first debate, Walter Mondale seemed more alert and sympathetic than Reagan, who at times seemed to lose his bearings. In their rematch, Reagan improved his performance, while Mondale turned in an undistinguished effort. Table 5.5 presents respondents' assessments of who won the debate broken down by party identification. Democrats, Republicans, and Independents all swung toward Reagan between the

Table 5.5. Impressions of Which Candidate Won the Reagan-Mondale
Presidential Debates, by Party Identification

	Republican (%)	Democrat (%)	Independent/Other (%)
First debate			
Reagan won	34.3	11.6	25.9
Mondale won	38.2	74.5	54.0
Neither/both/don't know	27.5	13.9	20.1
Total	100.0	100.0	100.0
N	280	310	278
Second debate			
Reagan won	69.0	21.6	40.2
Mondale won	9.2	45.8	23.9
Neither/both/don't know	21.8	32.6	36.0
Total	100.0	100.0	100.1
N	229	319	264

Source: CBS News/New York Times. First presidential debate: File 11 (October 7 and 9, 1984) and second presidential debate: File 12 (October 21 and 24–25, 1984).

first and second debates. Among Republicans, 38.2% named Mondale the victor of the first debate, but only 9.2% dubbed him the winner of the second debate. Fully 54% of Independents thought that Mondale won the first debate, and only 23.9% thought he won the second. Among Democrats, the corresponding percentages are 74.5% and 45.8%. From this pattern of opinion change, it seems apparent that the two debate performances produced analogous patterns of opinion change among the three partisan groups. Partisans do sympathize with their party's nominee, but they also change their assessments in a manner consistent with unbiased learning.

Scandals

Allegations of wrongdoing are the lifeblood of partisan politics. The offending party does its best to deny all charges, minimize their significance, and divert attention to other issues. Other parties, sensing an opportunity to turn the misstep to their advantage, seek to keep the scandal in the public eye and, if possible, widen its scope to include other misdeeds. Nowhere is this better illustrated than in the Whitewater scandal, in which allegations of financial misconduct by the Clintons led to a protracted and wide-ranging series of investigations, committee hearings, court battles, government reports, and eventually impeachment proceedings. For the majority of time he served as president, but with particular verve after the Republicans gained control of Congress in 1995, Bill Clinton and his associates were under investigation by a special counsel. Predictably, Democratic leaders assailed the protracted investigation as a baseless witch-hunt, while Republican leaders maintained that administration officials obstructed justice in order to avoid prosecution.

The turning point in this scandal came when the media reported that President Clinton had engaged in an extramarital affair with a White House intern, Monica Lewinsky. The news broke in January of 1998, just a few days after Clinton had testified in a sexual harassment suit brought against him that he had had no such sexual liaison. These reports were based on tape recordings of Lewinsky's description of her sexual relationship and plans to conceal it, but Clinton vigorously denied the allegations, stating, "I did not have sexual relations with that woman . . . I never told anybody to lie." By April, Clinton's denials seemed to be forcing a stalemate, with 47% of the public believing that an affair had occurred and 37% thinking not (Time/CNN poll, April 8–9, 1998). But the credibility of his claims eroded as the public became increasingly aware of the evidence that implicated the president. After Clinton was subpoenaed by a grand jury and Lewinsky admitted the affair in return for immunity in July, 60% of the public believed the allegations of an affair, and just 24% did not (Time/CNN poll, July 30, 1998). Still, there was reason for doubt, as many believed that Lewinsky had fabricated the story in order to draw attention to herself. Three weeks after this poll, however, Clinton appeared on national television to admit to a relationship that was "not appropriate" and "wrong."

The steady drumbeat of charges and denials in round-the-clock coverage of the scandal would seem to provide ample opportunity for partisans of all stripes to hew to information they found congenial. Yet Table 5.6 shows no evidence that Democrats and Republicans polarized as new evidence and theories were unveiled. Instead, what we see is that all three partisan categories move in the same direction to a similar degree over time. Republicans, who long regarded Clinton as personally untrustworthy, were prone to think the worst. As new information became available, their cynicism rose from 70% to 84%. Democrats, who encountered the Lewinsky scandal with the prior belief that Clinton was a compassionate and intelligent leader who was being persecuted for political reasons, also became more skeptical of Clinton's rendition of the facts, 32% to 46%. Both sides, of course, took very different views of what sorts of punishments were in order for these misdeeds, but it would be incorrect to

Table 5.6. How Partisan Views of the Lewinsky Scandal Unfolded over Time

Date of Survey	Republicans	Independents	Democrats
April 8–9, 1998	70%	49%	32%
N	263	301	371
May 18–19, 1989	75%	59%	40%
N	357	402	405
July 30, 1998	84%	61%	46%
N	209	269	265

Source: Time/CNN polls conducted by Yankelovich partners.

Note: Entries are the percentage of each partisan group who believed that Clinton had an affair with Lewinsky. The question read to respondents was as follows: "It has been alleged that while he was president, Bill Clinton had an extramarital affair with Monica Lewinsky, a former White House intern. Clinton has denied this charge. Which do you tend to believe— that Clinton had an extramarital affair with Monica Lewinsky, or that he did not have an extramarital affair with her?" Earlier Yankelovich polls on this topic used slightly different question wording.

say that partisanship prevented both sides from updating their beliefs in a rational manner.

The same point holds for the most famous of all American scandals, Watergate. On June 17, 1972, five men, including a security director for Nixon's reelection campaign, were arrested on charges of breaking into Democratic National Committee headquarters. They and others connected to the campaign were indicted in September and convicted in January, shortly after Nixon's landslide reelection victory. In February, the Senate established a committee to investigate. That summer, the former White House counsel, John Dean, told the committee of the president's efforts to cover up the incident, and another White House aide revealed the existence of Nixon's secret tape recordings. At this point, 60% of the public in surveys conducted by the Harris Poll expressed the view that Nixon was involved in the cover-up. Confidence in Nixon gradually eroded, but particularly damaging was the March 1974 indictment against seven former aides in which Nixon was named as an unindicted coconspirator. In late July, the Supreme Court ruled unanimously that Nixon must turn over the tapes to the special prosecutor, and the House Judiciary Committee voted to approve an impeachment article that charged Nixon with obstructing justice. By this point, 74% of the public had come to believe that Nixon had obstructed justice. Shortly after this last poll, Nixon announced his resignation.

Table 5.7. Evolution of Partisan Perceptions of Nixon's Role in Watergate

Date of Survey	Republicans	Independents	Democrats
August 18–19, 1973	37%	61%	71%
N	391	319	739
November 12–15, 1973	38%	67%	77%
N	367	366	638
May 4–7, 1974	52%	79%	86%
N	269	434	625
July 31–August 2, 1974	55%	76%	82%
N	319	448	725

Source: Harris surveys, studies 2344, 2351, 7485, and 2427.

Note: Entries are the percentage of each partisan group who said they believed that Nixon knew about the Watergate cover-up in response to the question: "Do you feel that President Nixon knew about the attempt to cover up White House involvement in Watergate while it was going on, or do you think he did not know about the cover-up?" All interviews were conducted face-to-face.

What do we find when we track party identifiers across the four polls conducted between August 1973 and August 1974 (see Table 5.7)? As expected, Republicans were at every point more skeptical of the allegations against Nixon than were Democrats. Nevertheless, Republicans were moved by the mounting evidence of Nixon's involvement, ranging from the conviction of his close associates to the testimony of eyewitnesses to his unwillingness to relinquish potentially damaging evidence. In a year's time, the proportion of Republicans who believed that Nixon was part of a cover-up rose from 37% to 55%. This change paralleled the evolution of opinion in other partisan groups. Independents moved from 61% to 76%, and Democrats from 71% to 82%. Thus, it could hardly be said that Republicans refused to be influenced by untoward information about Nixon's involvement.

A SYNTHESIS

Party identification is a strong predictor of what people think about the parties' economic stewardship, a president's performance in office, or a candidate's performance in a televised debate. Yet when opinion is tracked over time to control for preexisting tastes and beliefs, different partisan groups seem to be similarly influenced by information. This parallel learning process accords with Page and Shapiro's (1992) observation that across a wide array of issues, the opinions of opposing ideological, social, and economic groups seldom polarize over time. It also accords with a good deal of evidence from laboratory experiments and studies of media use calling into question the robustness and magnitude of biases attributable to selective exposure and perception (Sears and Whitney 1973; Chaffee and Miyo 1983). Given the speed with which partisan evaluations change and the consistency of these changes across partisan groups, the stability of partisanship is attributable neither to widespread ignorance nor to perceptual distortion.

Public opinion seems to evolve in an unbiased fashion, and yet party identification responds very gradually, if at all, to sharp changes in political fortune. If identification is more tenacious than a Bayesian learning model would suggest, perhaps the difficulty lies with the way in which scholars such as Downs, Fiorina, and Achen have characterized partisan learning. Following Achen, we have focused entirely on the consequences of observing the parties' performance in office for purposes of making prospective judgments of performance. Party *identification,* however, concerns the way in which people *think of themselves.* ("In general, when it comes to politics, do you think of yourself as a Democrat, Republican, Independent, or what?") What matters is one's image of the social groups "Democrat," "Republican," and "Independent" and whether one includes oneself among them. Party performance doubtless contributes to the esteem in which partisan groups are held, such that Republicans were a less attractive object of identification in 1964 than 1984, but the fortunes of the Republican Party can change without much altering what comes to mind when people think of rank-and-file Republicans.

The stability of partisanship, in other words, may reflect the persistence of citizens' images of Democrats and Republicans. Citizens learn about which sorts of social, economic, or ideological groups affiliate with each party, while at the same time sorting out which group labels properly apply to themselves. Partisan instability among the young, by this account, results from the fact that they acquire a great deal of reference group information and are somewhat more susceptible to change in their prospective evaluations of party performance. In time, however, voters acquire a sense of who Democrats and Republicans are and whether these social group labels describe themselves.

Unlike the rational actor models that preceded it, our model of rational learning does not start with the assumption that actors seek to maximize political benefits of one sort or another. Nor do we suppose that the electorate develops a partisan attachment as a time-saving device, a cognitive shortcut designed to reduce decision costs. This argument succumbs to a functionalist fallacy. Although there can be no doubt that partisans have an easier time making up their minds about the electoral choices presented to them, it would be a mistake to dub this cognitive *function* a cause of party identification. In order for functions to count as causes, there must be some mechanism through which functions exert their influence. One kind of mechanism would be instrumental deliberation—people might reason that party attachments would be useful time-saving devices. Yet it is far from clear that forming a party attachment is an efficient or even necessary means by which to save cognitive resources. Partisans spend more, not less, time following politics. It strains credulity to suppose that as people grow busier they become more likely to form strong party attachments. Another mechanism is natural selection, which is sometimes used to explain why legislators engage in behaviors that improve their reelection chances, on the grounds that those who fail to do so lose their seats. But it would be absurd to apply an evolutionary argument to the electorate. It is difficult to imagine a circumstance in which voters would be weeded out on the basis of their inability to conserve cognitive energy.

Our model is agnostic about whether people seek to save time or even to form social attachments. We are satisfied by decades of social-psychological research on "minimal groups" showing that people readily form group attachments even when there seems to be little or nothing at stake (Tajfel 1978). Given the human penchant for embracing group distinctions, it seems unnecessary and potentially misleading to explain party identification with reference to instrumentalities of various sorts. Suffice it to say that in the process of making sense of themselves and their surroundings, people form self-conceptions that tend to be consonant with their attitudes toward various social groups.

In and of itself, this model need not imply stable party identification. Voters' perceptions of which social groups affiliate with each party could change, as could the esteem in which they hold those groups. One might argue, however, that perceptions of which groups affiliate with the parties evolve very slowly because, barring a dramatic secular realignment, it is difficult for citizens not employed by polling firms to update their impressions of the social bases of partisanship. The effortless assimilation of social stereotypes that begins in childhood is quite different from the learning that must occur in order for one to detect *changes* in the political allegiance of social groups. It is not surprising, therefore, that group stereotypes in general should be resistant to change (Hilton and von Hippel 1996).

By the same token, one might argue empirically that feelings toward social groups—as opposed to political figures or institutions—tend to be quite stable over time. Putting both observations together suggests that the dynamics of party identification might be approximated by a tipping model. People maintain their partisan identities as long as their image of the partisan groups remains intact. But when secular realignment is afoot, the public image of the partisan groups shifts, which in turn produces a shift in party identification and perhaps further alters perceptions of partisan groups. The next chapter presents a case study of this kind of secular realignment, the movement of Southern whites to the Republican Party after decades of disaffection with the hegemonic Democratic Party.

Chapter 6 Party Realignment
in the American South

Having demonstrated that people maintain their party attachments over time and having ruled out the notion that defensive psychological mechanisms are responsible for this pattern, we now return to our central hypothesis: Party attachments tend to be stable because the social group imagery associated with the parties tends to change slowly over time.[1] Once a person's party attachments take root, they are seldom disrupted by new conceptions of the partisan groups and the social coalitions that they comprise.

Note that party identities, in our view, are not inherently stable. Rather, their stability hinges on the way that partisan groups are perceived. How groups are evaluated and linked with political parties tends to persist over time, but change can and does occur from time to time. To appreciate the role of group imagery in maintaining party ties, it is therefore useful to identify unusual instances in which group stereotypes changed dramatically. If our hypothesis is correct, these changes should precipitate a shift in party attachments at both the individual and aggregate levels. Individuals would be expected to alter how they categorize themselves vis-à-vis the partisan groups; aggregate change would reflect both individual-level change and the replacement of existing cohorts, who may still harbor older conceptions of the parties, with new cohorts, who have a new understanding of partisan group labels.

The American South represents a vivid illustration of how an exogenous shock to the electoral system—the enfranchisement of blacks through the Voting Rights Act of 1965 and their subsequent incorporation into the Democratic Party—can set in motion changes to the social imagery of the parties that ultimately produce a party realignment. Excluding blacks from power had since the 1890s been the guiding rationale behind the one-party politics of the South (Key 1949). Even as the Supreme Court signaled the end of de jure segregation of schools and the civil rights movement gained momentum as a national political cause, Southern whites bent on maintaining racial hierarchy still controlled the electoral system. The Democratic Party had long embodied a coalition of the whole among whites. Ironically, augmenting the Democratic Party with large numbers of newly enfranchised Democrats in 1965 had the long-term effect of undercutting its dominance.

This chapter begins by charting the extent and timing of Southern change from the early 1950s to the late 1990s. Using both cross-sectional data and fragmentary panel data, we trace the evolution of Southern partisanship and compare it with trends in the non-South. Next, we estimate how much of the apparent change in Southern party identification reflects individual conversion as opposed to the replacement of older, more Democratic cohorts with younger, more Republican ones. This exercise is important because it establishes several important facts about Southern realignment upon which the second, interpretive half of this chapter relies. Roughly half of the Southern realignment is due to cohort replacement, not individual-level change. Individual-level change occurred gradually over an extended period. The pace of change accelerated not in 1964, when Barry Goldwater's states' rights position on civil rights enabled him to win decisively in the Deep South, but in 1965, after the enactment of the Voting Rights Act, which brought large numbers of blacks into the Democratic Party. It accelerated again in the early 1980s as the image of the Republican Party in the eyes of Southerners began to change, buoyed by the popularity of Ronald Reagan and the activism of conservative religious movements with which the Republican Party had come to be aligned. This pattern of Republicanization continued into the 1990s, as the national Republican leadership became increasingly Southern. Yet, the entire process of convergence between non-South and South took decades, underscoring the fact that partisan imagery fades slowly, particularly when politicians in the declining party work steadfastly to keep it alive.

The second half of the chapter examines competing explanations of partisan change in the South. Some of these theories interpret partisan change as a long-term process of economic and cultural integration of the South. Other theories stress the role of issues rather than of groups, contending that whites deserted the Democratic Party in favor of a Republican Party that was more congenial to their conservative tastes. Related to the latter argument is the contention that the institutional vitality of the Republican Party itself played a role in attracting Republican adherents. Each of these perspectives, in our view, contributes to the explanation of partisan change and often in ways that are compatible with our theoretical perspective, which stresses the role of social identities.

THE PACE OF PARTISAN CHANGE

To appreciate the pace and timing of partisan change in the South, it is useful to return to Converse's (1966b) classic essay "On the Possibility of Major Political Realignment in the South." The bulk of this essay was written before the 1964 election, when one could confidently point to the fact that deeply conservative states such as Mississippi and Alabama had voted decisively against Nixon, Eisenhower, and their Republican forebears. Converse marveled at the remarkable stability of Southern party attachments, notwithstanding the prediction in wide currency since 1948 that the Bible Belt would soon bolt from the Democratic Party:

> It has long been obvious against the backdrop of national politics that the historical link between the South and the Democratic Party has become quite implausible from an ideological point of view. The facts are commonplace. The nominal coalition between northern and southern wings of the Democratic Party has lost much of the rationale it once had and has ceased to function in Congress at all on a fair range of major issues. The marriage has remained tolerable to each party on rather expedient grounds, such as easy presidential votes for the northern wing and congressional seniority for the southern. On most other counts, however, the grounds for divorce have become overwhelming. Hence it has not been unreasonable to look for the development of a South as solidly Republican as it once was Democratic. . . . Yet if individual partisan conversion is occurring in a manner which systematically favors one party over the other in the South, the phenomenon is so weak that it very nearly eludes any [panel] analysis for the 1956–1960 period. (pp. 213, 225)

A year later this conclusion seemed less secure. In a footnote added in early 1965, after Goldwater had won a remarkable 87% of the vote in Mississippi and 69% in Alabama, Converse qualified this conclusion and speculated that Goldwater's states' rights position may have created Republican converts in the Deep South (p. 241), even if the South as a whole, however, did not shift its party allegiance in 1964. Although the 1964 election provided "a supreme test of the capacity of the civil rights issue to touch off fundamental and rapid partisan realignment in the South" (p. 241), it only slightly accelerated the gradual partisan convergence between non-South and South.

Converse's analysis seemed secure through the 1970s, when Wolfinger and Arseneau (1978) and Beck (1977) argued that Southern partisan change could be explained as a function of interregional mobility and generational replacement, not individual-level conversion. But growing evidence of partisan change after the mid-1960s began to turn academic assessments around. The turning point in scholarly opinion occurred when Miller (1991) demonstrated that age cohorts of Southern whites drifted toward the Republican Party in numbers too large to be explained by sampling error or transitory period effects.

Some amount of the change must be due to partisan conversion, but how much and when did this trend begin? Tables 6.1 and 6.2 present the distribution of partisanship for non-Southern and Southern respondents in National Election Study surveys from 1952 to 1998. Even when we examine the more finely grained seven-point measure of party identification, we find remarkably little movement in partisanship among non-Southerners. Decades of generational replacement in the population, three foreign wars, several dramatic swings in party fortunes, three significant minor party bids for president, fluctuating economic conditions, and substantial changes in social mores scarcely altered the proportions of Democrats and Republicans. Without denying the significant electoral repercussions that might result from minute changes in the distribution of party identification, we would call attention to the strong resemblance between partisanship at the beginning and end of this forty-six year period.

Granted, some trends are discernible in the distribution of party identification in the non-South. Apparent from Table 6.1 is the pattern of "dealignment" (Clarke and Stewart 1998; Ladd 1982; but see Keith et al. 1992)—the gradual decline in self-identified Democrats after 1964 and the concomitant rise in Independents and "leaning" partisans that occurred through the 1970s. In 1964, for example, strong and weak Democrats represented 47% of the sample, compared with 37% in 1976; all shades of Independents (Independents plus leaning partisans) made up 25% of respondents in 1964 and 39% in 1976. The growth of Independents then receded, followed by the much-heralded "realignment" toward the Republican Party (Norpoth 1987; Petrocik 1987). In 1976, strong

Table 6.1. Party Identification of Non-Southerners, 1952–98

	1952	1956	1958	1960	1962	1964	1966	1968	1970	1972
Democrat										
Strong Democrat	18	18	24	19	22	23	17	18	18	14
Weak Democrat	23	20	22	23	23	24	27	24	23	24
Independent										
Leaning Democrat	11	8	8	8	8	11	9	10	12	12
Independent	7	10	8	9	8	8	12	10	12	13
Leaning Republican	8	10	6	8	6	6	7	9	7	11
Republican										
Weak Republican	16	16	19	16	18	16	18	17	18	15
Strong Republican	17	18	14	17	15	13	10	12	10	12
N	1,356	1,294	1,319	1,395	917	1,184	983	1,155	1,081	1,968

Source: National Election Studies cumulative file.

Note: Data (percentages) are weighted and include respondents of all races. The non-South is states other than South Carolina, Georgia, Alabama, Mississippi, Louisiana, Virginia, North Carolina, Tennesssee, Arkansas, Texas, and Florida.

Table 6.2. Party Identification of Southerners, 1952–98

	1952	1956	1958	1960	1962	1964	1966	1968	1970	1972
Democrat										
Strong Democrat	38	32	39	25	30	41	23	27	25	19
Weak Democrat	38	36	29	34	29	28	32	31	26	32
Independent										
Leaning Democrat	7	4	5	3	5	5	9	10	8	9
Independent	2	6	7	12	8	8	12	11	15	15
Leaning Republican	4	6	3	3	7	5	8	10	10	9
Republican										
Weak Republican	7	10	12	10	14	6	8	7	9	9
Strong Republican	4	7	5	12	7	6	8	4	7	7
N	373	396	418	469	320	352	280	376	409	688

Source: National Election Studies cumulative file.

Note: Data (percentages) are weighted and include respondents of all races. The South comprises South Carolina, Georgia, Alabama, Mississippi, Louisiana, Virginia, North Carolina, Tennesssee, Arkansas, Texas, and Florida.

1974	1976	1978	1980	1982	1984	1986	1988	1990	1992	1994	1996	1998
17	14	14	16	17	16	16	16	18	16	14	17	19
19	23	25	23	24	19	21	17	20	18	19	20	19
15	13	15	12	12	12	11	11	12	16	14	15	16
15	15	14	13	12	10	12	11	9	11	12	9	11
10	11	10	11	8	13	12	14	12	12	11	10	10
16	16	14	15	16	17	16	16	18	15	15	16	15
9	10	8	9	11	14	12	15	11	12	16	13	10
1,754	2,114	1,602	1,118	969	1,567	1,433	1,370	1,347	1,684	1,172	1,084	826

1974	1976	1978	1980	1982	1984	1986	1988	1990	1992	1994	1996	1998
21	19	19	23	29	20	23	21	26	22	18	21	20
28	32	26	26	25	24	25	21	18	18	19	19	19
10	10	13	10	8	9	11	14	13	11	13	13	10
17	15	14	13	9	15	12	10	14	14	8	10	10
7	7	9	8	9	12	9	12	11	13	12	15	11
11	11	11	13	12	11	13	10	10	12	14	13	19
6	7	7	7	7	9	8	12	7	10	15	10	11
679	713	622	459	414	631	687	629	588	762	597	608	430

and weak Republicans made up 26% of the sample, a figure that grew to 31% at its high water mark in 1994.

The trends in the South are more pronounced. In the 1950s, Democrats outnumbered Republicans by at least four to one. By the late 1960s, the proportion of Democrats diminished as a larger share of the population called itself Independent. The gradual erosion of Democratic partisanship continued through the 1970s and accelerated in the mid-1980s, when the proportion of Republicans began to grow. In 1998, the proportion of Independents had subsided to levels of the late 1960s, while Republican identification reached a new high water mark of 30%.

Tables 6.1 and 6.2 give us a sense of how the two regions compare, but they gloss over important differences between groups within each region. The story of the Republican realignment in the South is primarily about the changing attachments of whites, and so a more informative comparison would look at whites in the South and elsewhere. Even then, the trends that emerge from aggregate data raise questions about over-time comparability. Ideally, we would like to be able to track the partisan composition of a large, representative sample of *individuals* over a long time, but this is simply not feasible. Instead, we are forced to make the most out of two less-than-perfect sources of information: pooled cross sections of survey data spanning the period 1952–98 from the NES and a series of panel studies conducted between 1956 and 1998, most of which are also from the NES.

The pooled cross sections enable us to track cohorts, but not individuals, over time. The problems with this approach are well-known. There is no guarantee that a fifty-year-old Southern respondent interviewed in 1980 was in the population of forty-year-old Southerners in 1970; this respondent could have been living elsewhere in 1970.[2] To mitigate this problem, we have restricted many of the analyses to respondents who live in the same region in which they were raised.[3] As a shortcut we refer to these groups as "native" white Southerners and non-Southerners, but strictly speaking it is not that they were born in the region in which they now live, but that they "grew up" there. Focusing on whites raised in the South does not fully resolve the problems of drawing inferences from pooled cross sections, but it places the data analysis on somewhat firmer footing than examining samples of *current* residents.

The convergence between the two regions is illustrated in Figure 6.1, which graphs *average* party identification using pooled cross-sectional surveys from 1952 to 1998. In this figure, party identification is scored from 1 to 7, where 1 represents a strong Democrat and 7, a strong Republican. If Democrats and

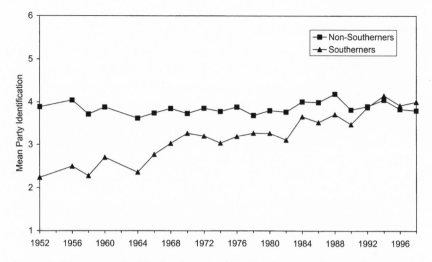

Figure 6.1. Mean party identification for native white Southerners and native white non-Southerners, 1952–98.

Republicans were evenly balanced, the mean would be 4.0. Anything below that line represents a net Democratic advantage. Focusing on native white respondents, Figure 6.2 shows the dynamics over the period 1952–98 in the South and the rest of the country.

The two time trajectories look fundamentally different. Outside the South, there is little change over time to speak of, but the South is a very different story. As political commentators since the 1948 election have predicted, the Democratic Party has gradually lost the allegiance of Southern whites. In 1952, fully 78% of native Southern white respondents described themselves as Democrats. Even amid the Goldwater candidacy of 1964, Democrats still accounted for 73% of the sample. After the Voting Rights Act of 1965, which simultaneously enfranchised black voters and rekindled interparty competition in the South (Black and Black 1987), the proportion of Democrats declined markedly. By the 1972 election, 51% of Southern whites were self-identified Democrats. The erosion of Democratic support slowed during the next decade but resumed during the 1980s and 1990s. By the century's end, whites in the two regions had become nearly indistinguishable in terms of average party attachments.

These regional trends among whites can be summarized statistically through a linear regression of party identification on the year during which the respondents were interviewed. A positive slope indicates that partisanship is becom-

Table 6.3. Rates of Partisan Change Using Cross-Sectional Surveys of Native
Whites in the South and Non-South, 1952–98

	Time Coefficient	Adjusted R^2	N
Southern whites			
Party identification on time	0.039	0.067	7,071
	(0.002)		
Party identification on time,	0.020	0.091	7,071
controlling for birth year	(0.002)		
Non-Southern whites			
Party identification on time	0.003	0.000	25,856
	(0.001)		
Party identification on time,	0.007	0.002	25,856
controlling for birth year	(0.001)		

Source: American National Election Studies, 1952–98.
Note: The samples were restricted to whites who currently lived in the region where they were raised.

ing more Republican over time. For non-Southern whites, this regression produces a slope of 0.003, implying that the region became 0.14 scale points more Republican over the forty-six-year period (see Table 6.3). The average rate of change for Southern whites is more than ten times as large. The slope of 0.039 implies that the average white Southerner became 1.8 points more Republican between 1952 and 1998.

These statistical results merely restate the trends apparent from the preceding figures, but in so doing they also provide a benchmark for regression analysis that tries to account for generational replacement. One way to grapple with the complications of cohort replacement is to control for the respondent's birth year in the regression of partisanship on time. This statistical approach is not completely satisfactory because one cannot disentangle the separate effects of time, birth cohort, and changes in partisanship related to maturation and life-cycle changes (Abramson 1979). Nevertheless, the exercise enables us to derive a rough sense of how much individual change might be occurring before we turn to the panel surveys discussed below. Outside the South, the slope coefficient associated with time grows from 0.003 to 0.007. Evidently, the Democratic inclinations of younger cohorts outside the South conceals a bit of Republican drift over time. For Southern respondents, this pattern is reversed. Controlling for birth year reduces the effect of time from 0.039 to 0.020, indicating that approximately half of the overall change is due to generational replacement and half to accumulated individual change.

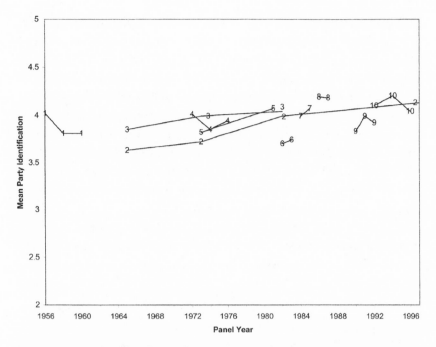

Figure 6.2. Mean party identification for native non-Southerners in ten panel studies: The numbers at each of the plotted points are used to denote the panel surveys: 1 = NES 1956–60; 2 = students 1965–82–97; 3 = parents 1965–82; 4 = NES 1972–76; 5 = Political Action Panel 1973–81; 6 = NES 1982–83; 7 = NES 1984–85; 8 = NES 1986–87; 9 = NES 1990–92; 10 = NES 1992–94.

To understand how generational replacement could have such profound effects in the South, consider the magnitude of the partisan differences between older and younger cohorts, as gauged by the NES. In 1952, 82% of white Southerners born before 1900 were Democrats, and this cohort of adults constituted 34% of all native Southern whites in the sample. Forty years later, this cohort had vanished from our surveys. The age cohorts that have since entered the electorate have diluted the Democratic composition of the Southern white population. Before 1964, 76% of the 50 native Southern white respondents aged twenty-one to twenty-four described themselves as Democrats. By contrast, during the period 1978–98, just 27% of the 365 Southerners aged twenty-one to twenty-four called themselves Democrats.[4] In sum, decades of NES surveys span a period in which older, ardently Democratic generations have been replaced by younger Southerners, who are much less likely to identify as Democrats.

While emphasizing the role of cohort replacement, the analysis of pooled cross sections also assigns an important role to individual conversions. The average white Southerner moved nearly one-fifth of a scale point every decade along the seven-point scale, slightly more if we consider only surveys conducted after 1964. This rate of change seems plausible; still, the fact that we do not actually follow individuals over time is cause for concern. A more cautious way of assessing the amount of individual-level change is to track respondents over time using surveys that track a group of respondents over successive years. The ten such panel studies at our disposal collectively span the period 1956–97. Our aim is to catch Southerners in the act of changing their party affiliations, if only to corroborate the results of our previous analysis.

Figures 6.2 and 6.3 display the mean levels of party identification among Southern and non-Southern respondents in each wave of the ten panel surveys, each of which is represented by a line segment. Non-Southerners show few

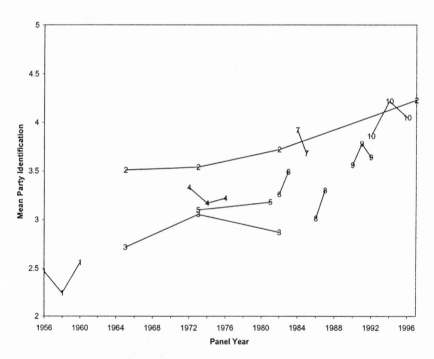

Figure 6.3. Mean party identification for native white Southerners in ten panel studies: The numbers at each of the plotted points are used to denote the panel surveys: 1 = NES 1956–60; 2 = students 1965–82–97; 3 = parents 1965–82; 4 = NES 1972–76; 5 = Political Action Panel 1973–81; 6 = NES 1982–83–97; 7 = NES 1984–85; 8 = NES 1986–87; 9 = NES 1990–92; 10 = NES 1992–94.

signs of movement, drifting faintly in the Republican direction after the mid-1980s. The Southern pattern is more complex. Clearly, the means *for different surveys* drift upward with time, but this type of movement is consistent with an interpretation of either cohort replacement or individual conversion. When we chart partisan change within surveys, the pattern is somewhat more ambiguous, but there seems to be a general tendency for respondents to grow more Republican from interview to interview.

This inference is confirmed by the regression analysis reported in Table 6.4. When we simply regress Southern party identification on time, the results suggest fairly substantial partisan change: The estimated effect of time is 0.036

Table 6.4. Rates of Partisan Change Estimated Using Panel Surveys of Native Southern Whites

	Model 1	Model 2	Model 3
Time	0.036* (0.003)	0.020* (0.005)	0.019* (0.005)
Students, 1965–82	—	0.91* (0.16)	0.36 (0.20)
Parents, 1965–82	—	0.16 (0.15)	0.19 (0.16)
NES 1972–76	—	0.50* (0.15)	0.33* (0.15)
Political Action Panel	—	0.35* (0.16)	0.11 (0.17)
NES 1982–83	—	0.48* (0.23)	0.23 (0.24)
NES 1984–85	—	0.86* (0.25)	0.49 (0.26)
NES 1986–87	—	0.18 (0.24)	−0.21 (0.24)
NES 1990–92	—	0.59* (0.22)	0.17 (0.23)
NES 1992–96	—	0.92* (0.24)	0.44 (0.25)
Born 1888–98	—	—	0.23 (0.36)
Born 1899–1909	—	—	0.12 (0.34)
Born 1910–20	—	—	0.03 (0.33)
Born 1921–31	—	—	0.25 (0.33)
Born 1932–42	—	—	0.48 (0.34)
Born 1943–53	—	—	0.71 (0.34)
Born 1954–64	—	—	0.83* (0.35)
Born 1965–75	—	—	0.96* (0.38)
Constant	1.52 (0.07)	1.38 (0.09)	1.23 (0.31)
Adjusted R^2	0.043	0.058	0.069
N	3,795	3,795	3,795

Note: Table entries are unstandardized regression coefficients with standard errors in parentheses. The dependent variable was party identification, coded zero (Strong Democrat) to six (Strong Republican). The NES 1956–60 Panel Study was the base category for the interpretation of the dummy variable for each survey. The cohort born in 1887 or earlier was the base category for the interpretation of the dummy variable for each cohort.
*$p < .05$ (two-tailed).

(with a standard error of 0.003). This estimate is quite similar to the estimate of 0.039 that we obtained from the cross-sectional data. But when we add an additional set of dummy variables to designate each panel survey on the grounds that these surveys differ in terms of sampling design and method of administration, the effect of time appears to be a more modest 0.020 (SE = 0.005) but in line with our previous cross-sectional results. To assess the robustness of these results, we also included control variables marking each birth cohort. As expected, the older birth cohorts were significantly more Democratic, but controlling for birth cohort does not change the overall pattern of results. On the basis of both the cross-sectional and panel results, our best guess is that Southern whites changed their party attachments at a rate of approximately one-fifth of a scale point per decade.

These results can be refined in three ways. First, the preceding analysis is based on the assumption that partisan change is constant across time. This is a problem because it appears that change was greater during the 1960s and 1980s than during the 1970s. Second, the rate of change is assumed to be the same for young respondents and old respondents. Third, by lumping together the Deep South (South Carolina, Georgia, Alabama, Mississippi, Louisiana) and Rim South (Virginia, North Carolina, Florida, Tennessee, Arkansas, and Texas), we overlook important nuances that give clues about the reasons for change.

To examine nonlinear time trends, we estimated the effect of time and functions of time (time squared, time cubed, etc.) on party identification using the pooled cross-sectional surveys. We then compared the results for regressions of party identification on time and functions of time up to the fourth power, with and without controls for birth year. The most notable result is that the pace of change slowed during the 1970s and accelerated after 1982. Even so, the history of the South after Ronald Reagan took office indicates how long it can take for realignments to unfold. At this maximum rate of individual-level conversion, the average respondent is expected to take roughly fifty years to move a single point along the seven-point partisan continuum.

To get a more nuanced sense of how different age groups reacted to the changing party system, we tracked mean partisanship for three cohorts across time. For each cohort, we focused on change through 1994, as that represents a peak of Republican identification among Southerners. The oldest cohort, including respondents born from 1920 to 1935, remained extremely Democratic for years after the disruptions that the party experienced in 1964, 1972, and 1980. The respondents in this cohort had a mean party identification of 2.68 in

1956, and thirty-two years later in 1988, had a mean party identification of 3.19—a rate of change of 0.016 per year. This shift represents a decline in the percentage of respondents who were Democrats from 67% to 43%—substantial, but not rapid considering the long time span and considering that these respondents tended to be more conservative in many ways than their younger Southern counterparts. This cohort continued to drift toward the Republican Party after 1988. By 1994, mean party identification for these respondents rose to 3.51. Although 49% still identified themselves as Democrats, Republican identification had increased from 14% to 28%.

As one compares the preceding cohort with the 1936–51 cohort, one first sees that the younger group entered the electorate far more Republican than did the 1920–35 cohort. In 1972, the first year when this younger cohort was fully in the sample, its mean party identification was 3.58, compared with a mean of 2.98 for the 1920–35 cohort in that year. In 1994, this cohort had a mean party identification of 3.52, exhibiting virtually no movement over the course of twenty-two years. Unlike its older counterpart, the 1936–51 cohort came of age politically after the emergent two-party South had begun to take shape.

Members of the youngest cohort that we examined, respondents born from 1952 to 1966, entered the electorate with very strong Republican inclinations that became stronger over time. The first survey in which these respondents were all of voting age was conducted in 1984, and their average partisanship was 3.99. Although this group appears not to have moved noticeably from 1984 to 1990, it shifted markedly with the rising fortunes of the Republicans in 1994. The mean surged to 4.62 in 1994, ending at 4.33 in 1998. Consistent with our earlier characterization of partisan instability among young adults, this cohort seems to have been unusually responsive to the growing stature of the Republican Party.

The analysis of age cohorts suggests the importance of both initial partisan ties and the process of equilibration by which these initial ties adjust to accommodate new perceptions. If realignment were simply a matter of people finding a party that best suits them ideologically, we would not find younger Southern whites to be sharply more Republican than their older, often more conservative counterparts.[5] Nor would it be clear why the election in 1964 should produce such a dramatic reaction at the voting booth, indicating that the electorate was fully aware of and deeply impressed by the differences between the candidates, yet fail to alter Southern party identification. The different trajectories of the three Southern cohorts alerts us to the special role that group images and attachments play in the explanation of Southern realignment. The oldest cohort formed its party attachments in reference to a long-standing one-party system that later experienced fundamental changes. The middle cohort entered the electorate with a new set of perceptions about who Democrats and Republicans were, perceptions that were much more in line with the way that the party coalitions would later develop after the 1970s. Unlike the youngest cohort, the middle cohort's party attachments had taken shape before the succession of Republican Party victories culminating in the 1994 election.

Finally, a more detailed account of change in Southern white partisanship requires some attention to regional differences within the South. Before the 1960s and continuing until 1972, the presidential voting patterns of the Deep South—Alabama, Georgia, Mississippi, Louisiana, and South Carolina—ran somewhat counter to the patterns of the Rim South. Whereas peaks of Rim South Republican voting occurred in 1928, 1952, 1956, and 1960, defections from Democratic voting in the Deep South did not occur in any of those years—with some minor exceptions such as Louisiana's vote for Eisenhower in 1956. Instead, the Deep South's defections led to third-party votes for the Dixiecrats in 1948 and George Wallace in 1968 and for the Republican Goldwater in 1964. Although Tennessee, Florida, and Virginia voted for Nixon in 1960, Johnson in 1964, and Nixon in 1968, Georgia, Alabama, Mississippi, and Louisiana voted for Kennedy in 1960, Goldwater in 1964, and Wallace in 1968. In sum, the Deep South's stronger Democratic ties were expressed in stronger support for Democratic candidates as long as those candidates could be trusted not to disrupt the foundations of Southern politics.

Race provided the rationale for the one-party system, and initially it was in the parts of the South—Rim and urban—where race was less paramount politically that Democratic identification was less prevalent. Table 6.5 shows the breakdown of party identification among whites in the Rim and Deep South. Because of the paucity of respondents in each of the regions, we have aggregated the data by decades. In the 1950s, whites in the Rim South were predominantly Democrats, but the Deep South was overwhelmingly so. During the 1960s, both regions moved toward Independence, and the Rim South began to acquire a slight Republican tinge. The 1970s saw the proportion of Republicans grow markedly in the Rim South, moving the region toward an equilibrium that would persist into the 1980s and 1990s. The Deep South lagged behind until 1984, when Republican identification began to grow. By the 1990s, whites in the Deep South had become slightly more Republican than their Rim South counterparts. Despite its greater conservatism, the Deep

Table 6.5. Party Identification by Decade in the Deep South and Rim South

	1950–58	1960–68	1970–78	1980–88	1990–98
Deep South					
Democrat	87	66	51	43	28
Independent	9	23	36	36	39
Republican	5	11	13	22	32
N	260	302	769	480	401
Rim South					
Democrat	66	55	42	40	34
Independent	17	25	35	36	38
Republican	17	19	23	25	28
N	752	1,219	1,730	1,667	1,812

Source: American National Election Studies.

Note: The Deep South includes respondents from South Carolina, Georgia, Alabama, Mississippi, Louisiana. The Rim South encompasses Virginia, North Carolina, Florida, Tennessee, Arkansas, and Texas. Values are percentages.

South maintained stronger attachments to the Democratic Party until decades after the demise of Jim Crow.

COMPETING PERSPECTIVES
ON PARTISAN CHANGE

The transformation of Southern party attachments may be explained from many theoretical vantage points. Before the occurrence of the realignment, observers of Southern politics advanced the argument that the South's economic development and integration with the rest of the country would gradually bring middle-class interests into alignment with their Republican counterparts in the non-South. Key (1949) in *Southern Politics in State and Nation,* Heard (1952) in *A Two-Party South?* and others foresaw an emergent coalition among "urban," "metropolitan," "progressive," and "business-oriented" Southern Republicans. The first signs of this small but growing force came in 1920 (when Tennessee voted for the Republican candidate, Warren Harding) and appeared more regularly in the 1940s and 1950s in presidential voting, if only because there were so few Republican candidates for other offices. It is generally thought that it was the more "progressive" and well-to-do elements of the urban Rim South that showed this presidential Republicanism. In presidential elections from 1936 to 1960, the percentage of Republican votes in urban areas exceeded for the first time the percentage in the traditional mountain Republican areas of the South. With less of a stake in the traditional arrangements that gave controlling power to the black-belt whites, these voters' interests resembled those of their non-Southern business-oriented peers. Or stated in terms of social identity, although they may have identified themselves as Southerners, they also felt an affinity with those who considered themselves to be Republicans elsewhere: white, Protestant, and middle class.

Converse (1966) bolstered these arguments by pointing out that the correlation between social status and party identification was gradually increasing over time. In the 1950s, Southerners in white-collar occupations were slightly *more* likely to identify as Democrats than their blue-collar counterparts, although fewer than 12% of all blue-collar Southern whites were Republicans. By the 1960s, this correlation was beginning to reverse itself and follow the non-Southern pattern, in which white-collar workers were more likely to call themselves Republicans than their blue-collar counterparts. By this account, politics of social class, for so long subordinated to the cause of racial hierarchy, poured forth after the demise of the one-party system. This argument is intuitively appealing but not without limitations. The correlation nowadays between social class and party attachments is not terribly strong in either the South or the non-South. Outside the South, Democrats outnumbered Republicans by about two to one among blue-collar whites in both the 1950s and 1990s. White-collar non-Southerners split about evenly between the parties. In the South, Republicans in the late 1990s held a four to three edge over Democrats among white-collar workers, whereas Democrats outnumbered Republicans about two to one among whites in blue-collar occupations. As Converse predicted, the occupational division now looks similar in both regions, but whereas white-collar workers in the South have found their natural class homes in the Republican Party, blue-collar workers have also dropped from 78% Democrat in 1952–60 to 38% Democrat in 1996–98.

Another way to think about the role of social class that helps account for regional convergence is the diffuse class imagery associated with the parties in the non-South and the South. Converse (1966: 221) observed that before the mid-1960s "the Democratic Party in the South had been quite generally the symbol of small-town middle-class respectability, much as the Republican Party has maintained this image in the small towns outside the South." The Democratic Party not only elected virtually all public officials in the region and therefore commanded the admiration and participation of high-status people, it symbolized the abiding principle of right-thinking citizens—white supremacy.

Even after Truman's integrationist policies drove Dixiecrats into revolt in 1948, Southern Democrats still saw their party in the 1950s as arguably committed to segregation by virtue of the power that the Southern delegation wielded within it. Goldwater's candidacy, the enfranchisement of black Democrats, Wallace's Independent candidacy in 1968, and the endorsement of Nixon by many Southern Democratic leaders in 1972 gradually chipped away at the middle-class respectability of the Democratic Party. When conservative Christian leaders became outspoken Republicans in the late 1970s and early 1980s, the Democratic Party was routinely castigated as the party of secular humanists. The allure of respectability eventually redounded to the benefit of Republicans, as their ranks were augmented by evangelical and fundamentalist Christians (Petrocik 1987).

This interpretation puts group imagery in the forefront and assigns a lesser role to economic development and the class interests that it engenders. How these group images become manifest and develop over time, of course, depends on a variety of contingent events. In the early 1970s, evangelical leaders such as Pat Robertson counseled their followers that politics was a dirty business that Christians should keep out of. A decade later, as the Democratic gains made in the aftermath of Watergate and Carter's election faded, political activism and evangelizing had become intertwined (Oldfield 1996). Some of the most interesting contingencies have to do with the decisions of Democratic leaders to stick with the party or switch. Some, such as George Wallace, argued that it was best to work within the Democratic Party and shape it to suit Southern tastes. Other prominent Democrats, such as Strom Thurmond (1964), John Connally (1973), Phil Gramm (1983), and Richard Shelby (1994), switched to the Republican Party. Other contingencies have to do with the growing prominence of Southern Republicans within the national party leadership. By the mid-1990s, for example, the Republican majority leader of the U.S. Senate, Republican speaker of the House, and chair of the Republican National Committee all hailed from the South.

Whether one chooses to call the organizational revitalization of the Republican Party a contingent fact or a foreordained consequence of new Republican strength in the electorate, the efflorescence of Southern Republican identification in part depended on the party's ability to field Republican candidates. Without them, Southerners would continue to associate Republicans with the non-South.

However attractive Eisenhower and Nixon may have been to some Southern voters from 1952 to 1960, their *party* remained largely moribund as a Southern

endeavor. In 1960, for example, sixty-four of ninety-eight Southern congressional seats, or 65%, went uncontested by a Republican candidate in the November election, and Republican state legislators were badly outnumbered in
or altogether absent from Southern statehouses. The Goldwater candidacy and
the passage of the Voting Rights Act gave new vitality to the Republican Party,
and by 1968 just 32% of Southern House seats went uncontested. In the mean-
time, Southern states, such as Arkansas and Florida, elected Republican gover-
nors. Interestingly, both the institutional development and electoral success
stalled in most Southern states during the early 1970s, coinciding with the
slowing pace of Republicanization of the electorate.[6] Significant Republican
inroads in state legislative delegations in Florida, North Carolina, and Virginia
receded, and Democrats continued to run uncontested in more than one in
four U.S. House seats. The Republican Party organizations of the South,
widely described during the 1970s as weak and incohesive (see Hadley and
Bowman 1995), rebounded in the 1980 election and after the 1982 recession. As
they elected larger and larger delegations of Republicans, they acquired the
kind of prominence and financial backing that made them a permanent fixture
of Southern political life.

A different interpretation of events places the electorate's ideological tastes,
rather than group attachments, in the foreground. Carmines and Stimson
(1989) argue that 1964 marked the beginning of a profound partisan division
over issues of race and that the Democratic Party's embrace of liberal racial
policies drove Southerners into the ranks of the Republican Party. In a similar
vein, one may argue that the left-leaning tendencies of the Democratic Party
made it vulnerable to an assortment of conservative attacks, stressing "family
values," patriotism, and Second Amendment rights. What drove the South
into the arms of the Republican Party was not the specter of secular humanists
as a group but rather anger over policies that banned prayer in schools, permit-
ted abortion, and denied tax breaks for parochial school tuition.

There can be no doubt that these issues were important to Southern voters,
and here it is important for us to distance our position from one of the central
arguments growing out of *The American Voter* (Campbell et al. 1960), "The
Nature of Belief Systems in Mass Publics" (Converse 1964), and *Elections and
the Political Order* (Campbell et al. 1966). In those works, issue voting of the
sort envisioned by Downs (1957) was downplayed on the grounds that the public had relatively weak opinions, little knowledge about where the parties stand
on these issues, and virtually no grasp of ideological terms or how to apply
them. An exception was carved out for racial issues, but even there the authors

were quick to point out that the parties seldom staked out distinctive positions.[7] Believing that issues have little effect on the vote, these authors inferred
that issues should have even less effect on deeper attachments such as party
identification.

Although we tend to assign less weight to issue-based explanations of realignment than many scholars, it is not because we are skeptical of the public's
ability to cast votes on the basis of issues. The success that Democrats continued to enjoy when running for state office attests to the importance of tailoring
one's platform to fit the conservative tastes of the electorate, something that
Democratic presidential candidates cannot do credibly without jeopardizing
the support of their core constituencies.[8] The electorate may lack an apprecia-
tion for ideological nuance and detailed information about what the candidates
stand for, but conservative constituencies nevertheless tend to elect like-
minded public officials. The reasons for this correspondence are several, but
perhaps chief among them is the fact that campaigns provide cues as to which
interest groups are pulling for each side (Brady and Sniderman 1985; Lupia
1994). If a candidate is denounced by the Christian Coalition and endorsed by
labor unions, voters can infer the candidate's stands on a variety of issues. Much
of what would ordinarily be termed issue voting reflects the importance of
group-based cues in shaping political preferences.

What about the role of issues in shaping Southern party identities? To the
widespread opinion that the conservatism of the region inevitably meant a Republican ascendancy we would add a number of important qualifications.
First, throughout much of American history, the political parties have been
ideologically heterogeneous. Just as the 1920s saw an unlikely alliance between
conservative Republicans and progressive Republicans, the New Deal forged a
remarkable coalition among Southerners, labor unions, cities, and recent immigrants. Conservative Southern Democrats in the early 1970s could plausibly
take the view that the Democratic Party was still their party; better to pull it
rightward than bolt to a Republican Party that they still associated with the
non-South. Even as late as 1972, when the National Election Study began asking respondents to label themselves using the ideological categories liberal,
conservative, or moderate, 50% of Southern conservatives called themselves
Democrats. A person may choose to vote for candidates on the basis of what
they stand for, but a person may identify with a party despite policy disagreement in the hopes that these tensions will subside.

Once a critical mass of people begin to shift parties, change in the parties' social imagery gains momentum.[9] As conservative, devout Southerners became

reticent about calling themselves Democrats, they less and less defined the social imagery of the party. As older party stereotypes faded, self-designated conservatives in the South gravitated steadily toward Republican affiliation. Between 1972 and 1978 the proportion of Southern conservatives who identified as Democrats dropped from 50% to 35% and dwindled still further to 30% in 1980. After pausing briefly in 1982, the decline resumed, so that by 1996 just 17% of Southern conservatives identified as Democrats. If this were simply a matter of the Democratic Party becoming more liberal in relation to the Republican Party over time, we would expect to see a similar trend in other parts of the country. But outside the South the percentage of conservatives describing themselves as Democrats has held steady over time: 20% in 1972, 16% in 1984, and 17% in 1996. Even Southerners who describe themselves as liberals have distanced themselves from the Democratic Party: 59% called themselves Democrats during the 1970s, as opposed to 52% in the 1990s.

Issue-based realignment and social group–based realignment are thus deeply intertwined. Both perspectives would lead us to expect that after the demise of the one-party system, liberals and conservatives gradually sorted themselves into different parties over the next three decades. In part, this pattern reflects the fact that conservatives are more at home in a party that espouses conservative issue positions. It also reflects the fact that conservatives are more at home in the company of other conservatives, and group affinities may be as important as ideological proximity. Survey data suggest that both processes were at work. As the Republican image improved, Republican identification became increasingly prevalent among all segments of the ideological continuum. Compare, for example, the relationship between party identification and "ideological proximity" for two years, 1972 and 1996.[10] As the preceding discussion would lead us to expect, the relationship among non-Southerners between ideological proximity and party identification remained constant over time. In the South, native white Southerners who perceived themselves to be ideologically closer to the Republican Party became much less likely to call themselves Democrats (50% to 5%). But so, too, did those who described themselves as equidistant from the parties (48% to 20%) as well as an even larger group, those who were unable to convey a clear sense of their ideological location vis-à-vis the parties (54% to 43%). The decline in Democratic affiliation and corresponding growth in identification with the Republican Party is related but not reducible to simple ideological affinity.[11]

Distinguishing issue evolution from evolution in group imagery is difficult, and both interpretations contribute to the explanation of partisan change in the South.[12] The most important facts that seem to militate in favor of the latter concern the pace and locus of partisan change. First, the persistent differences among age cohorts reflect the impressions they formed of the parties as they entered the electorate rather than their ideological proclivities. If we suppose that racial attitudes play an especially potent role in shaping policy opinions among Southern whites, it cannot be the case that younger cohorts are more conservative than their older counterparts. Younger white Southerners are more Republican not because they are more conservative but because their attachments formed during a period when Republicans were more likely to be regarded as an attractive social group. Second, although Southern whites voted Republican in large numbers in a string of elections for president and other offices dating back to the 1950s, party attachments changed very slowly; moreover, they continued to change gradually even after 1984, by which point Republican ballots were routinely cast for candidates at all levels of government.

The most persuasive fact militating in favor of the issue evolution perspective is the growing correlation between party attachments and ideology over time. In 1972, the correlation between the three-point party identification scale and the seven-point liberal-conservative self-placement scale was 0.19 among respondents of all races living in the South, compared with 0.31 outside the South. By 1996, both regions had experienced some ideological polarization in party attachments, and these correlations were 0.54 for the South and 0.51 for the non-South. As noted earlier, some of what passes for ideologically based choice of parties is group based, as people seek out partisan groups that harbor liberals or conservatives, and the growing correlation between liberalism-conservatism and party reflects cohort replacement as older conservative Democrats pass away. But issue-based realignment must be given its due. In the South, the disruption of the party system created an unusual circumstance in which ideological orientations could express themselves as whites gradually formed new partisan identities.

The interrelated processes of group perceptions and ideological choice created a new macropartisan equilibrium in the South. With the rehabilitation of the Republican image and the accumulation of a critical mass of younger Republicans and conservatives, the process of partisan adjustment has largely run its course. Conservatives in the South are now as firmly entrenched in the Republican Party as their non-Southern counterparts, and much the same may be said of the sizable aforementioned group of Southerners lacking a clear sense of ideological proximity. There are still gains to be made among the older generation, but these are small and diminishing parts of the Southern electorate. As the new social images of Republicans and Democrats stabilize, the high rate of partisan conversion, which has made the South so distinctive, will subside.

SUMMARY

Most studies of party identification, particularly those that focus on the United States, are situated in the politics of normal times. Southern politics since World War II has not been normal. The key political institutions of the South were swept away with the end of de jure segregation. The essential rationale for the peculiar politics of the solid South had been to disfranchise and disempower black voters, and the institutions created to limit black participation did so with remarkable effectiveness. As late as March 1965, only 7% of eligible black voters in Mississippi were registered (Grofman, Handley, and Niemi 1992). In addition to specific instruments of disfranchisement such as the poll tax and literacy tests, the maintenance of a one-party system hinged on the psychological connection between Democrats and white supremacy. This sectional definition of the Democratic Party naturally conflicted with the national Democratic Party's growing liberalism, but the logic of coalition politics prevailed. Through much of the New Deal it was useful to both national and Southern Democrats to maintain an arrangement that ceded to Southerners control over race relations in their region. By August 1965, Democrats in control of the presidency and Congress brought white control of Southern electoral institutions to an end, mandating an end to racially biased voting and registration requirements and introducing a regime of federal enforcement of race-neutral election procedures. By 1968, 60% of the black voting-age population in Mississippi were registered. As blacks poured into the Democratic Party, Southern politics was thrown permanently off the foundations laid in the late nineteenth century.

As our perspective on party identification would lead us to expect, this political disruption expressed itself immediately at the voting booth but altered self-conceptions much more gradually. The solid South thereafter became a dubious source of Democratic support in presidential elections. In 1952, 1956, and 1960, Southern states routinely gave majorities to liberal non-Southern Democratic presidential candidates (Adlai Stevenson and John Kennedy). No non-Southern Democratic candidate thereafter (Hubert Humphrey, George McGovern, Walter Mondale, or Michael Dukakis) has won a majority of the popular vote in any Southern state. Yet inhabitants of states that repudiated Democratic candidates by large margins continued to call themselves Democrats. Only over the decades to follow, through a gradual process that involved both individual-level conversion and cohort replacement, do we see appreciable movement in party attachments.

By the century's end, the balance of white Republicans and Democrats in the South mirrored the long-standing pattern in the non-South. In the past, each region perceived the parties in different terms. Southerners associated the Republican Party with the forces of Reconstruction, and non-Southerners associated it with business, farmers, and Protestantism. In the South, the Democratic Party was the party of states' rights and segregation, and in the non-South it was the party of cities, labor, and immigrants. For a variety of reasons—economic integration, migration, mass communication, the extension of federal power—the non-South's conception of the parties gradually spread southward.

Profound changes in party imagery having run their course, the pace of partisan conversion appears to have slowed to the near-standstill characteristic of party identification in the non-South. The stabilization of partisanship, of course, comes as small consolation to the Democratic Party. The generation that was largely beyond the reach of the period effects of the mid-1960s, those older than thirty in 1965, are now in their sixties. And although this generation has remained distinctively Democratic in identification, it comprises an ever smaller share of the Southern voting-age population and has failed to pass its partisan proclivities on to its offspring. The decidedly more Republican generation now reaching middle age can be expected to maintain its Republican affiliation. Moreover, it can be expected to transmit these partisan sympathies to the next generation in a political context that recognizes the Republican Party as a worthy representative of Southern interests.

Chapter 7 Partisan Stability outside the United States

The thesis that party attachments form a stable part of citizens' self-conceptions draws support from a wide range of American panel surveys. The question arises as to whether this claim extends beyond the borders of the United States. Although many countries, particularly in the West, feature more disciplined and ideologically distinct political parties, a great many scholars have expressed skepticism about whether the concept of party identification is equally fruitful when applied outside the United States (see, for example, Kaase 1976: 99–100; LeDuc et al. 1984; Thomassen 1976; and Budge and Farlie 1976; for defenses of the applicability of party identification, see Cain and Ferejohn 1981; Heath and Pierce 1992; Heath and McDonald 1988; and Johnston 1992). The doubts stem, first, from qualms about the stability of party attachments in countries such as Great Britain, Germany, or the Netherlands. Second, it is thought that party identities are overshadowed or encompassed by other identities, such as social class, religion, or language. To make the case that party identification enriches our understanding of electoral behavior in countries other than the United States, we must show that party identification is more stable and genuine there than is commonly thought and that its influence is more than a mere reflection of other social identities.

To do so, we must first grapple with the special methodological concerns that arise in political systems that have several political parties. When several parties compete for voters' affections and do so on the basis of diverse appeals—ideology, region, religion, language, or the magnetism of particular leaders—voters may conceivably identify with more than one party simultaneously. If respondents are shoehorned into response categories that allow for just one object of identification, conventional measures of partisanship may give a misleading picture of attitude change. This problem is just one of several concerns about response error. The more parties and the more response options available to respondents, the more likely it is that response error will produce an apparent switch in party identification. To complicate matters further, surveys of partisanship outside the United States have sometimes worded questions about partisanship in ways that shade answers in the direction of electoral support or ideological affinity rather than group identification. Because measurement error may produce altogether misleading statistical conclusions, the first sections of this chapter deal with the question of how to draw reliable inferences from potentially problematic data. We then analyze a wide array of panel surveys and find a number of parallels between U.S. partisanship and partisanship in other countries. In the countries in which panel data have been collected, partisan identities appear to be stable over time and related to, but not identical with, the vote.

In addition to demonstrating the cross-national portability of party identification, this chapter examines the conditions under which party attachments break down. Two instances in particular command our attention: Canada and Italy during the 1990s, both of which experienced profound changes in the nature of party competition. Panel surveys, for example, suggest that the sovereignty issue destabilized Canadian party attachments, particularly in Quebec. Thus, the Canadian case illustrates how social identities associated with language and region can displace party identities. The Italian case illustrates how, after the sudden disappearance of long-standing parties and the proliferation of new ones, the electorate's attachment to new parties is unusually fragile. Deep party attachments take time to form—a proposition with important implications for the new democracies that have arisen since the end of the Cold War. American party identification should be viewed as distinctive yet broadly typical of attachments in stable party systems.

SKEPTICISM ABOUT PARTY IDENTIFICATION
OUTSIDE THE UNITED STATES

Although party identification is quite arguably the most successful explanatory construct in political science, it has had difficulty establishing itself beyond the borders of the United States. Although American political parties and their denizens would seem to be less vivid and vital objects of identification than their European counterparts, political scientists frequently characterize party identification as a peculiarly American phenomenon. Outside the United States, it is argued, voters do not identify with political parties, or at least they do not identify with parties in the same way that Americans do. This argument rests on an interrelated set of empirical claims. LeDuc (1981: 267) contends that "the American electoral environment appears to be unique in its ability to combine stable party identification with instability of vote, a phenomenon observed in no other case." Elsewhere, LeDuc argues, party identification "displays a marked tendency to travel with the vote rather than to be independent of it." Why is European partisanship so labile? Ironically, it is the very coherence of European party politics that makes party identification flimsy and epiphenomenal. Shively (1972: 1,222) explains that "if the social or economic conflicts in which a voter is involved are sufficiently clear; and if the position of parties or groups of parties with regard to these conflicts is sufficiently clear; then there is no need for the voter to develop lasting ties to any party per se, and he will not do so." In other words, because American parties do not reflect the deep-seated divisions that beset other countries, they represent a *more* psychologically salient and penetrating form of identification.

What is the empirical basis of these challenges? The evidence most commonly used to question the durability of partisan attachments outside the United States has been party-switching rates: the percentage of citizens who state that they identify with a party but when reinterviewed some time later report identifying with a different party. Table 7.1 presents rates of party switching observed in recent surveys in the United States, Great Britain, Germany, and Canada. A glance at the first column of figures would seem to indicate that partisanship is less stable in Europe and Canada than in the United States. Only 4% of Democrats or Republicans switched parties between 1992 and 1996, whereas 17% of British Tory, Labour, or Liberal identifiers from 1992 reported identifying with a different party in 1997. The Canadian and German surveys also suggest a much higher party-switching rate than in the United States.

This conventional way of presenting the data seems to underscore American

Table 7.1. Comparison of Party Switching Rates in the United States, Great Britain, Canada, and Germany

	Percentage Switching *Parties* between Waves	Percentage Switching *Responses* between Waves
United States (NES 1992–96)	4.4	33.0
Great Britain (British Election Study, 1992–97)	17.0	27.0
Canada (Canadian Election Study, 1992–93)	28.2	42.0
Germany (German Election Panel Study, 1990)	13.4	35.5

Note: The first entry for the United States is the percentage of partisans (Democrats or Republicans) who switched to the opposing party from 1992 to 1996. The second entry also counts switches to or from Independence as a change in party (using responses to the first portion of the standard Michigan branching question format). The British data report the percentage of Labour, Tory, or Liberal identifiers from 1992 who identified with a different party in 1997. The second column reports this percentage, including also those who switched to or from a minor party or "no preference." The Canadian data report the percentage of Liberal, Progressive Conservative, New Democratic Party (NDP), Bloc Québécois, or Reform Party identifiers from 1992 who identified with a different party in 1993. The German data report the percentage of Social Democratic Party (SPD), Christian Democratic Union (CDU)/Christian Social Union (CSU), Free Democratic Party (FDP), and Green Party identifiers from the first wave of the survey who identified with a different party in the fourth wave of the survey. Again, the second-column figures include those switching to or from a minor party or "no preference."

exceptionalism, but a closer examination of the data provides reason for caution in drawing firm conclusions about the relative stability of party identification across countries. Notice that the rate of switching observed in the United States depends critically on how one treats movement to and from Independence. If one examines only switches from Democrat to Republican or vice versa, the party-switching rate in the United States is extremely low. If one also considers switches to or from Independence, however, the switching rate becomes much higher—creating the misleading impression that party attachments in the United States are subject to frequent change. By the same token, the switching rate outside the United States is elevated if we consider switching to and from minor parties and "no preference." Indeed, when calculated in this way, the switching rate looks similar across countries. Arbitrary choices about how to compute switching rates make all the difference. The more response categories one considers, the higher the switching rate.

Skepticism about the applicability of party identification outside the United

Table 7.2. Party Identification and Vote Choice in Great Britain
and the United States

	U.S. Vote Choice (Congressional Vote)			British Vote Choice (Parliamentary Election)		
	Stable	Variable	Total	Stable	Variable	Total
Party Identification						
Stable	76	16	92	75	8	83
Variable	2	6	8	4	13	17
Total	78	22	100	79	21	100

Source: Butler and Stokes (1969). The American data are drawn from the National Election Study of 1956–58–60. The British data are drawn from the 1963, 1964, and 1966 waves of "Study of Political Change in Britain, 1963–1970."

States stems also from the relative stability of voting preferences and party attachments. This theme was made prominent by Butler and Stokes (1969), who drew a contrast between partisanship in the United States and Great Britain, arguing that the latter "travels" with the vote. Butler and Stokes's (pp. 41–42) key piece of evidence for this claim is presented in Table 7.2. Notice that across similar time intervals, a higher proportion of British respondents than American voters changed their party identification (17% as opposed to 8%), even as a similar proportion changed their vote choice. Furthermore, approximately one in eight British voters changed their party identification and vote choice in concert (13%), whereas only 6% of American voters did so. Twice as many American respondents as British respondents changed their vote choice while maintaining their partisan identity (16% as opposed to 8%). If a defining feature of partisanship is its durability in the face of conflicting stimuli, the patterns evident in this table appear to belie the notion that many British voters have strong party attachments. Butler and Stokes thus conclude that "the British voter is less likely than the American to make a distinction between his current electoral choice and a more general partisan disposition" (p. 43).

Such findings have led numerous scholars to doubt the usefulness of party identification for explaining political behavior outside the United States. Tellingly, however, none of the individual-level studies showing partisan instability or responsiveness to short-term forces has allowed for the distorting influence of measurement error. When one takes this problem into account, it turns out that party identification in the United States has much more in common with partisanship in other countries than is commonly thought. But to appreciate these parallels, one must first grapple with a series of methodological problems that create superficial cross-national differences.

ANALYTICAL PROBLEMS ASSOCIATED
WITH MULTIPARTY SYSTEMS

It is sometimes quipped that one advantage of studying electoral politics in the United States is that federal elections are timed to coincide with the administration of the National Election Study. In fact, social scientists who study American electoral politics enjoy a number of advantages that become apparent only as one looks at the United States in a comparative perspective. Some have to do with the mechanics of measuring party identification in surveys. The collection of survey data has been easier in the United States than in countries such as Italy, where during the Cold War respondents were reluctant to disclose their party affiliations (LaPalombara 1987). Similarly, the concept of party identification—the sense that one thinks of oneself as belonging to a social group composed of fellow partisans—is easier to translate into a survey question in the American case. The United States has commonly used nouns, Democrat and Republican, to describe the leading partisan groups. In other polities, nouns describing partisan groups may not exist, forcing the researcher instead to ask about membership in or support for a political party, which are somewhat different constructs.

Practical difficulties become more acute as one grapples with the problem of representing party attachments along something other than a unidimensional continuum. Multiparty systems, such as those found in Britain, Germany, Canada, and Italy, potentially give rise to complex partisan identities. These systems feature three and sometimes four or more significant parties. Although these parties can in some cases be arranged along a left-right spectrum, it is unclear whether *identification* with the various parties can be depicted accurately along a single dimension. It is conceivable that voters may be attracted to different parties for different reasons and identify with more than one party simultaneously. Liberal Party adherents from British Columbia may also identify with the Canadian Alliance (formerly known as the Reform Party), whereas those from Quebec may harbor a degree of psychological attachment to the Bloc Québécois. Survey questions that ask respondents to state the *one* party with which they identify may miss these important nuances and distort the assessment of partisan stability in a multiparty context—one may maintain one's Liberal allegiance even as one's affinity for the Canadian Alliance grows. This intuition can be expressed by a mathematical representation of the process by which partisanship is measured. Before generalizing the model to encompass multiparty systems, let us first consider a relatively simple case: the two-party system found in the United States.

Models of the Survey Response

As mentioned in Chapters 1 and 2, it has long been conventional to envision American partisanship as a single dimension, ranging from Democratic to Republican identification. Implicitly, Democratic identification is assumed to coincide with the absence of Republican identification, and vice versa. Similarly, Independents are assumed to harbor an equal (and relatively weak) degree of identification with both parties. By this interpretation, responses to the stem question of the standard party identification scale follow an ordinal measurement process. Let ρ represent an individual's underlying degree of Republican identification (or, equivalently, lack of Democratic identification). For purposes of exposition, let ρ range from zero to one, where one represents maximal Republicanness. The process by which underlying partisanship is translated into one of the three survey response categories may be modeled as follows:

Model 1:

Democrat	if $\rho < \alpha_1$
Republican	if $\rho > \alpha_2$
Independent	if $\alpha_1 \leq \rho \leq \alpha_2$

where $0 < \alpha_1 < \alpha_2 < 1$, α_1 and α_2 being cutpoints that determine which response category a person selects.

The resulting three-point scale transforms the continuous variable ρ into a series of ordered categories, as shown in Figure 7.1. The thresholds separating Democrats and Republicans from Independents may be wide or narrow depending on how the question is worded. As we saw in Chapter 2, offering respondents the option of calling themselves Independents reduces the ranks of partisans, whereas a question format that forces respondents to volunteer their stance as Independents causes many more people to label themselves as Democrats or Republicans.

This unidimensional depiction changes as we relax the assumption that Democratic partisanship is equivalent to the lack of Republican partisanship. Denote the degree of Democratic identification δ (ranging from zero to one)

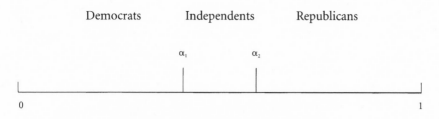

Degree of Republican Identification (ρ)

Figure 7.1. One-dimensional representation of party identification.

and relax the requirement that $\rho = 1 - \delta$. One's survey response now hinges on the relative strengths of the two attachments.

Model 2:

Democrat   if $\delta > \rho + \alpha_1$

Republican   if $\rho > \delta + \alpha_2$

Independent otherwise, where $0 < \alpha_1, \alpha_2 < 1$

Figure 7.2 presents a graphical depiction of the measurement process. The upper triangle consists of Democrats; the lower triangle, Republicans. Independents comprise the strip that divides the two triangles. Note that α_1 and α_2 are thresholds representing the difference in the relative strength of attachment to the parties that is necessary before a respondent states an identification with either party, as opposed to declaring his or her "Independence" of party ties. Figure 7.2 highlights one of the important shortcomings of the party identification measure, namely, that it captures only certain kinds of change, while other patterns of change go undetected. Denote the location of voter $i\,(R_i, D_i)$. When a person withdraws his or her attachment to one party and bestows it on another, the unidimensional measurement of party identification works well. The Democrat located at (0, 0.3) is dubbed a Republican when this underlying location shifts to (0.3, 0). But when attachments toward both parties grow simultaneously, the unidimensional model fails to record the change. The Democrat whose location moves the same distance, for example, (0, 0.7) to (0.3, 1), continues to be dubbed a Democrat. Similarly, the Independent whose underlying location shifts from (0, 0) to (0.5, 0.5) remains an Independent in the eyes of the standard party identification measure despite having become more closely identified with both parties (see Weisberg 1980).

Model 2 calls attention to two potential measurement problems. First, mea-

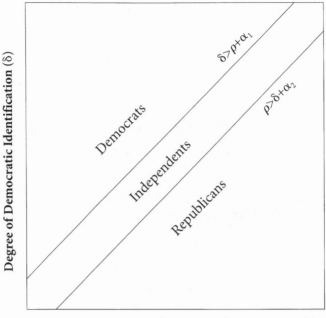

Degree of Republican Identification (ρ)

Figure 7.2. Two-dimensional representation of party identification.

sured partisanship that appears stable over time can mask underlying partisan change. Second, the three categories of partisanship may each be more heterogeneous than anticipated by model 1. Conceivably, Democrats consist of both Republican-haters located at (0, 0.7) and more conciliatory partisans located at (0.3, 1). Model 2, in other words, makes allowance for the possibility that individuals identify to some degree with more than one party simultaneously.

Before generalizing this model further to incorporate more than two parties, we should say a few words about the applicability of model 2 to partisanship in the United States. Seldom has party identification been measured on a party-by-party basis, the exception being a 1990 Times-Mirror national survey of U.S. adults (Green and Schickler 1993). Respondents were asked how well the terms *Democrat, Republican,* and various other group labels described them.

The response options were offered in the form of a scale ranging from one to ten.[1] Analysis of these data support the view that Democratic identification is the opposite of Republican identification. For example, when one regresses the two self-description items on a list of independent variables (1988 presidential vote, ideology, education, age, and dummy variables for gender, race, the South, and Catholic), the predicted self-description scores correlate at -0.972. Much the same conclusion emerges from the correlations between the seven-point Gallup party identification measure and the two self-description items. Republican self-description correlates at 0.776 with party identification, compared with -0.781 for Democratic self-description. In sum, party-by-party measures of identification behave very much as a unidimensional representation would predict.

The Survey Research Center measure of party identification may perform adequately in the United States, where partisanship falls largely along a single underlying dimension, but the range of potential problems becomes larger as we consider other political systems. Questions that follow the standard format ask respondents to name *the* party with which they identify. As we suggested above, respondents may identify (to some extent) with more than one party simultaneously. Furthermore, in a multiparty system, it is plausible that respondents will differ in the spatial alignment they attribute to the parties. The manner in which respondents are assigned to partisan categories may therefore produce a distorted image of partisan change and stability.

To see why the standard measure might produce distortions, consider a three-party system in which individuals have some level of identification with each party, again ranging from zero to one. The process by which these levels of identification are translated into a survey response may be depicted as follows:

Model 3:

Party 1, if $A > B + \alpha_1$ and $A > C + \alpha_1$

Party 2, if $B > A + \alpha_2$ and $B > C + \alpha_2$

Party 3, if $C > A + \alpha_3$ and $C > B + \alpha_3$

Independent, otherwise

Suppose a respondent's partisanship changes from (0.70, 0.65, 0.10) to (0.60, 0.65, 0.10). If $\alpha_k = 0$, the SRC measure detects a switch from Party 1 to Party 2. On the other hand, a more substantial change from (0.70, 0.15, 0.10) to (0.20, 0.15, 0.10) produces no corresponding change in survey response. Nor, for that matter, does a change from (0.70, 0.65, 0.10) to (0.70, 0.10,

0.65). It should be clear from these examples that the rate of party switching—the most frequently used index by which partisan stability is gauged (Clarke and Kornberg 1992; Clarke, Stewart, and Whiteley 1994; Richardson 1991; LeDuc et al. 1984; Mughan 1981)—offers a crude and possibly misleading picture of underlying partisan change. Converse and Pierce (1992) point out additional shortcomings of party-switching rates: Among other things, these indices will tend to underestimate the stability of attachments to small parties, such as the Liberal Democrats in Great Britain and the Free Democratic Party (FDP) in Germany, that take up a relatively narrow portion of the underlying partisan space.

Measuring Multidimensional Attachments

Models such as these help to explicate the potential complexity of the measurement process, but the extent of multiple identification is ultimately an empirical question. What happens when people are presented with the opportunity to indicate their identification with each party in the political system? In an effort to answer this question, we conducted a survey experiment in Italy at the beginning of 1998. Italy provides an especially interesting context for such a study because its party system has experienced flux since the early 1990s. In the wake of Communism's fall in the Soviet Union and Eastern Bloc, the Italian Communist Party dissolved. In 1991, corruption investigations began, eventually ensnaring thousands of politicians in the major parties and causing the dissolution of the formerly dominant Christian Democratic Party and Socialist Party. A year after reforms in the election system in 1993, the new center-right Forza Italia Party was swept into power in 1994 only to lose control of the government two years later. Thus, by the time we conducted our survey in 1998, Italy had experienced several years of political upheaval in its party system. The formerly dominant Christian Democratic Party and the Socialist Party had disappeared, replaced by an assortment of small center and center-left parties and the more formidable center-right Forza Italia. On the far left were the remnants of the Communist Party, which had split into the Communist Refoundation Party (Rifondazione Comunista) and the more moderate Social Democratic Party (PDS, later called DS, or Democrats of the Left). The Social Democratic Party was the largest component of the center-left Olive Tree coalition (Ulivo), which arose to garner legislative seats as the result of Italy's two-tiered system of legislative elections. The Olive Tree coalition for a time resembled a parliamentary party, and many Italians seeking a "bipolar" electoral system wished to see it absorb all of the left parties into a single unit. The Greens (Verdi) attracted voters concerned with environmental issues or disenchanted with left-right politics. Finally, on the far right stood Alleanza Nazionale (the National Alliance) and the smaller Fiamma Tricolore, which worked in alliance with Forza Italia and the Northern League (Lega Nord), which commanded a certain amount of regional allegiance from voters in Lombardy. In all, the survey presented respondents with no fewer than sixteen parties.

Survey respondents were randomly assigned to two groups. One version of the survey instrument presented 992 respondents with a standard list of party names:

> Usually, speaking of politics, some people think of themselves as "of" certain parties, some people think of themselves as of other parties, and some people of no party. Would you, more than other parties define yourself as . . . ?

Respondents were presented with a list of parties, from which they could choose one or select the options of "other party" or "no party." The other version of the survey posed this question to 927 respondents but asked about each party, one at a time. For example, the first question asked about Forza Italia, the second, about Alleanza Nazionale, and so forth. At the end of this sequence of questions, respondents were also asked whether they defined themselves as "of" no party at all. Thus, the two formats are broadly comparable. The party-by-party question format invites respondents to name as many parties as they like; the party list allows just one answer.

Table 7.3 reports the distribution of responses to the two party-identification questions. The similarity of the two sets of responses suggests that concerns about multiple identifications may be unwarranted, even in a party system with as much fragmentation and overlap as Italy's. Very few respondents—just one in ten—expressed identification with more than one party. Identification with minor parties did tend to increase somewhat when multiple identifications were probed, but the differences were slight. Those who identified with one of the larger parties seldom harbored multiple attachments. None of the ninety-eight Forza Italia identifiers expressed identification with the Communist Refoundation or PDS, two identified with the Olive Tree coalition, and just thirteen identified with the more ideologically proximate Alleanza Nazionale. On the left, shared identification was also unusual. Just one of ninety-nine identifiers with the Social Democrats identified with the Communist Refoundation, and none with the parties on the right. As expected, the greatest amount of overlap seems to exist between the Social Democrats and the Olive Tree coalition, but even here we find that just 15% of those who identified with

Table 7.3. Italian Party Identification as Described
by Alternative Survey Measures

	Party-by-Party Questioning (%)	Single List (%)
Forza Italia	10.6	8.2
Alleanza Nazionale	13.7	11.8
Christian Democratic Center (CCD)	2.8	1.1
Christian Democratic Union (CDU)	1.2	0.4
Panneliano	0.3	0.4
Social Democratic Party (PDS)	10.7	12.6
Rifondazione Comunista (RC)	5.8	7.5
Verdi	4.0	2.3
Rinnovamento Italiano	0.8	1.3
Italian Popular Party (PPI)	2.6	2.0
Lega Nord	4.1	3.2
Fiamma Tricolore	0.8	0.4
Socialisti	0.2	0.8
Patto Segni	0.1	0.1
Ulivo	15.0	16.2
Polo	5.6	3.9
Other	0.3	0.0
No party	30.5	27.7
Total	109.1	99.9
N	927	992

Source: Italian Panel Study, wave II.

Note: Party-by-party wording: "Usually, speaking of politics, some people think of themselves as 'of' certain parties, some people think of themselves as of other parties, and some people of no party. Would you, more than other parties define yourself as . . ." (Present each party one at a time; at the end of the list, respondents could indicate their identification with "no party.")

List wording: "Usually, speaking of politics, some people think of themselves as 'of' certain parties, some people think of themselves as of other parties, and some people of no party. Would you, more than other parties define yourself as . . ." (Present list of parties, from which respondents could choose one or select a "no party" option.)

the Social Democrats also identified with the Olive Tree coalition. As we shall see below, identification with Italian political parties was unstable during this time, but that does not seem to be because people were identifying simultaneously with several parties.

Without comparable experimental results from other countries, we cannot say whether multiple identification is a serious practical concern or merely an arcane theoretical issue. Still, the fact that partisanship in systems as different as the United States and Italy show similar patterns suggests that multiple identities are more rare than is often supposed. Overlapping identities, however, are just one of several problems that command attention, and we now turn our attention to the validity of party identification measures and our inability to array the results along a single dimension for the purposes of statistical analysis.

Measurement Validity

One interesting feature of this Italian survey is that respondents were queried directly about their sense of belonging to a social group. Indeed, in an earlier wave of this panel survey, we experimented with alternative ways of phrasing the question, variously asking respondents whether they "defined themselves of" or "felt that they belonged to" each party. (As it turned out, the two variants of the questionnaire elicited nearly identical answers from the two groups). Seldom do surveys lavish this much attention on measurement nuances. Unfortunately, several surveys that purport to measure party identification do not focus respondents' attention on social group attachment. The German surveys we will analyze below ask respondents whether they "lean toward a particular party over the long term," even if they might occasionally vote for a different party.[2] British and Canadian surveys have used the important phrase "think of yourself," but notice the complication that arises when the parties are used rather than partisan nouns. For example, in the Canadian panel study of 1992–93, respondents were asked,

> Thinking of federal politics, do you usually think of yourself as a Liberal, Conservative, N.D.P., Reform Party [in Quebec, "Bloc Québécois"], or none of these?

The list begins well, using the phrase "a Liberal," which seems to refer to a social group. The list ends, however, with "Reform Party," which refers to an organization rather than a group. These subtle concerns about question wording illustrate the difficulty of drawing attention to group imagery in the space of a short, intelligible question.

A related problem concerns the extent to which the respondent's attention is

directed away from vote intentions. As Flanigan, Rahn, and Zingale (1989) observe from their repeated in-depth interviews with voters during the course of
the 1988 presidential election, respondents are sometimes unsure about whether
the questions refer to party voting or group identity. These researchers occasionally found respondents reflecting on their voting history or intentions
when gauging their sense of party attachment. For this reason, Converse and
Pierce (1992) stress the importance of providing the respondents with cues
about the proper focus of their introspections, with wording that advises respondents to think about their long-term attachments and to ignore their current or prior vote preferences.

A powerful example of the importance of question wording is the trajectory
of party identification in Britain during the 1990s. The conventional question
used to gauge party identification in Britain reads, "Generally speaking do you
think of yourself as Conservative, Labour, Liberal Democrat (or Nationalist),
or what?" Surveys using this wording (see below) show a marked shift in identification with the Tories after 1992, with the departure of Margaret Thatcher,
the advent of Tony Blair as leader of the Labour Party, and Labour's decisive
victory in the 1997 national elections. The alternative wording, used by Bartle
(1999), draws a distinction between party identification and voter support,
while fleshing out the "or what" option: "Many people think of themselves as
Conservative, Labour, Liberal Democrat (or Nationalist), even if they don't always support that party. How about you? Generally speaking do you think of
yourself as Conservative, Labour, Liberal Democrat (or Nationalist), or don't
you think of yourself as any of these?" Both questions were used to gauge party
identities in a series of monthly polls from 1999 through 2000, and the differences between them are quite striking. Using the standard wording, Labour
shows a substantial lead over the Conservatives, 44% to 27%. The alternative
wording places them at a much more comparable 31% to 23%. Yet both surveys
find *identical* proportions of respondents intending to vote Labour and Tory,
47% versus 24%. It would appear that the standard wording invites many nonidentifiers to call themselves partisans, often on the basis of their vote intentions. This interpretation is strongly supported by the relationship between
party identification and vote intentions in the two surveys. Of those categorized as Tories by the standard measure, 88% intend to vote Conservative, as
opposed to 71% classified by the alternative question. Comparable figures for
Labour are 83% and 56%. Given these measurement problems, the construct of
party identification may not be to blame if, as Shively (1972: 1,223) puts it,
"what is often reported as 'party identification' in other countries is simply an

expression of immediate vote choice." It will therefore be all the more impressive if partisanship should prove to be stable in these panel surveys.

The distinction between partisanship and vote choice plays an important role in debates about party identification. Budge and Farlie (1976: 123) contend that "it is the very predictive success of party identification in these other contexts, relative to the American, that leads one to suspect its empirical independence of voting choice, its conceptual antecedence, and its explanatory capacity." We have just seen that this concern may stem in part from measurement problems; the link between vote intentions and party identification is not overwhelming when the latter is measured in ways that focus respondents' attention away from electoral support. Still, the possibility remains that vote intentions nevertheless rub off on party attachments, although in the context of U.S. elections, we have found little evidence that this occurs (Green and Palmquist 1990). Presumably, this concern is appropriate when party identification is measured at the same time as vote preference. Under such circumstances, we cannot be certain that party identification is influencing the choice rather than simply reflecting it. The situation is different when party identification is measured at one point in time and used to explain voting behavior years later; the time sequence resolves doubts about "conceptual antecedence." Consider, for example, voting behavior in Britain during the period 1974–79. In February 1974, respondents were asked about their party identification, and these responses were used to predict vote preference in a pair of 1974 elections as well as the 1979 election. As shown in Table 7.4, party attachments have a powerful predictive effect within the context of a single survey: 89% of those who declared themselves to be Tories in February 1974 also intended to vote Tory at that time. This number may seem suspiciously high, but note that 89% of these respondents also expressed a preference for Margaret Thatcher five years later. A similar story can be told for Labour: Of those who identified with Labour in 1974, 80% voted Labour in 1979. Party identification remains a powerful predictor of the vote several years into the future. This predictive success should not be viewed as a strike against the concept of party attachment. Doing so puts one in the peculiar position of saying that identification with the Liberal Party has more validity because self-identified Liberals defected from their party in droves in the 1979 election.

Gauging Partisan Stability
with Noisy Measures

Leaving aside concerns about multiple identification and the validity of the party identification measures, the problem of unreliable measurement re-

Table 7.4. Party Identification as a Vote Predictor in Great Britain

	Percentage Voting for That Party in February 1964	Percentage Voting for That Party in October 1966	Percentage Voting for That Party in 1970
Party the respondent identified with in February 1963			
Tory	84	79	88
Labour	88	90	78
Liberal	59	49	26
	Percentage Voting for That Party in February 1974	Percentage Voting for That Party in October 1974	Percentage Voting for That Party in 1979
Party the respondent identified with in February 1974			
Tory	89	84	89
Labour	88	88	80
Liberal	78	68	44
	Percentage Voting for That Party in February 1992	Percentage Voting for That Party in October 1997	
Party the respondent identified with in 1992			
Tory	92	64	
Labour	90	90	
Liberal	78	53	

mains. Any attempt to extract information about party identification from surveys in which respondents are presented with lists of alternatives contains some degree of measurement error. As mentioned in Chapter 3, these errors may arise from misread or misunderstood questions, coding mistakes, or an inability on the part of respondents to gauge their own partisan sentiment. Because of response error, reported partisanship may fluctuate from one moment to the next even though party attachments are truly stable. The problem of measurement error may be especially serious in a multiparty electoral system because the number of response options offered to interviewees is larger.

How should researchers address the problem of measurement error when measuring partisanship in multiparty systems? Currently, no standard method exists for differentiating true partisan change from change due to measurement error in data of this kind. When party identification falls along a single dimension, as in the American case, correcting for survey error is a relatively straightforward undertaking. (Or, to be more precise, the straightforwardness of the enterprise became apparent to us over a period of years, as we conducted a series of studies that, fortunately, corroborated our initial estimates.) In the U.S. case, estimation is simplified by assuming a linear relationship between a person's true partisanship and reported partisanship. The problem of assessing the degree of response error becomes much more complex when the partisanship measure consists of a series of unordered categories, in which case the translation from true partisanship to observed partisanship may be highly nonlinear.

In order to accommodate the possible nonlinearity in the data, we analyze existing measures of party identification as though they were a series of dichotomous variables: Does respondent i most strongly identify with party j, or not? The dichotomous indicator of identification with a given party (for example, Labour) can be analyzed across successive waves of a panel survey. With the use of techniques first elaborated by Heise (1969) and since adapted to the analysis of ordinal data (Babakus, Ferguson, and Jöreskog 1987; Sharma, Durvasula, and Dillon 1989; Rigdon and Ferguson 1991), the pattern of correlations over time can then be used to assess the degree to which individuals maintain their relative positions with respect to a given party as well as the reliability of the dichotomous indicator of partisanship (DIP).

A practical drawback of this statistical approach is that several waves of panel data are required before interesting parameters may be estimated. With three waves of data, the Heise method of analyzing over-time correlations can estimate only the reliability of the measure administered during the second wave; estimating trait stability requires the restrictive assumption that the measurement reliabilities remain constant over time (Wiley and Wiley 1970). By contrast, with four waves of data, the Heise model can estimate the R-squared, net of measurement error, from a regression in which the third-wave response is regressed on the second-wave response without assuming constant reliability over time. For this reason, the analyses that follow involve panels that have at least three waves of interviews, with emphasis on four-wave panels that require less restrictive statistical assumptions.

Before applying this technique to actual survey data, we evaluated its accuracy using simulated data. These statistical simulations, discussed in Schickler and Green (1997), indicate that the DIP analysis performs quite well: Across an array of different assumptions about the degree of polarization in the party system, the reliability of partisanship measures, and the underlying stability of individuals' partisanship, it gives an accurate rendering of partisan stability in a three-party system.[3] This finding contrasts sharply with the poor performance of party-switching indices, which simply gauge the proportion of respondents who give the same answers in successive interviews. Switching rates cannot differentiate between two very different situations: unstable partisanship and highly reliable measurement versus stable partisanship and unreliable measurement. Despite the frequency with which switching rates appear in published work on partisan change in political systems outside the United States, we regard them as potentially quite misleading and much inferior to the DIP analysis.

SURVEY DATA AND POLITICAL CONTEXT

We use data from five four-wave panel surveys to reassess the evidence on the stability of partisanship in Great Britain, Canada, and Germany before turning to panel data from Italy. We chose these three countries because they are the only places outside the United States for which we were able to find panel surveys with four waves of partisanship data (see Guchteneire, LeDuc, and Niemi 1991, 1985). We also analyzed four three-wave panel surveys from Great Britain, Canada, and Germany.[4] The results from the three-wave panels are substantively the same as the results from the four-wave surveys, which suggests that the stronger assumptions associated with the statistical analysis of three-wave panels are not unwarranted.

The British data are drawn from a 1963–64–66–70 panel survey, a 1974–74–75–79 panel, and a 1992–94–95–97 panel, each of which spans periods of dramatic change in party fortunes.[5] The first two surveys used nationally representative samples of adult citizens; the 1992–97 panel included an oversample of Scottish residents, but the results reported below are weighted to be representative of adult British citizens. The first wave of the 1963–70 panel interviewed 2,009 respondents in the summer of 1963, nearly a year and a half before the October 1964 general election. Approximately 1,500 respondents were reinterviewed after that election, and 1,163 of these respondents were interviewed immediately after the March 1966 election. After the June 1970 election, 718 of the respondents from the first three waves were interviewed for a final time. The period 1963–70 saw a Labour government, led by Harold Wilson, take charge after defeating the incumbent Tories in the 1964 election. Labour gained only a slim majority in 1964, but Wilson called a new election for March 1966, and Labour won a substantial majority. Labour's popularity eroded after 1966, partly because of difficult economic times, although the party recovered in time to make the June 1970 election competitive. Nonetheless, the Conservatives triumphed in 1970, and thus the 1963–70 panel spans a period during which the fortunes of the parties were twice reversed.

The first wave of the 1974–74–75–79 survey interviewed respondents in February 1974 after the first general election of that year. The Tory government of Edward Heath, elected in 1970, was by 1974 plagued by the international oil crisis and labor unrest. Nonetheless, Labour gained only a narrow plurality of seats in the February 1974 election and formed a single-party minority government under Wilson. Labour called a new election in October and made sufficient gains to enjoy a bare majority in Parliament. The second wave was conducted after the October 1974 election. A third wave of interviews was administered after the referendum on entry into the European Common Market in June 1975. The 1975 survey was administered through a mail-back questionnaire, and the other interviews were done in person. The Labour government's popularity fell considerably during its term—partly because of continuing economic troubles—and the party was defeated in May 1979 by Conservative leader Margaret Thatcher. The final wave of interviews was conducted after the May 1979 election. Thus, the 1974–79 survey spans one change in the governing party and a significant reversal of party fortunes.

The first wave of the 1992–94–95–97 panel took place after the April 1992 general election, in which the Tories, led by John Major, once again emerged triumphant. But the Tories lost considerable support over the ensuing five years. The second wave of the survey took place in spring 1994, after the European elections. The third wave was administered a year later, in the aftermath of local elections in which the Tories suffered noteworthy losses. The final wave of the survey took place in spring 1997, following Tony Blair and his Labour Party's overwhelming victory in the general elections. Coming after a period during which Labour moderated its most extreme stances of the 1970s and early 1980s, the 1992–97 survey covers a period during which Blair transformed the Labour Party into the more moderate "New Labour," revamped the image of the party in ways that emphasized its middle-class constituency, and catapulted the party from its low point of 1992 to an immense majority in Parliament five years later.

Our German data are from a 1989–90–90–90 panel survey.[6] Interviews were conducted during November–December 1989, May–June 1990, October–November 1990, and December 1990. The final wave followed the December 1990 election. The German data are from a stratified multistage random sample of voting-age West German citizens. The 1990 elections were a setback for the Social Democratic Party (SPD) and the Green Party and a significant victory for the governing Christian Democratic Union/Christian Social Union (CDU/CSU) parties and their coalition partner, the FDP. The SPD appeared to have a reasonable chance to win the election in 1989, on the basis of its gains in several states. But the combination of economic prosperity and the government's successful negotiation of reunification with East Germany made the 1990 election a difficult one for the opposition SPD and Greens.

The Canadian data are from a 1983–84–88–88 panel study using a nationally representative sample of adult citizens.[7] Interviews were first conducted in 1983, then after the September 1984 federal elections, and before and after the November 1988 federal election. This survey brackets a period marked by dramatic swings in the popularity of the Progressive Conservative Party. The panel's first wave was conducted in 1983 while the Liberals were still the governing party, as they had been for most of the previous twenty years. The Conservatives convincingly defeated the Liberals in the 1984 elections but then suffered a severe drop in popularity once in power. The Conservatives rebounded strongly in the months leading up to their victory in the 1988 election. This revival was in part due to Prime Minister Brian Mulroney's use of the issue of free trade with the United States (Clarke and Kornberg 1992); therefore, this Canadian panel spans one change in government, as well as marked shifts in the Conservatives' popularity.

More tumultuous was the period covered by the three-wave 1992–93–93 Canadian panel survey, which saw the rise of regional parties rooted in dissatisfaction with the federal government. The Bloc Québécois was formed in 1990 to pursue independence for the province of Quebec after the failure of the Meech Lake Accord. The party won 49% of the vote in Quebec in the 1993 election and won 54 of the 295 seats in Parliament—becoming the official opposition party to the victorious Liberals. Reform, founded in 1987 and based in the west, captured the support of many Conservatives dissatisfied with the party's efforts to pacify Quebec and concerned about the dismal state of the economy. It drew upon a long tradition of western dissatisfaction with perceived mistreatment from Ottawa before transforming itself into the Canadian Alliance in 2000 in an effort to broaden its nationwide appeal. In 1993, the party won 16% of the vote nationally and 52 seats in the Parliament, a victory that came at the expense of the Conservatives, who received 16% of the vote but just 2 seats. The growing regional fragmentation of the Canadian party system distinguishes it from the British and German cases.

Italy during the 1990s is another dramatic example of a party system in flux. The fall of the Soviet Union coupled with a corruption scandal of immense proportions brought about the disintegration of the large parties of the post-war era. The Christian Democrats, who had previously accounted for the plurality of Italian party identifiers, splintered into several center and center-right parties, with the lion's share of its erstwhile adherents gravitating to the newly formed Forza Italia, headed by the media magnate Silvio Berlusconi. On the left, the former Communist Party reconstituted itself as the Communist Refoundation, with more moderate elements of the party becoming the PDS (later, the DS), to which some former adherents to the scandal-plagued Socialist Party gravitated. As in Canada, regional movements (the Northern League, or Lega Nord) gained new vitality as well. Our three-wave panel study charts Italian politics from May 1997 to January 1998 to December 1998, in the aftermath of the restructuring of the party system. The first wave comes more than a year after the electoral defeat of Berlusconi by a left coalition (Olive Tree, or Ulivo) headed by Romano Prodi. The last wave comes shortly after Prodi's ouster from within his own coalition, which replaced him with PDS head Massimo D'Alema.

This survey is unusual in that it was administered to a panel of respondents who participated in weekly surveys distributed over the Internet. These respondents were given a computer and Internet access in return for their participation, and they remained in the panel for one to four years. Although not an entirely representative sample of the Italian public, the party attachments of the respondents to this survey match closely the attachments of respondents from more conventional telephone surveys. More important for our purposes, this panel enables us to gauge how stable a set of individuals' attachments are over time.

The Distribution of Partisanship over Time

Parties in Britain, Germany, and Canada share several important features. In each case, two major parties have long attracted a substantial majority of identifiers (see Tables 7.5A through 7.5F). In Britain, roughly 80% of the respondents identified with Labour or the Tories in each wave of the 1963–70 panel (Table 7.5A), whereas 75 percent did so in the 1974–79 panel and in 1992–97 (Tables 7.5B and 7.5C). This relatively slight decline, along with evidence of a

Table 7.5. Frequency Distribution for Partisanship in Great Britain, West Germany, and Canada

A. Great Britain, 1963–70

	1963	1964	1966	1970
Conservative	36.7	37.7	35.7	42.6
Labour	44.1	42.4	43.3	40.1
Liberal	9.9	13.3	12.3	9.9
Other party	0.0	0.3	0.7	0.6
No party	7.0	5.1	6.5	6.0
Don't know	2.3	1.1	1.4	0.9

B. Great Britain, 1974–79

	1974 (February)	1974 (October)	1975	1979
Conservative	34.3	33.3	35.5	37.7
Labour	40.6	40.9	38.5	39.1
Liberal	13.5	14.5	9.4	13.0
Other party	2.0	2.8	2.4	1.2
No party	6.6	6.6	13.5	7.0
Don't know	3.0	1.8	0.7	1.9

C. Great Britain, 1992–97

	1992	1994	1995	1997
Conservative	44.2	33.4	31.5	35.0
Labour	30.1	35.8	39.0	40.1
Liberal	13.8	16.2	14.4	15.6
Other party	2.9	3.5	3.0	2.8
No party	7.8	7.8	8.9	5.7
Don't know	1.1	3.3	3.1	0.9

D. West Germany, 1989–90

	November 1989	May 1990	October 1990	December 1990
SPD	34.8	39.1	37.5	34.6
CDU/CSU	32.5	32.7	36.1	37.0
FDP	3.2	2.9	3.2	4.3
Green	5.4	4.1	4.5	4.0
Republican	2.0	0.9	1.3	0.7
Other	0.2	0.3	0.2	0.2
No party	17.0	16.3	14.2	18.5
Don't know	3.1	1.7	1.5	0.2
Refused	1.8	1.8	1.5	0.2
Not applicable	0	0	0	0.2

Table 7.5. (*Continued*)

E. Canada, 1983–88

	1983	1984	1988 Preelection	1988 Postelection
Liberal	31.8	32.2	31.2	33.0
Progressive Conservative	32.8	34.6	32.6	34.8
NDP	8.8	12.2	10.6	12.4
Social Credit	1.2	1.0	0.6	1.2
Other	2.0	1.8	2.6	2.8
Refused	4.4	2.2	2.4	2.0
Don't know	4.8	2.6	6.4	3.4
Independent	2.4	1.4	1.2	0.4
None	11.8	12.0	12.4	10.0

F. Canada, 1992–93

	October 1992	September–October 1993	November 1993
Liberal	26.8	24.7	30.8
Progressive Conservative	18.4	20.6	15.7
NDP	10.9	7.6	7.9
Reform	3.7	4.6	7.2
Bloc Québécois	8.2	11.4	14.0
Other	0	0.3	0.4
None	26.1	26.6	21.9
Don't know	4.5	3.3	0.7
Refused	1.4	0.9	1.4

Note: Values are percentages. Table 7.5A, $N = 705$; 7.5B, $N = 724$; 7.5C, $N = 1,235$; 7.5D, $N = 869$; 7.5E, $N = 500$; 7.5F, $N = 1,312$.

substantial reduction in the mean strength of partisanship for identifiers, is often cited as evidence of the demise of partisanship in Britain (Crewe 1983; Schmitt 1989; Clarke and Stewart 1984). It will be interesting, therefore, to examine whether the stability of party identification fell off in Britain during the 1970s. The SPD and CDU/CSU together account for approximately 70% of the German respondents, with nearly another 20% falling in the "no party" or "don't know" categories (Table 7.5D). The two main parties in Canada—the Liberals and Progressive Conservatives—account for roughly 65% of the Canadian respondents in the 1983–88 data (Table 7.5E), with an additional 15% to 20% responding with Independence, "none," or "don't know." By the time of the 1993 elections, the share of the Liberals and Conservatives had fallen substantially in Canada, to well below 50% of the respondents (see Table

7.5F). Although some of this change is probably attributable to the different question wording used in the 1992–93 survey (Johnston 1992), much of the movement is due to the growth of the Reform Party and Bloc Québécois as viable alternative parties, largely at the expense of the Progressive Conservatives.

In each country there are serious, institutionalized alternatives to the two dominant parties. In Germany, the centrist FDP has often held the balance of power in coalition governments, allying with either the SPD or the CDU/CSU. In the 1980s, the Green Party emerged as an alternative for those disaffected by the established parties. The Greens won 5.6% of the vote in the 1983 election and 8.3% in 1987—just behind the 9.1% of the third-place FDP. The Greens, facing many internal fissures, fell to 3.9% of the vote in the 1990 all-German election. Meanwhile, the FDP gained ground, finishing with 11.0% of the vote in 1990. In Britain, the Liberal Democrats account for 9% to 14% of the respondents in the 1963–70 and 1974–79 periods. Like the FDP, the Liberal Democrats are regarded as a centrist alternative to the two dominant parties; but unlike the German case, the British electoral system does not afford the Liberal Democrats the same opportunities to become part of governing coalitions. The single-member district, plurality voting system in Britain makes it more difficult for minor parties to win seats than in the German system of modified proportional rule. The Canadian New Democratic Party (NDP)—the most significant third party in Canada before the emergence of Reform and the Bloc Québécois—is perceived to be situated to the left of the Liberals and Progressive Conservatives. Although the NDP lagged behind the Liberals and Conservatives in federal identification during our 1983–88 panel, the party won 19% of the vote in 1984 and 20% of the vote in the 1988 election. The NDP fell to a mere 7% of the vote and nine seats in 1993 and has been eclipsed by the rise of the Bloc Québécois and Reform/Canadian Alliance.

Before turning to evidence of individual-level change, fluctuations at the aggregate level warrant attention. The 1963–70 British data show a gain in Tory identification from the third to fourth waves of the survey. Conservatives trailed Labour 36% to 43% in 1966 (and by similar margins in the first two waves) but enjoyed a 43% to 40% advantage immediately after the 1970 election. This increase in Conservative identification—which actually began soon after the 1966 election and peaked over a year before the 1970 election (Butler and Stokes 1974)—corresponds to troubled times for Wilson's Labour government and led up to the Tories' 1970 triumph. At the opening of the 1974–79 panel, the Labour Party again enjoyed a six-point edge in identification over the Conservatives. This advantage was cut in half by the time of the June 1975 Common

Market referendum and was reduced to a mere 1.4 points by 1979. The Tories gained identifiers over the next several years, so that by the opening of the 1992–97 panel, they enjoyed a substantial lead over Labour. This advantage disappeared by 1994, however, and gave way to a five- to seven-point Labour advantage in 1995–97. As noted above, some of this apparent change may reflect the failure of the survey question to distinguish between party identities and vote preference. Nevertheless, it seems clear that Labour enjoyed more adherents in the late 1990s than before. Tellingly, Labour's surge in identification coincides with a dramatic change in its social imagery after Blair's attempts to broaden the party to build up its middle-class constituency. In 1992, 54% of the British public felt that the Labour Party was "good for one class" rather than for all classes, whereas only 14% held that view in 1997.[8]

The German data capture the CDU comeback that allowed it to hold on to power in the 1990 election despite early indications of increased SPD strength. Over the course of thirteen months, the CDU/CSU gained 4.5 points, whereas in December 1990 the SPD found itself in virtually the same place it had been in November 1989. Finally, the Canadian data show little evidence of aggregate instability in the share of identifiers for the Liberals, Conservatives, or NDP from 1983 to 1988. However, this masks a precipitous drop in Conservative identification not long after the party's 1984 election victory (Clarke and Kornberg 1992). By the time of the 1988 preelection survey, the Conservatives had regained nearly all of the ground lost in the 1985–87 period, whereas the Liberals had ceded all of their post-1984 gains. The magnitude of aggregate partisan change between 1984 and 1988 provides an intriguing opportunity to investigate the relationship between aggregate and individual-level stability. Our results show that partisan attachments were loosened significantly in the 1980s in Canada, paving the way for even greater change in the early 1990s, when identification with the Conservatives faltered and Reform and the Bloc Québécois emerged as important alternatives.

PARTISANSHIP IN STABLE PARTY REGIMES

We analyzed the data by creating dummy variables for identification with each of the major parties, based on the partisanship question. For example, a West German respondent who in the first wave claimed to identify with the SPD would be coded as one for the SPD dummy variable in that wave, and all others would be coded as zero. To estimate the stability of "SPD Partisanship," we used weighted least squares on the matrix of polychoric correlations of the SPD dummy variables from each wave. This analysis produces estimates for the effect of SPD partisanship in wave two on SPD partisanship in wave three, for the measurement error variance in waves two and three, and for the R-squared value in wave three.[9] It is important to emphasize that this method does not assume that respondents harbor multiple identifications but merely allows for the possibility.

Table 7.6 presents the estimates for the four-wave studies conducted in Britain, Germany, and Canada. The estimates for the stability of partisanship are broadly consistent with expectations drawn from American data (see Chapter 3). For example, in previous work (Green and Palmquist 1994), we calculated two-year equivalent R-squared values for each American survey and

Table 7.6. Partisan Stability in Great Britain, West Germany, and Canada

Panel	Party	Approximate Time Between Waves 2 and 3	R^2, Wave 2 to Wave 3	Measurement Error Variance	
				Wave 2	Wave 3
Great Britain,	Labour	2 years	0.957	0.036	0.033
1963–64–66–70			(0.020)	(0.056)	(0.057)
($N = 705$)	Tory	2 years	0.961	0.029	0.045
			(0.021)	(0.057)	(0.057)
Great Britain,	Labour	8 months	0.996	0.037	0.057
1974–74–75–79			(0.012)	(0.054)	(0.056)
($N = 724$)	Tory	8 months	0.975	0.052	0.036
			(0.015)	(0.055)	(0.055)
Great Britain,	Labour	1 year	0.984	0.045	0.037
1992–94–95–97			(0.012)	(0.042)	(0.042)
($N = 1,235$)	Tory	1 year	0.963	0.018	0.030
			(0.013)	(0.042)	(0.042)
Germany,	CDU	5 months	0.956	0.031	0.097
1989–90–90–90			(0.023)	(0.053)	(0.055)
($N = 869$)	SPD	5 months	0.944	0.104	0.065
			(0.030)	(0.056)	(0.054)
Canada,	Liberal	4 years	0.836	0.041	0.075
1983–84–88–88			(0.045)	(0.074)	(0.071)
($N = 500$)	Progressive Conservative	4 years	0.736	0.005	0.078
			(0.052)	(0.076)	(0.073)
	NDP	4 years	0.897	0.117	0.000
			(0.050)	(0.080)	(0.069)

Note: Analysis of four-wave panel studies using dummy variables for party. Numbers in parentheses are standard errors.

found an average R-squared value of 0.94. Replicating that analysis using the DIP measures for non-U.S. data also yields a median R-squared value of 0.94. This similarity is quite remarkable.

The British results are particularly striking: They show an extremely high level of stability in the relative locations of voters, something of a surprise given Butler and Stokes's (1969) famed turnover tables. The R-squared value for the Labour dummy variable in Britain is 0.957 over two years (1964–66) and is 0.996 over eight months (1974–75), whereas the Tory dummy variable has an R-squared value of 0.961 over the two-year period and of 0.975 over the eight-month period. These results suggest that once the partisanship item is purged of random measurement error, knowing that a respondent was a Tory in 1964 explains 96% of the variance in whether the respondent was a Tory in 1966. The finding of similarly high R-squared values for identification with Labour (0.984) and with the Tories (0.963) in 1994–95 (waves two and three of the 1992–97 panel) may seem surprising, given the substantial gain by Labour in that period. Recall, however, that the Heise model assesses the extent to which individuals maintain their relative locations even as the electorate as a whole drifts toward one party. Evidently, as we argued in Chapter 5, partisans tend to move in parallel in response to political and economic developments.

Although our German panel reveals slightly lower estimates for partisan stability, the estimates are still quite similar to results based on American data. (When one takes into account the standard error associated with these estimates, one discovers that the German and U.S. patterns are not statistically distinguishable.) The R-squared value for the CDU/CSU dummy variable is 0.956, and the R-squared value for identification with the SPD is 0.944. Again, these results indicate that German respondents tend to maintain their relative positions in terms of the degree to which they identify with the major parties.

The 1983–88 Canadian data provide evidence of greater volatility. The Liberal dummy variables show reasonably high stability: The R-squared value of 0.836 over the four-year period is only slightly lower than one would expect on the basis of the U.S. data. It corresponds to an R-squared value of 0.914 over the course of two years. The Conservative dummy variables, however, show considerably more instability. The estimated R-squared value of 0.736 implies an R-squared value of 0.858 for two years.

This raises the question of whether Canadian partisanship has always been more unstable than in other countries. Evidence from the two Canadian three-wave panels provides some answers. (See Table 7.7 for these results and estimates for the British and German three-wave panels.) The 1974–80 Canadian

Table 7.7. Partisan Stability in Great Britain, West Germany, and Canada

Panel	Party	Approximate Time Between Waves 2 and 3	R^2, Wave 2 to Wave 3	Measurement Error Variance, Wave 2
Great Britain, 1969–70–74 ($N = 463$)	Labour	4 years	0.837 (0.063)	0.034 (0.074)
	Tory	4 years	0.901 (0.049)	0.041 (0.073)
	Liberal	4 years	1.000 (0.080)	0.191 (0.137)
Germany, 1986–87–87 ($N = 1,311$)	CDU	1 month	0.890 (0.034)	0.024 (0.044)
	SPD	1 month	0.939 (0.037)	0.048 (0.045)
Canada, 1974–79–80 ($N = 822$)	Liberal	1 year	0.980 (0.038)	0.090 (0.058)
	Progressive Conservative	1 year	1.000 (0.024)	0.070 (0.051)
	NDP	1 year	0.845 (0.075)	0.008 (0.065)
Canada, 1992–93–93 ($N = 1,312$)	Liberal	1 month	0.881 (0.057)	0.059 (0.051)
	Progressive Conservative	1 month	0.873 (0.058)	0.078 (0.053)
	NDP	1 month	1.000 (0.027)	0.053 (0.048)

Note: Analysis of three-wave panel studies using dummy variables for party. Numbers in parentheses are standard errors.

survey shows partisanship to have been quite stable: The R-squared value over one year (1979–80) for the Liberal dummy variable is 0.980, and for the Progressive Conservatives is 1.000. By contrast, the 1992–93 panel shows considerable instability. The R-squared value for the Liberals over the course of a single month (with an election intervening) is 0.881, and that for the Progressive Conservatives is 0.873. Taken together with the results from the 1983–88 panel study, these estimates suggest that the Canadian party system was becoming destabilized in the mid-1980s and that individual-level partisan stability in Canada has fallen considerably from its prior levels. The sharp differences between the Canadian evidence on the one hand and the British and German data on the other offer the potential for many insights into the conditions under which partisanship changes. We consider this issue in more detail below in our discussion of party systems in flux.

Do these results depend on the particular way we have chosen to analyze these data? To check the robustness of our results, we augmented our model to account for the strength of respondent partisanship. We turned the dummy variable for identification with each party into an ordinal scale in which very strong partisans, fairly strong partisans, and not very strong partisans were distinguished from nonidentifiers with that party. We also constructed scales of partisanship in which identifiers with a given party were scored a value of two, leaners toward that party were scored one, and nonidentifiers with that party were scored zero. In each case, the results were essentially indistinguishable from results obtained using dichotomous indicators. This finding is encouraging because it speaks to the robustness of our estimates. It is also consistent with our results from Chapter 3, where we show that estimates for the stability of American partisanship are not very sensitive to scaling assumptions once measurement error is taken into account.

We also constructed scales of partisanship comparable in some respects to the standard American partisanship item. We used two different types of measures here. For the first, we put the two main parties on either end of a partisanship scale and coded respondents who did not identify with a party in the middle. For the second measure, we used an ordering that corresponds roughly to the ideological orientations of each party (see Converse and Pierce 1992).[10] The results from these analyses were quite similar to those obtained when the dichotomous indicator of partisanship was used (see Schickler and Green 1997).

In addition to assessing the stability of partisanship, our analyses also provide estimates for the measurement error in the partisanship item. Because the variance of each item is standardized to one (since the analysis is based on polychoric correlations), the reliability of each item is simply one minus the measurement error variance. The median reliability for the dichotomous indicator of partisanship in the four-wave surveys is 0.96, which is slightly higher than the median reliability estimate when Green and Palmquist's (1994) American data are reanalyzed using polychoric correlations. The consonant reliability estimates are encouraging: If we found considerably more measurement error outside the United States than in U.S. data, we would have to question the validity of our method for assessing and correcting response error in survey data.

A CLOSER LOOK AT AN UNSTABLE PARTY
SYSTEM: ITALY DURING THE 1990S

It is a sad commentary on the prescience of the discipline that political scientists have never conducted a multiwave panel study spanning a period of party realignment. Like photographers who use copious quantities of film but never seem to have their cameras loaded at just the right time, survey researchers have yet to capture substantial partisan change while it is occurring. The 1956–60 NES panel survey came too early to record the Democratic realignment of blacks, and the 1972–76 NES panel survey came too early to record the final stage of the Republican realignment of Southern whites. Outside the United States, only the 1992–93 Canadian panel study shows evidence of substantial partisan instability (realignment may be too strong a term to describe it); the other panel studies track periods of persistent party attachments. One of the most dramatic party realignments in recent years, the collapse of the Italian party system during the early 1990s, largely eluded pollsters. Until 1997, the only surveys conducted that asked about party identification interviewed cross sections of the population. The first panel study to track Italian party identification did not come along until 1997, by which time Italians had already begun to settle into the new array of parties.

Nevertheless, this panel survey provides a unique look at party attachments during a period of flux. As noted above, the survey began a few years after the disappearance of the Christian Democratic Party, Socialist Party, and the traditional Communist Party. To put these results in perspective, consider the differences in the distribution of party identification across the three waves of the panel survey. In waves one and two, respondents were invited to say whether they identified with one or more parties, named one at a time. During wave two, the list was expanded at the end to include two coalition groups—which seemed at the time to be nascent parties—Ulivo and Polo. Although these groups appear at the end of a lengthy inventory of questions (so that it seems unlikely that the change in question format would affect the standing of parties asked before), these new parties seem to have cut into the center right (Forza Italia) and center left (PDS). Even though respondents were encouraged to name more than one party with which they might identify, attachment to Forza Italia dropped from 14.4% to 7.3%, and PDS declined from 22.3% to 14.2%. Conversely, as Table 7.8 indicates, Ulivo drew heavily from former PDS and Communist Refoundation (RC) identifiers to become an object of identification for 16.2% of the sample.

Table 7.8. Changes in the Distribution of Party Identification over Time in Italy

	Party-by-Party Questioning		Selections from a List of Parties	
	Wave I (%)	Wave II (%)	Wave II (%)	Wave III (%)
Forza Italia	14.4	7.3	7.5	11.9
Alleanza Nazionale	17.5	15.2	12.2	14.4
Christian Democratic Center (CCD)	3.3	2.3	0.6	1.3
Christian Democratic Union (CDU)	0.8	0.5	0.3	0.6
Panneliano	0.8	0.5	1.3	1.3
Social Democratic Party (PDS)	22.3	14.2	10.7	14.1
Rifondazione Communista (RC)	11.1	7.1	7.2	6.0
Comunisti Italiani	N/A	N/A	N/A	2.2
Verdi	5.3	4.3	2.2	2.2
Rinnovamento Italiano	1.0	0.5	0.9	0.3
Italian Popular Party (PPI)	4.1	3.5	0.9	1.6
Lega Nord	3.0	4.1	4.7	4.7
Fiamma Tricolore	1.3	0.8	0.3	0.3
Socialisti	1.3	0.5	0.9	0.6
Patto Segni	0.3	0.0	N/A	N/A
Ulivo	N/A	16.2	13.2	7.5
Polo	N/A	5.3	4.7	N/A
Other	0.3	0.0	0.0	0.6
No party	25.1	26.1	32.3	30.4
Total	111.9	108.4	99.9	100.0
N (respondents present in both waves)		395		319

The fortunes of Ulivo waned between waves two and three, however. Tracing party identification as measured by a standard list format, we see that the proportion of Ulivo identifiers declined from 13.2% to 7.5%, with a corresponding revival of the PDS. The same revival occurs on the right, although in Table 7.8 the trend is confounded by the fact that the Polo coalition was dropped from the list because of an oversight in the printing of the survey. Fortunately, we had asked the party identification question in open-ended form to a subsample in waves two and three. Only 1.3% of the sample ($N = 1,384$) in wave three volunteered identification with Polo, as opposed to 2.2% in the previous interview ($N = 975$). Anticipation of "bipolarism" between large coalitions on the left and right, which seemed to be in the air during wave two, had dissipated by wave three, and respondents withdrew their attachments from the coalitions and returned to the parties that comprised them. This fragmentation, particularly on the Left, later brought the right back into power in the 2001 elections.

The correlations between party identification over time tell an interesting story of how attachments waxed and waned during this period. At one extreme (literally), were respondents attached to the rightist Alleanza Nazionale. As shown in Table 7.9, identification with Alleanza Nazionale was highly stable between the second and third waves of this survey. By contrast, identification with the RC was highly unstable. The RC was the remnants of the old Communist Party (the stalwarts who did not want to transform it into the PDS) and was flanked on its right by the much larger PDS and the increasingly viable Ulivo coalition. By wave three, it was challenged also on the left by the upstart Communist Party of Italy. As Table 7.9 shows, the correlation between partisanship in waves one and three drops off dramatically, suggesting that respondents' attachments to RC changed sharply. Somewhere between these two extremes lies Forza Italia, which shows one-year correlations well below what we commonly observe for other countries but higher than for the mercurial RC. The most interesting pattern of all is that of identification with the PDS. In wave two, Ulivo challenged the PDS for voters' attachments. The disruption is evident in the weak correlation between PDS identification in waves one and two. As the challenge by Ulivo subsided, the correlation actually rises, so that there is a stronger correlation between waves one and three than between waves two and three.

These results nicely illustrate the unusual patterns of party attachments found in rapidly evolving party systems. Some political parties, such as the rightist Alleanza Nazionale, remain stable because they are sufficiently de-

Table 7.9. Stability of Party Identification toward Italy's Four Largest Parties

	Polychoric Correlation, Wave I and Wave II	Polychoric Correlation, Wave I and Wave III
Alleanza Nazionale	0.875	0.859
Forza Italia	0.818	0.806
PDS	0.580	0.789
Rifondazione Comunista (RC)	0.840	0.688

Note: $N = 319$. The wave one measure is the party-by-party measure shown in Table 7.3. Partisanship in waves two and three was measured using a list of parties, from which respondents picked the one with which they identified most. The stability of partisanship was gauged by the degree to which the correlation declined with time.

tached from party formation and splintering. Others, such as the leftist RC, are in a thicket of incipient parties and watch their adherents come and go. Still other parties, such as the PDS, are fortunate enough to find their itinerant identifiers return home. Evidently, the social images of the new partisan groups have not solidified to the point at which citizens have internalized them into their self-conceptions. For many Italians, particularly on the left, whether one *is of* the PDS, Ulivo, or one of several smaller parties remains unsettled.

TO WHAT EXTENT DOES PARTY IDENTIFICATION TRAVEL WITH SHORT-TERM EVALUATIONS?

In our view, Italy is a notable exception to the generalization that party attachments are typically stable and insulated from short-term forces. Unlike Italy, Britain, Germany, and pre-1990s Canada were relatively stable across both short and long time spans, a finding that goes against the notion that citizens readily adjust their partisanship to changes in government popularity, candidate evaluations, or voting behavior. To this point, however, we have not directly assessed the effect of these short-term forces on party identification. We have examined this link between short-term forces and partisanship using a variety of data sets, but for the sake of brevity, we will focus on the 1983–88 and 1992–93 Canadian panel studies and the 1974–79 British survey. The most recent Canadian survey coincides with a period of upheaval in the party system. The 1974–79 British panel is also a promising test case because it covers a period during which there was a major reversal of party fortunes: The Labour Party's 1974 victories were followed by the Tory sweep in 1979 that brought Margaret Thatcher to power.

We first examine how evaluations of the Labour Party's handling of inflation and unemployment and attitudes toward the Labour Party's leader affected British party identification in 1979. The former variable is an index created by summing responses to survey questions asked in October 1974 and after the 1979 election. Attitudes toward the Labour Party leader were measured by approval, on a ten-point scale, of Harold Wilson in 1974 and James Callaghan in 1979. As in Chapter 3 and our earlier work (Green and Palmquist 1990; Schickler and Green 1995), we use pooled cross-sectional models to examine the interplay between short-term forces and party identification, but we also use an estimation technique that treats the data as ordinal rather than continuous. In each of the models, we use lagged values of party identification and the test variable (Labour's handling of inflation and unemployment and attitudes toward the Labour Party's leader[11]) as instruments for party identification and the test variable, which are assumed to influence each other at a given point in time.[12]

The results, presented in Table 7.10, provide little support for the view that party identification was responsive to short-term forces in Britain during this period. None of the estimated coefficients is statistically significant, and the estimates tend to be substantively small. For example, a change of one standard deviation in evaluations of the Labour Party's leader is associated with a corresponding shift of 0.145 of a standard deviation (SE = 0.216) in Tory identification, and a wrongly signed change of 0.222 of a standard deviation (SE = 0.796) in identification with the Labour Party.

For the 1983–88 Canadian panel, we assessed the effects of ratings of the Progressive Conservative and Liberal party leaders and evaluations of the performance of Brian Mulroney as prime minister on party identification in 1988. Again, we found no evidence that short-term forces affect party identification. For example, a shift of one standard deviation in evaluations of the Liberal and Progressive Conservative leaders in 1988 is estimated to result in a change of 0.085 of a standard deviation (SE = 0.562) in identification with the Progressive Conservative party and a move of 0.137 (SE = 0.238) in identification with the Liberal Party. As noted in Chapter 3, analysis of U.S. data using similar pooled panel methods reveals comparable small and insignificant effects of presidential approval and other short-term forces on party identification (see Green and Palmquist 1990).

Although these findings reinforce our confidence that party identification outside the American context is not a mere reflection of current political evaluations of leaders and parties,[13] our results for the 1992–93 Canadian panel show that partisan stability can be undermined in certain contexts, particularly when competing forms of identity become highly salient. We first estimated the effects of evaluations of the Progressive Conservative and Liberal party leaders on party identification. Jean Chretien was the Liberal Party leader throughout the period; Mulroney was still the Conservative leader when the first survey wave was administered, but Kim Campbell had taken over by the time of the second wave. Although Campbell was, at least at first, considerably more popular than Mulroney, we find only mixed evidence that changing evaluations of the party leaders affected partisanship. The estimates of leadership evaluations' effects on identification with the Progressive Conservatives are uniformly negligible in size and statistically insignificant. Turning to the Liberals, however,

Table 7.10. Estimated Effects of Short-Term Forces on Party Identification in Great Britain and Canada

Alternative Specifications	Time Span	Effect of PID_{t-1} on PID_t	Effect of Short-Term Forces$_t$ on PID_t	N
A. Britain, Tory identification				
Callaghan evaluation	5 years	0.857	0.145	717
	(waves 2–4)	(0.148)	(0.216)	
Approval of Labour's				
handling of inflation	5 years	0.965	−0.049	685
and unemployment	(waves 2–4)	(0.212)	(0.351)	
B. Britain, Labour identification				
Callaghan evaluation	5 years	1.000	−0.222	717
	(waves 2–4)	(0.552)	(0.796)	
Approval of Labour's				
handling of inflation	5 years	0.997	−0.096	685
and unemployment	(waves 2–4)	(0.281)	(0.451)	
C. Canada, Liberal identification, 1983–88				
Difference in ratings for	4 years	0.827	0.137	419
Progressive Conservative	(waves 2–4)	(0.142)	(0.238)	
and Liberal leaders				
Approval of Mulroney's	1 month	0.960	−0.046	493
performance	(waves 3–4)	(0.080)	(0.114)	
D. Canada, Progressive Conservative identification, 1983–88				
Difference in ratings for	4 years	0.777	0.085	419
Progressive Conservative	(waves 2–4)	(0.382)	(0.562)	
and Liberal leaders				
Approval of Mulroney's	1 month	0.949	−0.003	493
performance	(waves 3–4)	(0.130)	(0.150)	
E. Canada, Liberal identification, 1992–93				
Difference in ratings for	1 year	0.728	0.268	1,064
Progressive Conservative	(waves 1–2)	(0.075)	(0.136)	
and Liberal leaders				
Difference in ratings for	1 month	0.908	−0.025	1,064
Progressive Conservative	(waves 2–3)	(0.080)	(0.121)	
and Liberal leaders				
Difference in ratings for	13 months	0.655	0.323	1,064
Progressive Conservative	(waves 1–3)	(0.086)	(0.195)	
and Liberal leaders				
F. Canada, Progressive Conservative identification, 1992–93				
Difference in ratings for	1 year	0.794	0.138	1,064
Progressive Conservative	(waves 1–2)	(0.080)	(0.149)	
and Liberal leaders				

(*continued*)

Table 7.10. (*Continued*)

Alternative Specifications	Time Span	Effect of PID_{t-1} on PID_t	Effect of Short-Term Forces$_t$ on PID_t	N
Difference in ratings for Progressive Conservative and Liberal leaders	1 month (waves 2–3)	0.907 (0.070)	−0.057 (0.118)	1,064
Difference in ratings for Progressive Conservative and Liberal leaders	13 months (waves 1–3)	0.832 (0.090)	−0.238 (0.230)	1,064

Notes: Standard errors are in parentheses. Each row represents a separate regression analysis estimated using weighted least-squares on polychoric correlation matrices. All coefficients are standardized. Variables were recoded so that the short-term forces were expected to have a positive sign. The reliability of party identification (PID) was stipulated to be 0.975. This is a higher reliability than the typical estimate in Tables 7.6 and 7.7, thus providing a difficult test for the partisan stability thesis. When the reliability of the PID measure is stipulated to be 1.0, there still are no significant effects of short-term forces in either of the two four-wave surveys. The reliability of the measures of short-term forces has no effect on these estimates (see Green 1990). Substantively identical results were obtained when different combinations of survey waves were analyzed.

there is modest evidence that partisanship responds to short-term forces. In wave three, the estimated effect of evaluations of the party leaders on Liberal identification is 0.323 (SE = 0.195).[14] We should note, however, that these estimates are based on extremely conservative assumptions about measurement error: The variable of Liberal Party identification is stipulated to have a reliability of 0.975, whereas our analyses in Table 7.7 suggest that the true reliability is 0.941. Although this difference is small, fixing the reliability of the measure of Liberal Party identification to 0.941 diminishes the estimated size and statistical significance of the effects of leadership evaluations.

Still, there is reason to believe that partisanship did respond to political changes in Canada during the 1992–93 period. Given the vitality of regionally based parties, focusing on national-level results may obscure evidence for the importance of political forces that would be apparent when regional data are examined. When leadership evaluations are broken down by region, we find that estimates for the effects of the evaluations on Liberal Party identification are much higher in Quebec than in the rest of Canada. The Quebec estimates—although not statistically significant at conventional levels (because of the restricted sample size)—are two to three times the size of the estimates for the country as a whole. Furthermore, when the sample is restricted to those outside Quebec, evidence for the effects of leadership evaluations on party identification becomes negligible.

The leadership evaluation variable, however, is probably not the best indicator for the effect of the rising separatist tide in Quebec. Each wave of the 1992–93 panel asked respondents from Quebec whether they favored or opposed sovereignty for their province. We used the model discussed above to assess whether attitudes toward sovereignty affected identification toward the Progressive Conservatives, Liberals, and Bloc Québécois. Our estimates provide striking evidence that partisanship in Quebec was responsive to attitudes toward sovereignty. Not surprisingly, the coefficients for identification with the Bloc Québécois are the largest in value. A one–standard deviation change in approval of Quebec sovereignty in wave two generated a 0.511-unit change (SE = 0.172) in identification with the Bloc Québécois. A similar though somewhat smaller effect is found for identification with the Progressive Conservatives (0.254, SE = 0.127).[15] The results indicate that most of the change occurred between the first and second waves; none of the analyses of change between the second and third waves shows strong evidence that party identification continued to shift in response to the sovereignty issue.

On the whole, these findings provide good reason to believe that Quebecers during the 1990s responded to a changing political landscape by altering their party identification. Long-standing Canadian parties rose and fell as regional identities became increasingly salient rivals to partisan predispositions. Yet, the Canadian party system also illustrates how powerful old attachments can be. The election of 1993, which followed a period of erosion in Progressive Conservative identification, demolished the Progressive Conservative Party's parliamentary delegation, leaving it with just two seats in 1993. After this fiasco, identification with the Progressive Conservatives diminished rather slowly, falling from 15.7% in 1993 to 13.8% in 1997.[16] Although we have avoided use of the term *party loyalty* because it conjures images of party-line voting, here it seems especially apt.

SUMMARY

In this chapter we aimed to extend findings of partisan stability beyond the borders of the United States. The principal conclusion to emerge from our analysis of numerous panel studies is that once measurement error is taken into account, rates of partisan change in Britain, Germany, and pre-Mulroney Canada closely resemble those found in the United States. Of course, partisanship is nowhere found to be perfectly stable; in any given year, roughly 2% to 4% of the variance in partisanship is newly introduced. To treat partisanship as an exogenous predictor of the vote during a given election cycle represents a simplification. Yet it is precisely the kind of empirical approximation that can be useful to students of voting behavior, who must inevitably grapple with specification problems that are much thornier than the exogeneity of party identification.

One cannot fully understand partisan stability without examining the conditions under which partisan change occurs. As Converse and Pierce (1986) have argued, partisan attachments whither when parties die out or change names, an observation of special relevance to contemporary Italy. The disappearance or transformation of parties untethered many former partisan identifiers. The change in the parties was much more profound than mere electoral misfortune. Whereas the Conservatives in Canada dwindled into parliamentary obscurity but still retained their most ardent supporters, the Italian parties shed them by disbanding.

This line of argument may be extended to postrealignment periods, when attachments seem unusually fragile. In the late 1990s, the partisan groups on the Italian left had yet to develop powerful social group images, and incipient parties continually threatened to draw away a party's base. This pattern has interesting implications for new democratic regimes, which frequently begin with a profusion of small parties vying for voters. Not only may it take years for parties to sort themselves out into large blocs, but it may take even longer for voters to develop enduring attachments to the emergent parties. Although in former communist countries one finds a sizable number of hard-core communist identifiers—remarkable testimony to the persistence of both parties and party attachments—identifiers with newer parties tend to have less stable party attachments and less predictable voting patterns. The cohesiveness of the Communists has in many countries enabled them to compete effectively against a divided opposition.

Competing identities are another source of partisan instability. As we noted in the previous chapter, partisan change occurred among whites in the American South immediately after the passage of the Voting Rights Act in 1965, which enfranchised blacks and revitalized two-party politics. That race and regional identities can unseat partisan attachments within an environment in which new electoral rules or new parties are emerging is a thesis that comports well with our present findings concerning Canada from the early 1980s to the early 1990s. As separatist issues concerning region, language, and ethnicity grew in prominence and achieved institutional expression in the emergence of regional parties, partisan attachments to the major parties weakened. In effect, one set of group identifications rooted in nationality unseated another associated with party.

This hypothesis, too, has important implications for new democratic regimes. It is perhaps no accident that new democracies frequently witness the efflorescence of parties aimed at attracting the votes of farmers, regional ethnic groups, and conservative Christians. Each of these parties recognizes the potency of these social identities and seeks to parlay a social attachment into a party attachment. Although a common strategy, it is one that is difficult to execute. At its founding, a party must rely on its platform, leadership, and electoral prospects to draw a social group into its orbit. Yet, by appealing to a particular social group, the party in some ways limits its broader electoral prospects by alienating others, which in turn diminishes the party's chances of surviving long enough to become a viable object of identification. The long-term success of a party hinges on its ability to build a coalition of groups and to cement this coalition by creating partisan attachments that go beyond group attachment.

Chapter 8 How Partisan

Attachments Structure Politics

Party identification is an unending source of fascination for researchers who study how voters think, feel, and formulate decisions. Study after study examines how partisanship develops and expresses itself, and this book has tried to integrate and interpret this immense body of research. Our reading of the evidence suggests that the outstanding characteristic of party identification is its resemblance to other familiar forms of social identification. Like identification with a socioeconomic class, party identification reflects an awareness that one belongs to a social group. As with ethnic identification, the individual must decide whether to appropriate the group label as part of his or her self-description. And like religious identification, one's sense of group membership and attachment may develop for reasons that have to do with a person's social location (for example, the family in which one was raised, the person one chooses to marry) rather than the draw of the doctrine associated with the group. Although party identities are not as stable as religious identities over long stretches of time, the analogy is apt for those who track voters over the course of a campaign or presidential term. In both politics and religion, one's identification with the group may endure despite one's heterodox beliefs.

Characterizing party attachments as social identities helps explain why they endure amid changing political conditions. One's partisan self-conception is guided by a sense of who belongs to these groups and one's relationship to them. When the self is changing rapidly, as in young adulthood, partisanship is relatively malleable. Party attachments may also shift markedly when people acquire new information about which social groups support each party, a process that describes the acquisition of party identities among recent immigrants (Wong 2001). Sometimes an individual's group identities collide with one another. As we saw in Chapter 7, party attachments can be disrupted by the emergence of new parties that appeal to voters on the basis of linguistic, regional, or religious affiliation.

But ordinary politics and life experiences, which impinge neither on self-conceptions nor on the stereotypes associated with partisan groups, tend to leave little imprint on voters' party identities. It is not that voters steadfastly ignore politics or refuse to accept new information about how parties and their leaders are performing. As the vicissitudes in presidential approval demonstrate, these opinions may change rapidly. But one can change one's assessment of political leaders and their policies without revising one's sense of self or social location. In this crucial respect, opinions and identities are different.

Building the case for the distinctiveness of party attachments has been the central aim of this book. We recognize, however, that many who study electoral politics are primarily interested not in voter cognition but rather in the ways that voter psychology influences political outcomes. In their view, investigating the nature of partisanship is interesting insofar as it helps us understand why elections come out as they do. These readers have patiently waded through the foregoing chapters but now find themselves asking what the concept of party identification contributes to our understanding of electoral politics.

We devote the remaining pages to the topic of how party attachments shape the nature of electoral competition. First, using survey data from the 1996 and 2000 elections, we demonstrate the profound influence of party identification on how people vote. This influence is not reducible to issue-based affinity for the candidates' platforms. Although the candidates' issue stances can be crucial to how voters cast their ballots, party attachments remain influential even when ideological orientations are held constant. Nor does the influence of party identification disappear when we take into account how people evaluate the incumbent president. While by no means the sole influence on vote choice, party identification powerfully shapes how voters cast their ballots.

Second, we propose an interpretation of the strong relationship between party identification and voting that stresses the role of group attachment. Identification with parties imbues electoral choice with special significance. Elections affirm and empower the social groups that comprise the winning party. Even if Democratic policy objectives appeal to a Republican, he or she may still sense that when a Democrat wins an election it is a victory for minorities, liberals, union members, and Democratic partisans in general. To those who define themselves in partisan terms, elections represent more than simply a competition between candidates and rival platforms. Elections are also forums for *intergroup* competition. Individuals who identify with these groups are drawn into this competition. Their interest and level of emotional engagement increase as they embrace the team as their own. Although not irresistible, the desire to see one's team prevail powerfully influences the probability of casting a vote for the candidate of one's party.

This chapter closes with a discussion of the systemic implications of widespread party attachment. Because party identities change slowly and express themselves in elections at all levels of government, the distribution of party attachments in the electorate defines an equilibrium toward which electoral outcomes tend to gravitate. Moreover, by increasing the variance in voting proclivities within the electorate at a given time, party attachments dampen the electoral tides that would otherwise produce much larger electoral victories for the party favored by short-term forces. By contributing to the stability of electoral outcomes over time, party identification indirectly shapes politics. Politicians must adjust their behavior to the fact that unusual election outcomes are unlikely to endure.

THE ELECTORAL SIGNIFICANCE
OF PARTY IDENTIFICATION

In Chapter 1, we pointed out that despite the outpouring of scholarship on the declining influence of party identification, party attachments remain powerful predictors of vote choice. Initially, we made this point with reference to the simple bivariate relationship between party identification and vote choice, ignoring other determinants of voter preference. Taken at face value, the strong association between party identification and the vote seems to imply that people express their attachments to partisan groups by siding with candidates associated with their party. Party identification influences the vote by instilling a sense of group loyalty.

This interpretation is by no means uncontroversial. Party attachments are correlated with the other *P*s that shape voter choice: evaluations of the candidates' *performance* in office, *personal* traits, and *positions* on the leading issues of the day. One important challenge to the apparent association between party identification and the vote is that this relationship is a spurious reflection of the influence of issue stances on both party affiliation and votes. If one becomes a Democrat because one is a liberal, and one votes for George McGovern because one agrees with his liberal platform, the apparent congruence between party and vote choice gives the misleading impression that this vote is a manifestation of party loyalty. A similar line of argument could be advanced with respect to group interests. The economic and social interests that impel blacks to become Democrats also may be sufficient to cause them to vote against Ronald Reagan. Party identities may predict the vote, but what do they add to this prediction beyond what might be accounted for by other factors?

To gauge the genuine influence of party identification, critics propose a multivariate analysis in which the putative causes of party identification are controlled statistically. In operational terms, this regression model includes not only party identification but also covariates that capture voters' ideological orientations and their group interests. If a sequence of regressions reveals that the apparent influence of party disappears after one controls for factors that potentially cause party identification, the implication is that the correlation between party and the vote is spurious.

Although multivariate models are proposed in the spirit of providing a fairer assessment of party influence, they may inadvertently understate the influence of party attachments on the vote. The reason is that party identification may shape the variables that are used as covariates. Consider, for example, the link between the partisan groups with which people identify and the stances that they take on the issues of the day.[1] One possibility, consistent with the hypothesis that the correlation between the vote and party identification is spurious, is that people gravitate to the party that best matches their views on issues. Another possibility is that partisans absorb the party line. This hypothesis is illustrated rather dramatically when party leaders make sudden or unexpected changes in the party's official positions, precipitating a revision of their supporters' issue stances (Gerber and Jackson 1993). If party attachments inure people to certain ways of thinking about issues, controlling for the latter may overlook an important indirect channel through which party affiliation influences the vote.

Unfortunately, the process by which party attachments and issue stances influence one another is not observed directly. The analyst can do no more than speculate about which characterization is correct. Thus, when two scholars look at the same sequence of regression equations and note that the direct effect of party identification has fallen to zero, they may draw diametrically opposing conclusions. One may infer that party has no influence at all and that the apparent correlation between partisanship and the vote was a spurious reflection of the other covariates in the model. The other may conclude that party identification transmits its influence indirectly through one or more of these covariates.

For a period during the late 1970s and early 1980s, political scientists thought they could resolve these interpretive disputes by creating more elaborate models. Rather than rigidly assume that issues cause party or that party causes issues, these models tried to estimate the bidirectional causal flow between issues and party (Jackson 1975; Page and Jones 1979; Franklin and Jackson 1983). This strategy was abandoned after it became clear that the assumptions on which these statistical models rested were no more palatable than the all-or-nothing assumptions of unidirectional causality. The field of election studies never recovered from the resulting deadlock; since the mid-1980s, modeling the vote in individual-level survey data has receded in prominence as a scholarly activity.

Although the interpretation of any given regression will always be a matter of disagreement, a series of regressions offers an instructive way to place *bounds* on what we think party effects may be. The most generous assumptions attribute the correlation between party identification and other political attitudes to party. In this maximal account, people come to think of themselves as members of a partisan group and then assimilate the views of this group. To produce a maximal estimate, one regresses the vote on party identification, controlling only for background attributes such as ethnicity, age, sex, region, religion, family income, and educational attainment. Party in this model reflects one's sociological location and attendant socialization experiences, causes of voting behavior that express themselves through the group interests and fixed social-psychological orientations they engender (see Campbell et al. 1960: 24–37).

The minimal account controls for the two additional factors, respondents' views on policy questions and their evaluations of the incumbent's performance in office, on the grounds that voters gravitate toward the party that promises them the best package of policy and competence in office.[2] The measures of policy orientations capture the degree to which party attachments are formed on the basis of ideological affinity with a party. As we noted in previous chapters, scholars disagree about how ideological distance should be measured. The approach we take here is to measure how voters respond to a variety of policy questions and examine how these responses predict the choice between two candidates, one of whom is consistently more conservative than the other. Another approach is to use respondents' descriptions of where the candidates stand on each issue to create a summary measure of ideological proximity. Although it in theory provides a more precise measure of ideological affinity, the latter approach may lead to biased statistical results if respondents rationalize their vote preferences by pulling their preferred candidate close to them. This concern, in addition to the fact that perceived candidate stances are asked on only a portion of the NES items, led us to use issue positions rather than issue proximities.

The other factor, retrospective evaluations, arguably shapes party attachments insofar as people are drawn to the more capable party (Fiorina 1981). Impressions of the incumbent may measure ideological orientations as well. To see why, think back to the rational learning model presented in Chapter 5. To the extent that everyone shares a common perception of what the incumbent has done in office, the variability that we observe among individuals at any given time consists of two components. First, individuals differ because they assign different weights to various political issues and objectives. For example, compared with Democrats, Republicans may be distinctive in their concern for national defense and their eagerness to devote more resources to it, and at any point in time their evaluations of the incumbent president will reflect their conservative tastes. In some ways, approval is a more flexible and comprehensive measure of issue preferences than a long battery of questions about issues. The latter may omit issues that are on voters' minds. Moreover, statistical models that assess the link between issues and votes may fail to appreciate the idiosyncratic weights that respondents assign to each issue when deciding which candidate to support. Approval, on the other hand, measures how people have translated their political tastes—however defined and expressed—into an evaluation of the incumbent. Second, when asked about their evaluation of a president, who also serves as the leader of a political party, partisan respondents will tend to answer in ways that redound to the benefit of their own party. Those who belong to the same party as the president will tend to describe the administration's behavior in more positive terms than those in an opposing party. In the context of an interview concerning politics,[3] they will paint the economy in rosier hues even if the true economic perceptions that guide their patterns of consumption and investment do not differ from those of opposing partisans who occupy a similar economic station. Assuming that partisans are fooling others and not themselves, the partisan spin that respondents put on their answers should have no effect on their vote decisions, controlling for party identification. But this theoretical prediction may break down empirically because our measurement of party identification is not flawless. To the extent that our survey measures give an imprecise reading of party attachments, the apparent effects of presidential approval will be exaggerated. Presidential ratings would be given credit for their partisan tinge, and the effects of partisanship would be underestimated.

To be fair, measurement concerns cut both ways here. Any attempt to canvass the range of relevant issues or to capture what people think about them raises questions about coverage and measurement precision. To some extent these concerns are obviated when we control also for evaluations of the incumbent because these evaluations will reflect what people regard as the important evaluative dimensions. But even here, it remains possible that our best efforts to measure approval come up short, in which case the effects of party may simply reflect unmeasured or mismeasured psychological orientations that are correlated with party identification. In the empirical exercise that follows, we try to gauge issues and evaluations as extensively as the NES survey allows, bringing to bear no fewer than twenty-four different indicators of issue stances and performance evaluations. The measures tap liberal-conservative self-placement and opinions on abortion, environmental regulation, capital punishment, the scope of the welfare state, gun control, aid to blacks, health care, how to spend the budget surplus, whether English should be the country's official language, gay rights, feminism, and moral traditionalism.[4] Nevertheless, it is always possible that we have not gone far enough, and the reader must judge whether the inadequacies of measurement are a plausible cause for concern.

The focus of our initial empirical analysis is the 2000 presidential election. This election featured two standard-issue major party candidates. The Republican nominee, George W. Bush, centered his campaign around a proposal to roll back federal income tax rates and end the estate tax. The Democrat, Al Gore, emphasized the importance of maintaining and expanding medical and retirement benefits. Although both candidates were more centrist than most activists in their parties, their records and campaign themes appealed to people with different ideological tastes. Another attitude that shaped vote choice was one's assessment of President Clinton, whose personal misbehavior in office and ideological zigzags but strong economic record evoked mixed feelings within the electorate. Indeed, it was widely believed that Vice President Gore distanced himself from Clinton during the campaign in an effort to dampen the effects of these retrospective judgments.

The dependent variable in our regression models is whether a voter cast a ballot for Bush.[5] Because the dependent variable is dichotomous, we analyze the data using logistic regression; in effect, the model tries to assess how factors such as party identification change the odds of voting for Bush. Table 8.1 presents the sequence of logistic regression models. The first model, which includes only demographic predictors of the vote, provides a baseline against which to compare the more elaborate specifications that follow. This model is interesting in its own right in that it underscores the limited predictive power of membership in broad social and economic categories. Variables marking age, sex, union membership, income, education, region, religion, and ethnicity account for less than one-quarter of the variability in vote outcomes and forecast how people voted at a rate (68%) that is not vastly more impressive than a model that fits only an intercept to the data (53%). As students of voting behavior have long recognized, voters' objective membership in coarse social categories does not go very far in shaping electoral decisions.

Frustrated by their inability to explain individual variability with reference to sociodemographic variables, scholars during the 1950s turned increasingly to social-psychological variables, such as the voters' subjective sense of party attachment, to explain the vote. Many of the psychological orientations that they turned to, such as authoritarianism, proved to be sporadic or weak predictors of voting behavior. Party identification, on the other hand, has for decades been found to predict votes in a wide array of different types of elections. True to form, party identification greatly improves the accuracy with which our model predicts the 2000 vote. Whether measured as a seven-point scale or simply a three-point scale as in Table 8.1, the effects of party attachment are profound. The percentage correctly predicted climbs to 82%, and the R-squared, to 0.60. The logistic regression coefficient of 2.3 indicates that the log-odds of voting for Bush increased 2.3 for each one-unit movement along the party identification scale. To translate this statistic into more familiar probabilities, consider the example of an Independent whose demographic characteristics imply a 50% chance of voting for Bush. If this voter were to become a Republican, the probability of voting for Bush would rise from 50% to 91%.[6] Conversely,

Table 8.1. Effect on Vote Choice of Party Identification, Issue Preferences, Demographics, and Evaluations of Bill Clinton, 2000

Model	Logistic Regression Coefficient for Party Identification	Percentage Predicted Correctly	Nagelkerke R^2
1. Demographics only		68.0	0.243
2. Demographics and party identification	2.29 (0.16)	82.0	0.602
3. Issues and demographics		84.4	0.650
4. Issues, demographics, and party identification	2.04 (0.20)	88.2	0.750
5. Issues, demographics, Clinton ratings, and economic evaluations		89.0	0.767
6. Issues, demographics, Clinton ratings, economic evaluations, and party identification	1.57 (0.22)	91.4	0.803

Notes: Entries in parentheses are standard errors; $N = 962$. Estimates for party identification are all significant at a value of $p < .001$. The dependent variable in each regression was whether the respondent voted for Bush (1 = Voted for Bush; 0 = Voted for Al Gore or Ralph Nader). The party identification variable was scored 1 = Democrat, 2 = Independent, and 3 = Republican. When the seven-point party identification scale is used instead of the three-point scale used here, the coefficient in Model 2 is 1.02 as opposed to 0.72 in Model 6. The percentage predicted in Model 6 rises slightly to 91.5, and the R^2 becomes 0.811.

Demographic regressors included whether the respondent belongs to a household with a union member, sex, years of education, family income, and residence in the South. Dummy variables were used also to denote Protestants, Catholics, blacks, Latinos, Asians, and "other" race, as well as several age categories (eighteen to twenty-five, twenty-six to thirty-five, thirty-six to forty-five, forty-six to fifty-five, fifty-six to sixty-five, and older than sixty-five). The measures of issues included the following regressors: liberal-conservative self-placement, abortion, environmental growth at the expense of jobs, environmental regulations, death penalty, job guarantee, gun control, aid to blacks, government services, government's role in providing health insurance, whether to spend the surplus on tax cuts, whether to use the surplus for social security and Medicare, gays in the military, gay adoption, English official language law, women's equal role, and four "traditionalism" items (each entered separately: moral breakdown, adjust views to new conditions, importance of family ties, and tolerate different lifestyles). In each case, respondents who answered "don't know/haven't thought about it" were placed at the mean for that variable. Furthermore, a "missing data" dummy was put in for each issue item, coded one if the respondent had answered "don't know/haven't thought about it" for that item. Note that if the analysis were to omit missing data listwise, the N drops to 422, but the pattern of results remains the same. The coefficient for three-point party identification declines from 2.58 in Model 2 to 1.85 in Model 6.

Measure of performance evaluations included Clinton's job approval, his handling of economic affairs, a feeling thermometer rating of Clinton, and retrospective evaluation of the national economy during the past year.

changing this Independent into a Democrat would lower the probability from 50% to 9%. Controlling for voters' demographic profiles, the apparent effects of party identification are immense. These results provide an upper bound on the effects of party attachments on presidential vote choice.[7]

How do these results change when we control for other political opinions? Bringing to bear the entire arsenal of NES measures of ideological self-designation and policy opinions improves the predictive accuracy of the model. What voters think about leading policy issues strongly influences how they cast their ballots. Consider a voter who takes the most liberal position on each of our two dozen indicators of ideological orientation. Suppose that on the basis of this person's demographic characteristics and partisanship we estimate that he or she has a 1% chance of voting for Bush. Now suppose that he or she were suddenly to adopt the most conservative possible stance on every issue. His or her probability of voting for Bush rises to 99.9%. As it happens, just one person in our sample took the most liberal possible position on every issue, and no one took the most conservative stance. Few respondents, in fact, came close to these extremes. The views of the American electorate are by and large centrist, although the political activists who crowd the political stage are drawn disproportionately from the tails of the ideological spectrum. Still, the point remains that people with divergent political viewpoints vote in sharply different ways.

Surprisingly, the effects of party remain largely intact even after we take into account how people came down on the policy issues around which the campaign revolved. Comparing models 2 and 4, we see that the logistic regression coefficient associated with party identification declines from 2.3 to 2.0 after we control for two dozen indicators of how people stand on major policy questions. In other words, a relatively small fraction of the influence of party identification is potentially attributable to issue stances. Ideological proclivities and partisanship overlap somewhat but less than is often supposed, and each contributes to the predictive accuracy of the model.

This point bears emphasis because the debate between party and ideology is often framed as an all-or-nothing struggle between competing theoretical camps. *The American Voter* (Campbell et al. 1960), *Elections and the Political Order* (Campbell et al. 1966), and Philip Converse's enormously influential research (1964) contend that only a small fraction of the voting public is capable of casting an ideological vote. They lack genuine policy commitments, have little sense of how their convictions are related to the parties' ideological agendas, or are frustrated in their attempts to vote ideologically by candidates who deliberately take indistinct positions. Against the view that "forces not based on party loyalty that influence the decisions of the American electorate appear al-most wholly free of ideological coloration" (Campbell et al. 1960: 550), the in-tellectual progeny of *An Economic Theory of Democracy* (Downs 1957), such as Enelow and Hinich (1984) or Enelow, Endersby, and Munger (1993), assume that ideological reasoning lies at the heart of voter decision-making and omit party identification from their empirical analysis.

Our results suggest to us that issues and party attachments are distinct fac-tors that strongly influence vote choice. Although American politics is often caricatured as a string of meaningless competitions between ideologically in-distinguishable candidates, liberal and conservative voters evaluate presidential candidates quite differently. But how voters think about basic policy questions does not account for why Democrats and Republicans vote as they do.

It is easy to lose sight of the considerable ideological heterogeneity within each party. Despite the best efforts of the NES to measure ideological orienta-tions in copious detail, none of its surveys shows a particularly strong correla-tion between issues and party. Even with the most generous corrections for measurement error, no more than half of the variance in party identification can be traced to ideological proclivities.[8] To be sure, in other electoral systems one finds parties (usually small ones) that are closely associated with a particu-lar policy objective. But ideologically diffuse parties are also quite common. Historically, catchall parties such as the Democratic Party during the New Deal, Italy's Christian Democratic Party of the 1970s, or India's Congress Party comprised a diverse coalition of social groups and were quite ideologically het-erogeneous. Some people gravitated to these parties on the basis of what they stood for (and the affections of others were purchased through patronage), but many people developed attachments because these parties were emblematic of groups with which they identified politically. In Italy, for example, the Chris-tian Democrats symbolized a church-going anticommunist subculture within Italian society (LaPalombara 1987). The platforms of these parties evolved over time in response to the pressures of the political environment and changing power of the leaders within the party. As Converse (1964) points out, to the ex-tent that party attachments are passed from one generation to the next, the connection between party and ideology may become frayed. This fact does not preclude ideology from influencing vote choice, but it does help explain why party and ideology may often push the voter in different directions.

The last stop in this series of regressions introduces retrospective evaluations of the incumbent. The effects of partisanship remain substantial even when we further control for opinions about Bill Clinton and his record. From 1992 onward, Clinton's accomplishments and misdeeds were continual subjects of partisan debate, congressional hearings, and talk-show commentary. Rarely has a president been loathed as vigorously as Clinton was by his Republican detractors. Thus, the evaluations of Clinton, his job performance, and the state of the economy bring to bear the fullest possible range of grievances, including those that might plausibly arise from partisan attitudes. As one might expect, these retrospective evaluations improve the predictive accuracy of the model, such that 91% of the votes are correctly predicted. Nevertheless, the results of the logistic regression show that party identification continues to exert a strong influence. To get a feel for what an estimate of 1.6 means, picture a Democrat whose various demographic characteristics, issues stances, and performance evaluations predict a 17% chance of voting for Bush. If this person were to become a Republican but change none of his or her policy views or assessments of Clinton, the probability of voting for Bush would rise to 83%. This effect provides a *minimal* assessment of party influence on vote choice.

The range between the minimal and maximal estimate of how party identification influences vote choice is surprisingly narrow. Approximately 70% of the relationship between party identification and the vote persists even after controlling for an extensive array of political opinions. One can now understand why party identification has played such an important role in the study of presidential elections. For the price of one concise survey question, the researcher obtains a measure that provides enormous explanatory leverage without duplicating other constructs, such as performance evaluations or ideological location.

This is not to say that partisans invariably stick by their parties. Other factors besides party identification, such as the personal popularity of the candidates, shape vote choice as well. American politics is replete with sports figures, Hollywood stars, war heroes, and other celebrities whose accomplishments and magnetism attract votes from both parties. In addition, ideological heterogeneity within each party may lead to party defections. Too often, scholars expect an unrealistic confluence between identities and voting behavior and are disappointed when partisan defections occur. The point to bear in mind is that party profoundly alters the *probability* of voting for a candidate. Eisenhower received a great many votes from crossover Democrats, yet the probability of voting for Eisenhower was vastly greater for Republicans than for Democrats.

What party identification offers in explanatory power becomes more apparent when partisan attachments are measured before a presidential campaign. The 2000 NES preelection survey took place during the fall, and one may argue that party identification by that point came to reflect evaluations of the candidates, if not vote intentions. Although somewhat skeptical of this argument, we seek to obtain the most conservative possible estimate of party influence, and the best way to do so is to measure party identification well in advance of a campaign. This approach ensures that the effects of party stem from long-standing orientations toward partisan groups.

Several NES surveys have traced individuals over four-year periods, but one in particular tracked voters through two successive campaigns during which a presidential contender later stood for reelection. The 1992–96 NES panel survey followed 351 voters from the 1992 campaign, before Clinton was elected, to the 1996 election, when he sought a second term. Thus, party identification in 1992 antedates four years of retrospective evaluations of the Clinton administration. It also antedates the fundamental changes that occurred in Congress when the Republicans gained control of both houses after the 1994 elections. To predict the 1996 vote on the basis of 1992 party attachments, controlling for ideological and demographic factors, represents an especially steep challenge, particularly because this survey records an unusual amount of change in party identification around 1992.

Table 8.2 shows how party identification in 1992 predicted vote choice in 1996. The dependent variable is whether a voter cast a ballot for Bill Clinton (how one handles the small number of Perot voters makes little difference). Party identification again proves to be a strong predictor of the vote. With only demographic control variables in the equation, the effect of party identification is 1.6, which is the same estimate we obtained as the lower bound in the 2000 study. This figure drops a bit when issues are added but rebounds when controls are added for evaluations of Clinton and his performance in office. In the complete model, which predicts 89% of the variance in vote preferences, the logistic regression coefficient is 1.4. This estimate, which is statistically significant despite the small sample size, implies that holding demographic characteristics, ideological tastes, and evaluations of Clinton constant, Democrats and Republicans voted in sharply different ways. For example, two otherwise identical Democrats and Republicans would have 81% and 19% probabilities of voting for Clinton in 1996, respectively. This logistic regression coefficient, which is statistically indistinguishable from what we obtained from the 2000 study, reaffirms the basic conclusion: Voting behavior can be explained in part by reference to psychological orientations that take shape long before an election. Despite the tremendous fluctuations in party fortunes that occurred between the 1992 campaign and the 1996 election—the Democrats' first presidential

Table 8.2. Effects on Vote Choice of Party Identification, Issue Preferences, Demographics, and Evaluations of Bill Clinton, 1996

Model	Logistic Regression Coefficient for Party Identification	Percentage Predicted Correctly	Nagelkerke R^2
1. Demographics only		73.3	0.36
2. Demographics and party identification measured in 1992	−1.55 (0.23)	77.3	0.53
3. Issues and demographics		87.8	0.73
4. Issues, demographics, and party identification measured in 1992	−1.29 (0.34)	88.1	0.76
5. Issues, demographics, Clinton ratings, and economic evaluations		94.0	0.88
6. Issues, demographics, Clinton ratings, economic evaluations, and party identification measured in 1992	−1.42 (0.54)	93.8	0.89

Source: 1992–96 National Election Study.

Notes: Entries in parentheses are standard errors. $N = 351$. The estimates for party identification are all significant at $p < .01$. The dependent variable in each regression was whether the respondent voted for Clinton (1 = Voted for Clinton; 0 = Voted for Robert Dole or Ross Perot). The party identification variable was scored 1 = Democrat, 2 = Independent, and 3 = Republican, and is from the NES 1992 preelection survey. If the seven-point party identification scale is used instead of the three-point scale, the coefficient in Model 6 is 0.57 (SE = 0.22), the percentage predicted is 94.0, and the R-squared is 0.892.

Demographic regressors included whether the respondent belongs to a household with a union member, sex, years of education, family income, and residence in the South. Dummy variables were used also to denote Protestants, Catholics, blacks, Latinos, Asians, and "other" race, as well as several age categories (eighteen to twenty-five, twenty-six to thirty-five, thirty-six to forty-five, forty-six to fifty-five, fifty-six to sixty-five, and older than sixty-five). The measures of issues included the following regressors: liberal-conservative self-placement, abortion, environmental growth at the expense of jobs, environmental regulations, death penalty, job guarantee, gun control, aid to blacks, government services, government's role in providing health insurance, women's equal role, and four "traditionalism" items (each entered separately: moral breakdown, adjust views to new conditions, importance of family ties, and tolerate different lifestyles). In each case, respondents who answered "don't know/haven't thought about it" were placed at the mean for that variable. Furthermore, a "missing data" dummy was put in for each issue item, coded one if the respondent had answered "don't know/haven't thought about it" for that item. Measures of performance evaluations included Clinton's job approval, his handling of economic affairs, and retrospective evaluation of the national economy during the past year.

victory since 1976, their extraordinary defeat at the hands of Newt Gingrich in 1994, and their remarkable recovery in the months leading up to the presidential campaign—attachments that were formed before Clinton took office profoundly influenced how voters made up their minds in 1996.

INTERPRETING THE EFFECTS OF PARTY IDENTIFICATION

The results presented in the previous section reaffirm the findings of many previous election studies. Whether modeling the presidential vote (Miller and Shanks 1996) or elections for Congress (Koch 1998; Brown and Woods 1991; Lockerbie 1991) or state office (Beck et al. 1992; Atkeson and Partin 1995), researchers routinely find party identification to be a strong predictor of how voters cast their ballots. But how should one interpret this statistical relationship? How do party attachments influence the vote?

To address this question more systematically, let us first lay out some criteria that a valid interpretation of party influence must satisfy. First, the proposed causal mechanism must be consistent with the fact that party identification measured at one point in time influences elections several years later and under quite different political circumstances. If people are expressing an evaluation of the parties' attributes, it must be the sort of evaluation that is little affected by changing political conditions. In previous chapters, we saw that assessments of the parties' capacity to manage economic and foreign affairs often change rapidly, so an explanation that focuses on how voters evaluate these aspects of governance will not work. Second, the mechanism cannot rely solely on voters' policy aspirations. What people would have government do can go only so far in explaining why they affiliate with a partisan group (or even why they like or dislike a political party; see Campbell et al. 1960: Chap. 10). Party identities have profound effects among people with similar policy opinions. Third, an interpretation should provide an account for the expressive dimensions of partisan behavior. Partisans feel strongly about politics. Compared with Independents, partisans are much more likely to feel anger when thinking about leaders of the opposing party, to care which party wins an election, to follow news of a campaign, and to vote. To characterize party identification as a time-saving device that merely records one's current assessment of party capabilities fails to account for partisan affect. Partisans are less likely than Independents to avoid the cognitive costs of thinking about politics; on the contrary, they find politics engaging.

Our interpretation emphasizes partisans' sense that they are part of a team. Consider for the purposes of explication the most ardent partisans, whose sense of team membership is unusually acute but whose way of thinking is shared in lesser gradations by those with more ordinary party attachments. Partisans feel themselves to be part of the constant competition for public support and control of government that typifies party politics. Competition between political parties elicits some of the same reactions from the partisan as sporting events do from the avid fan. Partisans are drawn in by political competition in a way that nonpartisans are not. Like people who lack an allegiance to a football team but who nevertheless find themselves at a Super Bowl party, nonpartisans look on with a certain sense of indifference. They do not regard a victory of one side as a victory for themselves. Compared with partisans, Independents are much more likely in surveys to indicate that they do not really care which party wins, and studies of voter turnout consistently show that Independents vote at substantially lower rates than partisans. Whether we examine survey responses or rates of political participation, it is clear that partisans feel engaged by electoral competition. Like long-standing fans of a local sports team, they have a clear sense of which team to root for. Their team is embedded in how they think of themselves. They take an interest in political news in much the same way that sports fans follow the fortunes of various teams and players. The sports analogy aptly captures the manner in which partisan spectators get caught up in team competition, but partisan attachment often runs deeper than attachment to a sports franchise because embedded within parties are evocative social groups that each party calls to mind. Small wonder that polite conversation admits sports talk but excludes politics.

It may be argued that there is a further difference between sports and politics: Football fans win nothing of material significance when their team wins the world championship, whereas partisans may win desired policy outcomes. Again, we circle back to the hidden instrumental motives that might animate expressions of party loyalty. As noted above, however, party effects do not seem reducible to policy orientations. As Greenstein notes (1963: 27), this instrumental calculation may be more diffuse than any specified set of policy objectives. Partisans may simply sense that their own party's candidate has their best interests at heart. If this hypothesis were true, one would think that this evaluation would be reflected in evaluations of the incumbent's and the administration's performance. The fact that the effects of party identification persist even after controlling for these evaluations implies a slightly different interpretation. Partisans feel happier about having their allies in charge. This kind of evaluation is compatible with the notion that people perceive the parties to have distinct group bases (see Chapter 1 and Campbell et al. 1960) and that elections confer status and power on a party and its constituent social groups. This is not to deny that partisans are often enthusiastic about the putative policy benefits that their party will provide, but what the election means in terms of tangible outputs cannot fully account for the fact that partisan motives express themselves in elections for every office in which party labels are offered. It cannot simply be that partisans fear an untoward policy outcome should their opponents win office. Partisans would not want the opposing party to win election to a purely honorary office.

The sense of team membership and acute awareness of the ongoing competition between partisan groups structures the way that partisans look at politics. Partisans, as we saw in Chapter 2, do not put their attachments aside during the periods between elections; they know full well that the struggle rages on. Witness the gleeful outrage that ardent partisans feel at the news of misconduct by leaders of the opposing party. Partisans do not want their rivals to succeed in ways that curry favor with the electorate. Partisans do not want airports named after their opponents.

Conversely, partisans do not want their own leaders to become a liability to the team. In this respect, Democrats' withdrawal of support from Carter during the last years of his administration stands in telling contrast to Democrats' reaction to Clinton during the last two years of his first term. In both cases, liberals were angered by their president's move to the right, but Carter was regarded by Democrats as a weak leader and an electoral liability, whereas Clinton was tolerated as an unusually gifted campaigner during 1995–96 after the Republican takeover of Congress. At the end of his second term, Clinton's image among Democrats was tarnished more by the sense that his personal misbehavior propelled the Republicans to victory in the 2000 election than by outrage at the misbehavior itself.

Party identification predicts the vote because partisans pull for their team and the social groups that it symbolizes while at the same time rooting against the other party and its allied social groups. Although the expression of group attachment may be augmented by instrumental motives such as desired policy outcomes, party attachments have been expressed historically by large segments of the population who would seem to be out of step with the party's stated policy ambitions. Partisans derive what in rational choice parlance might be described as *expressive benefits* from supporting their team. Although one person's vote and campaign activities have scarcely more effect on political outcomes than the cheers of a sports fan have on the performance of the players (especially when the fan watches the sports events at home), these behaviors express the connection that a partisan feels toward the ongoing competition between parties.

This is not to deny that partisans sometimes vote against their party or abstain from voting altogether. A party's supporters often have diverse priorities and policy views, and as we noted in Chapter 2, partisans vary in their affection for the party and its leaders. Moreover, the people we dub partisans vary in terms of their sense of group attachment. The partisan motivation that we have described varies in potency from one person to the next, so when we speak of the effects of party identification, we are describing the average motive force across a spectrum of strong to weak attachment. Given partisan disaffection and varying levels of party attachment, the effects of party identification should be regarded in probabilistic terms. Describing oneself in partisan terms substantially alters the *probability* of supporting the party and its nominees. Although not insuperable, partisan motives are important determinants of how people behave politically.

THE SYSTEMIC IMPLICATIONS
OF PARTISAN VOTING

Those who endeavor to explain election outcomes sometimes express disappointment in party identification as an explanatory construct. The politics that they seek to explain are the fast-moving changes in party fortunes. They correctly point out that a slow-moving variable such as party identification rarely if ever accounts for dramatic interelection swings. Moreover, those who study the strategic behavior of politicians tend to find party loyalties drab and uninteresting. Candidates have a certain amount of flexibility in the sorts of issues they emphasize and the positions they take on questions of policy. But the party labels that candidates bear are relatively fixed. It is the rare politician who, like Eisenhower, can run as either party's nominee. Once a party's nominee is named, the strategic options available to candidates are relatively few in terms of how to describe their partisan coloration. They may choose to downplay their party ties during the campaign or stress their record in building bipartisan consensus, but in the end, voters in most jurisdictions will be presented with ballots with party labels printed next to the candidates' names. Party identification has little to offer as an explanation for short-term political change or the maneuvering that produces it.

Yet the effects of party identification on electoral competition and the politics that grows out of it are profound. First, the distribution and potency of party attachments dampen the over-time variability in election outcomes. Two-thirds of those who go to the polls in U.S. elections identify with a partisan group, an attachment that changes slowly over time. Election after election, party labels provide cues by which partisans evaluate the candidates on the ballot, and as we have seen, party identification exerts a powerful influence on voter choice. These facts imply that a large fraction of the electorate start each campaign with a strong proclivity to support one candidate or the other.

To understand how these factors stabilize election results, consider the hypothetical example shown in Figure 8.1. The top panel supposes that one hundred Republicans have a 27% probability (one logit below 50%) of voting for a Democratic candidate, whereas one hundred Democrats have a 73% probability (one logit above 50%) of voting for the Democrat. Thus, the Democratic candidate can expect to receive $100 \cdot 0.27 + 100 \cdot 0.73 = 100$ votes. Now suppose that national electoral tides favor the Democratic candidate, increasing support by one logit. Republicans vote Democratic at a rate of 50%, and Democrats up their support to 88% (two logits above 50%), producing a total of 138 votes. This political tide therefore produces an additional 38 votes. The effects of national tides are dampened when we increase the divide between the two parties, as in the lower panel of Figure 8.1. Suppose that Republicans stand two logits below 50% (giving them a 12% chance of voting Democratic) and Democrats stand two logits above 50% (giving them an 88% chance), producing 100 Democratic votes. Again, the national political tide shifts both groups one logit in the Democratic direction. The Democratic vote rises to 27% among Republicans and 95% among Democrats, raising the expected Democratic vote to $0.27 \cdot 100 + 0.95 \cdot 100 = 122$. Thus, the wider the partisan divide in the electorate, the smaller the vote swing produced by short-term forces.[9]

This line of argument often raises alarm among those who lament the decline of party attachments in democratic polities. In their view, as partisan feelings subside and "floating voters" comprise an increasing share of the electorate, election outcomes become more variable. In the United States, the modest decline in party identification among voters and the continuing strength of partisanship as an influence on vote choice makes any trend in volatility too subtle to detect. Indeed, in their longitudinal study of sixteen countries that experienced declines in party identification, Dalton, McAllister, and Wattenberg (2000: 40–41) found increased variability in election outcomes over time in all but three, one of which is the United States. Increasing electoral volatility

Expected Democratic Votes = 100*.27+100*.73 =100

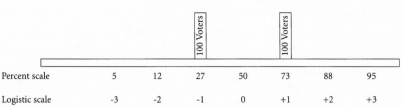

Expected Democratic Votes in the wake of a 1-logit shock= 100*.50+100*.88 =138

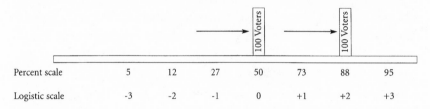

Expected Democratic Votes = 100*.12+100*.88 =100

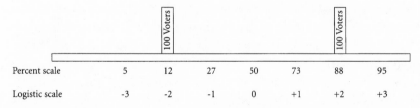

Expected Democratic Votes in the wake of a 1-logit shock= 100*.27+100*.95 =122

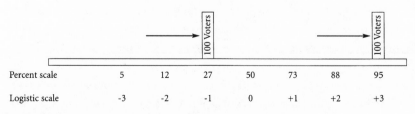

Figure 8.1. How partisanship dampens the effects of short-term forces.

may not be a live concern in the United States, but it seems clear both analytically and cross-nationally that elections involving large numbers of partisans produce outcomes that are less responsive to a host of influences, be they economic evaluations or the perceived personal merits of the candidates.

Second, party attachments create a formidable obstacle for would-be parties. Absent these attachments, new parties could grow around popular political figures and make significant inroads by invading the ideological turf occupied by the dominant parties. The dismal performance of third-party candidates in U.S. national elections—even in congressional races for which only one major party candidate is on the ballot—attests to the unwillingness of partisans to desert their parties in favor of like-minded candidates. Again, the comparative analysis of Dalton, McAllister, and Wattenberg (2000) is instructive. The secular decline in party identification has coincided with a rise in the average number of parties contesting elections, suggesting that the opportunity for new parties to make headway has increased over time.

Electoral institutions work in tandem with psychological processes to give a party system its particular flavor. Electoral systems that assign legislative seats on the basis of proportional representation tend to encourage greater numbers of parties, whereas first-past-the-post systems in which a single representative is selected from a given electoral district lead to fewer parties and often just two (Lijphart 1994). Empirically, it seems that the precise number of parties toward which an electoral system equilibrates is not fully determined by institutional incentives. Dalton's (2000) findings suggest that the strength of existing party attachments plays a role as well. Moreover, in a system such as that in the United States, electoral incentives alone do not determine *which* two parties will become preeminent, and indeed, the configuration of parties has shifted occasionally over the course of American history. That such realignments are relatively rare attests to the difficulty that a party faces in making inroads in an electorate whose party attachments are largely spoken for.

Third, party identification determines the equilibrium toward which election outcomes tend to return. Although the concept of a "normal vote" (Converse 1966) has gradually faded from the field of electoral studies, its basic insight remains correct. Knowing the partisan composition of the voting public provides a strong indication of where election outcomes will tend in the absence of short-term forces that favor one party. No election is ever wholly free from idiosyncratic factors that benefit one side or the other, but we see persistent differences in voting patterns in geographic areas that have different partisan complexions. State-level survey data, for example, indicate that in Kansas,

Republicans outnumber Democrats; in Massachusetts, Democrats outnumber Republicans; and in Ohio, the two groups are about equal in size (Erikson, Wright, and McIver 1993: 15). These distinct partisan equilibria express themselves in both presidential and congressional voting. Kansas consistently votes more Republican than Ohio, which consistently votes more Republican than Massachusetts.

The most striking illustration of how voting equilibria track party identification may be found in a longitudinal comparison of voting patterns in the South and the non-South. In Chapter 6, we demonstrated that the South became markedly more Republican after the mid-1960s, whereas little change occurred outside the South. To the extent that the partisan equilibrium shapes election outcomes, we should see different patterns of congressional election outcomes over time in response to changes in the partisan balance. House elections are particularly telling because the candidates have an opportunity to adjust their issue positions to conform to local tastes. As a result, House election outcomes reflect less the ideological distance between candidates and more the influence of party per se. The electoral advantages enjoyed by House incumbents can slow the process of change but cannot stop it. In the long run, a changing balance of party attachments will change the number of seats each party wins.

Figure 8.2 shows the relationship between average levels of party identification and the Republican share of the U.S. House delegations elected in the South and the non-South from the 1950s through the 1990s. Party identification is measured using a scale ranging from 1 (Strong Democrat) to 7 (Strong Republican). Each decade's data have been pooled, so that one point on the plot represents a region's average partisanship and degree of Republican representation. In the 1950s, the mean level of party identification was 2.6 in the South, and only 6% of the House delegates from the South were Republican. As mean partisanship rose steadily through the 1990s, the Republican share of the House delegation grew steadily. By the century's end, the South had become approximately as Republican in its identities and vote patterns as the non-South, whose equilibrium changed little during this period. Regression analysis of these data reveals that a one-unit change in mean party identification translates into a thirty-seven percentage-point increase in the proportion of seats won by Republicans.[10]

In sum, partisanship induces a powerful central tendency in election outcomes, dampening the electoral effects of short-term forces and causing deviant election outcomes to return to the norm. Whether the norm is balanced

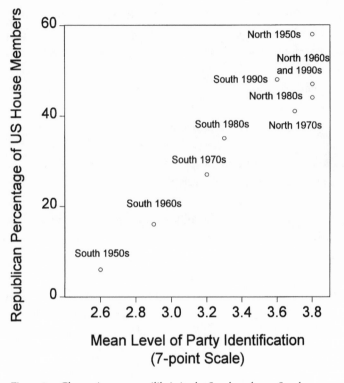

Figure 8.2. Change in party equilibria in the South and non-South, 1950s to 1990s.

or lopsided has a variety of political implications. When the partisan equilibrium is balanced, the victorious party is always in danger of regressing to the mean. Expecting that its electoral edge will dissipate, a party that comes to power in a balanced environment has a strong incentive to institute policy changes right away, before the opportunity passes, logic that doubtless impelled the massive Republican tax initiatives in the immediate aftermath of the 1980 and 2000 elections. Evenly matched parties also have an incentive to engage in partisan politics with an eye toward the future, when the reins of government may pass to the opposition. Contrast this situation with one in which the majority party enjoys a commanding partisan advantage. Under these conditions, the majority party moves with no particular sense of urgency or desire to placate the minority, which in turn senses that it has little to lose through riskier political tactics.[11]

The partisan equilibria within representatives' constituencies also have political implications. The seniority system, by which committee assignment and rank are typically determined in Congress, rewards constituents whose representatives enjoy flaccid political competition. Members of Congress from districts with lopsided partisan distributions are more likely to accumulate seniority (Wolfinger and Hollinger 1971; Gerber 1996). For decades, the seniority principle allowed safe-seat Southern conservative Democrats to hold a disproportionate share of powerful committee chairs in the House and Senate (Davidson 1980). The logic of selecting leaders who are insulated from electoral pressures also means that congressional party leadership is drawn disproportionately from safe seats (Cox and McCubbins 1993). The net effect is to enhance the political power of, and governmental resources flowing to, these constituencies (Rundquist, Lee, and Rhee 1996).

Party identification, in other words, shapes the strategic context within which electoral competition and legislative politics occur. In political systems such as that of the United States, where the parties may be counted "among the most enduring political institutions known to Western civilization" (Miller 1966: 248), the dependable divide between partisan groups confines political outcomes to a relatively small patch of well-traversed terrain. Election outcomes may wander outside that terrain, as in 1964 or 1972, but subsequent elections remind us of how quickly they may return. Party identification cannot account for the short-term factors that cause electoral outcomes to oscillate, but it does help us understand why parties so seldom consolidate and build upon landslide victories. The group affinities of the electorate tend to endure, whereas the special conditions that helped propel a candidate to an unusual margin of victory seldom do.

If party identification is so central to political outcomes, why do we not see political parties make more effort to recruit partisans? One possibility is that parties and their candidates have conflicting interests. In an effort to build winning coalitions, candidates often downplay party in their campaign messages. Much as they might like to see the ranks of fellow partisans grow, they do not wish to develop a reputation for pursuing a partisan agenda for fear of alienating their Independent and crossover supporters. It is the rare politician, such as Ronald Reagan, whose popularity enables him or her to bear the costs of party building.

The parties themselves have mixed motives. For example, recent immigrants constitute one of the largest groups of unaligned citizens in the United States, but parties have been slow in recruiting them, perhaps fearing that direct overtures to new citizens might undermine party support among people who are hostile to immigrants (Wong 2001). Each party comprises a delicate set of alliances among social groups, and for that reason, parties prefer to expand their support among their existing friends than to go out and make new ones. Changing the social imagery of the parties is a difficult and risky venture, and parties, like candidates, tend to focus their energies on more immediate and manageable tasks, such as winning over swing voters in particular elections.

Even if parties were to become more committed to the idea of expanding their bases of support, it is not clear that they have the capacity to do so. Over time, local party organizations have dwindled. Many of the campaign activities that parties formerly carried out are now subcontracted to private consultants, phone banks, and mailing houses. The growing professionalism of campaigns means a growing thirst for campaign funds, and national party organizations have increasingly focused their energies on securing donations. The net effect of these changes is a marked drop in the proportion of people who report working for political parties since the early 1970s (Putnam 2000) despite a resurgence in the proportion of partisans. As the number of activists declines, parties become less able to marshal recruitment campaigns.

The interaction between parties' organizations and the typical citizen has grown increasingly tenuous over time. For many new voters, the parties are not terribly different from clandestine organizations that one learns about through rumor. Yet voters are able to discern the social bases of partisan groups, and most eventually locate themselves within this group imagery. Therein lies the paradox of party identities. They continue to flourish and express themselves even as parties as organizations fade from voters' daily experience. Dalton and Wattenberg's (2000) phrase "parties without partisans" seems less apt than "partisans without parties."

This paradox may extend to a variety of social identities. Ethnic clubs have largely disappeared. Class-based organizations, such as labor unions and chambers of commerce, have receded in size and vitality over time. Religious organizations remain, but their role in the daily lives of the population has diminished over time. Arguably, the proportion of the population that identifies with ethnic, class, or religious groups has declined over time as well although it is difficult to say precisely how much, given the dearth of survey data charting social identities over time. Yet these attachments continue to profoundly influence social, economic, and political behavior because they structure the way that people categorize themselves in relation to others. We immediately recognize when somebody seems out of place on account of their class demeanor or ethnic background, just as we immediately register a reaction to such a person based on how we evaluate these group characteristics. Social categories may trace their origins to institutions, organizations, and the ideologies they helped foster, but their psychological sequelae take on a life of their own.

Appendix

Mean-corrected panel analysis enables one to estimate the time-series dynamics associated with individual-level partisanship. The term *mean-corrected* refers to the fact that the estimation procedure allows each individual to have an idiosyncratic equilibrium to which his or her partisanship returns in the absence of short-term influences. This technique is described in detail in Green and Yoon (2002).

Another approach is to describe the persistence of individual locations within the distribution of partisanship. This approach, which is known as *pooled panel analysis,* tracks individuals' relative standing vis-à-vis one another and ignores the way in which the group mean changes over time. The key statistic to emerge from this analysis is the disattenuated correlation between the true level of partisanship at successive time points. By eliminating the distorting influence of measurement error, this statistic tells us the degree to which individuals change their relative standing on a spectrum ranging from Democrat to Republican.

To see how pooled panel analysis distinguishes true change from measurement error, consider a single survey item, $y_{t,i}$, that measures party identification of N respondents at four points in time. This observed measure gives a potentially fallible representation of each person's true underlying partisanship $(\eta_{t,i})$. At each interview, the observed score can be expressed as a function of true partisanship $(\eta_{t,i})$, forces that lead to enduring partisan change $(\zeta_{t,i})$, and measurement error $(\varepsilon_{t,i})$. For the first time period,

$$y_{1,i} = \eta_{1,i} + \varepsilon_{1,i} = \zeta_{1,i} + \varepsilon_{1,i}$$

At the second point in time, party identification reflects past partisanship, new partisan attitudes, and new errors of measurement:

$$y_{2,i} = \eta_{2,i} + \varepsilon_{2,i} = \beta_{21}\zeta_{1,i} + \zeta_{2,i} + \varepsilon_{2,i}$$

The same process continues over time, with each new observation reflecting past influences and new sources of change.

$$y_{3,i} = \eta_{3,i} + \varepsilon_{3,i} = \beta_{32}(\beta_{21}\zeta_{1,i} + \zeta_{2,i}) + \zeta_{3,i} + \varepsilon_{3,i}.$$

$$y_{4,i} = \eta_{4,i} + \varepsilon_{4,i} = \beta_{43}(\beta_{32}\beta_{21}\zeta_{1,i} + \beta_{32}\zeta_{2,i} + \zeta_{3,i}) + \zeta_{4,i} + \varepsilon_{4,i}.$$

If we assume that the sources of mismeasurement are unrelated to the sources of real attitude change (that is, $\varepsilon_{t,i}$ is uncorrelated with $\zeta_{t,i}$), that the errors at one time are unrelated to errors at other times (that is, $\varepsilon_{t,i}$ is uncorrelated with $\varepsilon_{s,i, s \neq t}$), and that disturbances at one time are unrelated to disturbances at other times (that is, $\zeta_{t,i}$ is uncorrelated with $\zeta_{s,i, s \neq t}$), we can readily estimate the true correlation between party identification at time 2 and time 3. A consistent estimator of this correlation may be calculated from the observed variances and covariances of the four measures of party identification. Using COV() and VAR() to refer to covariances and variances, and dropping the individual subscripts for clarity, we note that

$$r_{\eta_2 \eta_3} = \frac{COV(\eta_2, \eta_3)}{\sqrt{VAR(\eta_2)VAR(\eta_3)}}$$

$$= \frac{COV(y_2, y_3)}{\sqrt{[VAR(y_2) - VAR(\varepsilon_2)][VAR(y_3) - VAR(\varepsilon_3)]}}.$$

The only unobservable terms in this equation are the variances of the two measurement errors, $\varepsilon_{2,i}$ and $\varepsilon_{3,i}$. A consistent estimator for the variance of $\varepsilon_{2,i}$ is

$$VAR(\varepsilon_2) \approx VAR(y_2) - \frac{COV(y_3, y_2)COV(y_2, y_1)}{COV(y_3, y_1)}.$$

$$VAR(\varepsilon_3) \approx VAR(y_3) - \frac{COV(y_4, y_3)COV(y_3, y_2)}{COV(y_4, y_2)}.$$

Thus, a variance-covariance matrix of four waves of partisanship data enables us to estimate the true correlation without distortion due to measurement error.

Covariance matrices, however, presuppose interval level measures of partisanship, and often partisanship is measured with just a few coarse categories (Democrat, Independent, Republican) or as a dichotomy (Social Democrat or not). Rather than impose an arbitrary metric on these variables, the analyst assumes that they have a variance of one and computes the correlations among the measures. Coarse categorization remains a nuisance but may be addressed by computing polychoric correlations rather than product-moment correlations. In our experience, the two types of correlations produce similar results when disattenuated.

Estimating the disattenuated correlation between true partisanship at waves two and three is a matter of forming an estimator based on the observed correlations among the survey responses at each wave. In the absence of sampling variability, it can be shown that

$$r_{\eta_2 \eta_3} = \frac{1}{\sqrt{\dfrac{r_{21} \cdot r_{43}}{r_{31} \cdot r_{42}}}}.$$

In short, to estimate the true correlation between partisanship at time 2 and time 3, we take the observed correlation and adjust it. This adjustment can be made using a hand calculator, although it can be made more statistically efficient if the estimates are obtained using somewhat more complex procedures. These procedures make use of the fact that this adjustment can be calculated in more than one way given the full set of correlations between measures. In technical terms, the system of equations used to generate these estimates is overidentified. When analyzing a matrix of polychoric correlations, it is conventional to use a weighted least-squares estimator.

The analysis of latent variables may be extended to cover regression models in which the disturbance terms $(\zeta_{t,i})$ are divided into two components, observed indicators of short-term forces and random disturbances. Short-term forces gauged in the first period are allowed to predict short-term forces in the next period. Moreover, short-term forces and party identification are assumed to influence each other at every point in time. This two-way causal flow allows for the possibility that partisanship shapes and is shaped by short-term evaluations.

A detailed description of this model and the manner in which it is estimated may be found in Green and Palmquist (1990), Green (1991), and Schickler and Green (1995). In brief, we posit a system of equations:

$$\text{Party Identification}_{2,i} = \gamma \, \text{Short-Term Forces}_{2,i}$$
$$+ \, \beta \, \text{Party Identification}_{1,i} + \zeta_{2,i} + \varepsilon_{2,i}$$

$$\text{Short-Term Forces}_{2,i} = \theta \, \text{Short-Term Forces}_{1,i}$$
$$+ \, \phi \, \text{Party Identification}_{2,i} + \zeta^*_{2,i} + \varepsilon^*_{2,i}$$

The key parameters of this system, β and γ, are estimated in a manner that takes into account the fact that Party Identification$_{1,i}$ is measured imprecisely. Based on an initial analysis of the reliability of the party identification term, a certain degree of measurement error is posited, and the remaining parameters are estimated using analysis of covariance software (LISREL 8).

Notes

CHAPTER 1: INTRODUCTION

1. The most detailed explanation of the concept of identification, and the one we find most instructive for our own conceptualization, appears on page 121 of *The American Voter:* "We use the concept here to characterize the individual's affective orientation to an important group-object in his environment. Both reference group theory and small-group studies of influence have converged upon the attracting or repelling quality of the group as the generalized dimension most critical in defining the individual-group relationship, and it is this dimension that we call identification."

2. The Gallup survey was conducted November 1 through November 5, 1953, and is available through the Roper archives. The 1997 data are drawn from the Roper Reports Survey fielded in October.

3. In the 1997 Roper survey, 62% of Democrats ($N = 383$) indicated that the term "big business" came to mind when they thought of Republicans. Republicans were described in this way by 48% of Independents ($N = 344$) and 52% of Republicans ($N = 235$). By contrast, 16% of Democrats, 18% of Independents, and 23% of Republicans used "big business" to describe Democrats. Interparty differences were similarly muted in the case of applying the term "minorities" to the parties: 53% of Democrats, 31% of Independents, and 42% of Republicans described the Democrats in these terms, whereas just

6% of Democrats, 4% of Independents, and 11% of Republicans used this term to describe Republicans.

4. The actual instructions read: "Here is a list of groups. Please read over this list and tell me the letter for those groups you feel particularly close to—people who are most like you in their ideas and interests and feelings about things."

5. These figures were calculated using the 1996 NES variables 1294, 1298, 1299, 1302, 1305, and 1307. The weighted number of respondents in the analysis is 1,696.

6. The proportion of partisans is even higher if we include the "closet partisans" who initially describe themselves as Independents but who later indicate that they feel "closer" to one of the parties. Keith et al. (1992) have demonstrated that these so-called Independent leaners display strong partisan orientations. As we point out in Chapter 3, the proportion of people who identify with one of two parties goes up considerably when those surveyed are not offered "Independent" as a response option.

7. Voting technology has also played a role in this change. The "party levers" on voting machines that once facilitated straight-ticket voting have largely disappeared.

CHAPTER 2: PARTISAN GROUPS AS OBJECTS OF IDENTIFICATION

1. The fact that ideological self-categorization and partisan self-categorization have gradually become more closely related may therefore be interpreted in different ways. One view is that partisans gradually sort themselves into the correct parties as they become aware of differences in the parties' issue positions. Another view is that when the parties make a special point of drawing the connection between themselves and certain social groups—for example, conservatives—partisans either adopt labels like "conservative" or cease to categorize themselves in the same partisan terms. Either way, the point remains that at any historical moment, the correlation between party and ideology may be weak or strong, depending on how coalitions have been forged over time.

2. It should also be noted that "party loyalty" is sometimes expressed in complex ways. Some Democrats in 1972 turned away from Democratic presidential nominee George McGovern because they thought that the themes of his campaign ran afoul of what the Democratic Party stood for (Page 1978). The point is both that party identification does not require party loyalty and that party loyalty need not entail straight-ticket voting: The loyalist may vote against his or her party's nominee on the grounds that this candidate does not personify the authentic values of the party.

3. Another such survey is the Times-Mirror Spring 1990 Political Update (see Green and Schickler 1993). A great many surveys, of course, have measured various partisan *opinions* during the course of an interview.

4. The increase from 0.62 to 0.65 is very close to what one would expect given the reliability of the SRC measure (0.88) and the basic self-regard measure (0.84) (see Green and Schickler 1993: 527).

5. The party identification question used by the Roper Starch organization reads, "Regardless of how you may have voted in the past, what do you usually consider yourself—a Democrat, a Republican, some other party, or what?" As Green and Schickler (1993)

point out, this version produces responses that correspond closely to those obtained using the traditional SRC wording.

6. In each election, reported turnout greatly exceeds actual turnout in the population. This discrepancy reflects both misreports of voting behavior and a skew in the panel sample toward more politically involved respondents.

CHAPTER 3: A CLOSER LOOK AT PARTISAN STABILITY

1. For purposes of exposition, we assume partisanship to be a continuous and unbounded scale. Later, we return to complications introduced by coarse categorization.

2. Conversely, if we insist on using the three-point categorization of party identification, we must turn to other statistical techniques. Fortunately, it turns out that alternative measures and statistical models lead to similar substantive conclusions.

3. This approach begins by treating the fixed effects as nuisance parameters and eliminates them by working with first differences of $y_{t,i}$ (where the first difference of $y_{t,i}$ is $y_{t,i}$ minus $y_{t-1,i}$). Although it is tempting to regress the first differences of $y_{t,i}$ on the first differences of $y_{t-1,i}$, ordinary regression will produce severely biased estimates. Arellano's instrumental variables estimator instead uses first differences of the $y_{t,i}$ and the regressor $y_{t-1,i}$ but uses levels of $y_{t-2,i}$ as instruments.

4. Green and Yoon (2002) present a complete description of these simulations.

5. Interestingly, we find approximately the same dynamic coefficients even though older respondents as well as those more interested in politics tend to have much more variance in their partisan attachments. This finding directly contradicts the interpretation offered by Erikson, MacKuen, and Stimson (1996: 12), who contend that partisan variability increases with age because individual time series have unit roots. On the contrary, individuals of all ages and levels of political interest seem to have autoregressive parameters of zero. Whatever causes the between-subjects variance in partisanship to grow over time or with increased interest in politics is not reducible to the behavior of explosive time series within subjects.

6. For estimating the parameters in these models, it is best to use panel studies with at least four interviews, but estimation with three waves is feasible; see Green and Yoon 2002.

7. The adequacy of the statistical assumptions used to generate these disattenuated correlations can be gauged by means of a goodness-of-fit test. Nonsignificant tests indicate that one cannot reject the null hypothesis that the model places the correct theoretical constraints on the data. Such results are interpreted to mean that observed departures from the expected covariances among the measures are attributable to sampling variability. As it turns out, nonsignificant chi-squared statistics turn up in each case. The p value for the 1980 NES panel is .09. Comparable statistics for the 1956–58–60 NES panel and the 1992–93–94–96 panel are .52, and .85, respectively.

8. Specifically, we must assume that the measurement errors at each point have the same variance. This is not an unreasonable assumption, but one cannot be sure that questions were asked and answered in similar ways over time.

9. This model fits the data reasonably well, with a nonsignificant chi-squared value of 15.0 with eight degrees of freedom ($p > .05$).

10. This correlation is calculated for the 260 respondents for whom we have valid data on short-term evaluations. The sample size is reduced because only half of the sample were asked to evaluate party competence in 1996.

11. Log-odds are computed from a two-by-two table by multiplying the northwest and southeast cells and dividing this quantity by the product of the remaining two cells, taking the natural log of the result. For example, in the first entry in Table 3.8, the log-odds is $\ln[(467\cdot74)/(33\cdot23)] = 3.82$.

12. This survey selected one of the parents at random for reinterview after 1965. Our analysis focuses on this parent, recognizing that the accuracy with which parents' party identification predicts children's party identification would be stronger were we to use both parents.

CHAPTER 4: PARTISAN STABILITY

1. Party identification in this example is measured during the preelection survey.

2. The starting point of 1953 coincides with the first consumer sentiment surveys, which will be used as predictors in the analysis below. This date also coincides approximately with the Gallup Poll's introduction of probability sampling, as opposed to the quota samples that had been used previously.

3. Both consumer sentiment and presidential approval are highly autocorrelated. The correlation between consumer sentiment at time t and consumer sentiment at time $t-1$ is 0.90. Dropping quarters in which a new president takes office, the correlation between approval and approval lagged one quarter is 0.84. For the entire sample, this correlation is 0.86. The autocorrelation for macropartisanship is also similar, in this case 0.92. Unlike consumer sentiment and presidential approval, however, the macropartisanship series reveals a significant second-order partial autocorrelation, a symptom of the imperfect reliability with which partisanship is measured in the aggregate.

4. The disjuncture between forecasts and outcomes is even more dramatic when the CBS polls are examined. Forecasts based on 1976–88 predict that macropartisanship at the close of 1999 would be above 70 when in fact this figure stood at 55.8.

5. Like Reagan, Roosevelt inherited an economy in disarray, and by the logic of the model of MacKuen, Erikson, and Stimson, its sub-par performance during the first Roosevelt administration should have penalized the Democrats.

CHAPTER 5: PARTISAN STABILITY AND VOTER LEARNING

1. Throughout our analysis, we will assume that the voters know the process by which the information they observe is generated (that is, the distribution of the error terms, the equation linking what they observe each period to the underlying parameter they wish to estimate) but do not know the values the errors take on and so therefore must use what they observe to make statistical estimates of what they are interested in. In principle, over time all the parameters that we assume the voters know could be estimated using the data

the voters observe. We will not analyze how our results might differ when the voters must also estimate those additional parameters, although it seems intuitive that after an initial period of learning, the situation will approximate that when the parameters are known from the beginning.

2. Two similar versions of the prosperity item were used. The first reads, "Looking ahead for the next few years, which political party do you think will do a better job of keeping the country prosperous—the Republican Party or the Democratic Party?" The other version is, "Which political party—the Republican, or the Democratic—will do a better job of keeping the country prosperous?" The war questions come in three formats: "Looking ahead for the next few years, which political party do you think would be more likely to keep the United States out of war—the Republican Party or the Democratic Party?" An earlier version reads, "Looking ahead for the next few years, which political party do you think would be more likely to keep the United States out of World War III—the Republican or the Democratic party?" A variant of the World War III reference reads, "Which political party do you think would be more likely to keep the United States out of World War III—the Republican Party or the Democratic Party?"

3. For readability, the graphs in Figures 5.1 and 5.2 have circles representing each survey's results and a line that represents the interpolated trends, based on a Kalman filter correction for sampling variability (see Green, Gerber, and De Boef 1999).

4. Logistic regression in effect transforms a given probability into a log-odds and examines whether different partisan groups experience the same changes in log-odds over time. Since the data indicate that most Republican partisans begin with a very unfavorable view of the Democratic Party's relative economic competence, even a small change in the absolute percentage of Republican partisans favoring the Democratic Party indicates an important shift in beliefs. An appropriate scale must be chosen for comparing effects across parties. A convenient choice is the logit (log-odds) transformation, which makes a change in probability from 0.50 to 0.73 equivalent to a change from 0.73 to 0.88.

5. *Valence issues* refer to policy outcomes that everyone wants, such as lower crime rates. *Position issues* refer to policy outcomes that some people want but others do not, such as increasing the role of prayer in public schools.

CHAPTER 6: PARTY REALIGNMENT IN THE AMERICAN SOUTH

1. To the extent that the parties and the groups that they embody remain stable points of reference, partisan change occurs because the individual's self-conception changes, something that occurs relatively infrequently and for reasons that typically reflect the particularities of a person's social environment.

2. A number of scholars have found migration to be a significant source of change in Southern partisanship before the Voting Rights Act (Converse 1966b; but see Petrocik 1987).

3. We excluded the 1954 and 1962 surveys because the NES surveys did not collect information about the region in which respondents were raised. Note that the information about where the respondents grew up is not available for 1998 either, but by that time the partisan behavior of native white Southerners and white Southerners who had moved in

from outside the region had almost completely converged. So in the analyses that follow when we consider only native Southerners or non-Southerners, we include all respondents in 1998 who lived in the particular region at the time of the interview. We have also analyzed Southern partisanship using the more stringent requirement that a respondent claim to have been born as well as raised in the South. The results were substantively the same as those reported here. We chose to use the less stringent criteria because information about place of birth is available in even fewer years than information about the region in which respondents were raised.

4. Outside the South, the comparable percentages are 41% before 1964 and 26% in the period 1978–98, suggesting a drop-off in Democratic identification among the young, but one that is much less pronounced than in the South. The net result is convergence among young whites in different regions. In later graphs, we show that Southern whites become slightly more Republican than non-Southern whites by the century's end. It should be noted, however, that Southern white Protestants continued to be less Republican than white Protestants outside the South.

5. The cohort differences in liberal-conservative self-identification are palpable in each decade, 1970–78, 1980–88, and 1990–98. The cohort born during 1920–35 has a mean rating that is 0.1 to 0.2 points more conservative than the 1936–51 cohort, which is in turn 0.2 to 0.3 points more conservative than the 1952–66 cohort. Yet each cohort becomes progressively more Republican. The relative liberalism of the younger generation is also apparent, although less striking, from policy questions dealing with whether government should guarantee employment or aid blacks.

6. Of course, there is a chicken-and-egg problem here, in that Southern Republicans are positioned to run strong races when there are incipient Republicans' votes to be won, and hence it is impossible to judge merely from the trend of electoral success and growing Republican attachment which is causing which. A state-by-state analysis linking the extent and timing of party development to attitude change is not possible with NES and CBS data, given the small number of interviews in each state. NES and Gallup surveys present additional problems because of their clustered sampling frame, which was not designed to be representative within states.

7. Converse (1966b) reports that in 1960, lower-status Democrats blamed desegregation on the Republican Party, in light of Eisenhower's enforcement of desegregation orders. Before 1964, "competition of both national parties to become associated with a strong stand on civil rights create[d] an ambiguous situation which voters [could] interpret to justify partisan shifts in either direction" (p. 233).

8. We reject the hypothesis that Southerners have split-party identifications; that is, they are Democrats when thinking of state and local politics and Republicans when it comes to national elections (Hadley 1985; Niemi, Wright, and Powell 1987). Converse (1966b) found little empirical support for this conjecture in the late 1950s, and as we point out in Chapter 2, the argument has not grown more empirically defensible over time. One should not be surprised when votes and party attachments diverge—they are influenced by different factors.

9. The best example of this process at work may be found in Dowd's (1999) study of African-

American partisan realignment from 1937 through the early 1960s. The shift toward the Democratic Party, which was initially the product of generational replacement, became increasingly a matter of individual conversion once a critical mass of black Democrats was in place.

10. This variable is measured using respondents' descriptions of themselves and the two parties along a seven-point scale ranging from liberal to conservative. Respondents are classified as being either closer to the Democrats, equidistant, closer to the Republicans, or unable to locate themselves or the parties on this scale.

11. A similar pattern over time holds for ideological proximity with respect to specific issues, such as aid to minorities.

12. Unfortunately, neither the NES surveys nor other surveys of which we are aware provide direct measures for assessing party images over time or testing their relative influence vis-à-vis issue stances. It is true that the NES has frequently asked respondents to discuss what they like or dislike about each party and to describe the differences they see between the Democratic and Republican parties. But roughly half of the survey respondents (and often more) opt out of these open-ended questions, and the remaining responses are so sparse as to defy any over-time analysis.

CHAPTER 7: PARTISAN STABILITY OUTSIDE THE UNITED STATES

1. The question wording for the self-description item was as follows: "Now I'd like to ask you a question about how you regard yourself. On a scale from 1 to 10, where '10' represents a description that is perfect for you, and '1' a description that is totally wrong for you, how well do each of the following describe you? . . . A Republican . . . A Democrat." The two self-identification measures correlate with one another at -0.587, but this number is most likely attenuated by random and nonrandom measurement error (Green 1988). Hence, our reliance on criterion measures such as vote intentions, party identification, and political background.

2. This alternative wording was adopted because literal translation of the Michigan item was thought to confuse party membership and subjective identity (Norpoth 1978). It reads: "Many people in the German Federal Republic lean toward a particular party for a long time although they may occasionally vote for a different party. How about you: Do you in general lean toward a particular party? If so, which one?"

3. It is possible to construct pathological examples that would cause this method of analysis to yield misleading estimates. For instance, suppose we were considering the case of two parties, as in model 2. Let $\alpha_1 = \alpha_2 = 0.02$, and place the Democrats at $(0.05, 0.10)$ and Republicans at $(0.75, 0.70)$. This perverse illustration suggests a *negative* correlation between a dummy variable scored one if the SRC measure dubs one a Democrat and the underlying degree of Democratic identification in this sample. It is not surprising, given this inverse correlation between the dummy variable and the criterion variable it purports to measure, that the pattern of over-time correlations can also be thrown off. Were the Democrats to shift to $(0.70, 0.75)$ and the Republicans to $(0.10, 0.05)$, no change would be registered in our DIP measures. We cannot, therefore, claim that the dummy

variable approach produces an unbiased assessment of partisan stability. As a practical matter, however, few difficulties are likely to arise when one uses dummy variables to assess partisan stability.

4. These surveys are the "British Election Study, 1969–1974" (Inter-university Consortium for Political and Social Research [ICPSR] No. 7869), the "German Election Panel Study, 1987" (ICPSR No. 9078), the "1974–1979–1980 Canadian National Election and Quebec Referendum Panel Study" (ICPSR No. 8079), and the "1992–93 Canadian Election Study, Incorporating the 1992 Referendum Survey on the Charlottetown Accord" (ICPSR No. 6571).

5. These surveys are "The Study of Political Change in Britain, 1963–1970," the British Election Panel Study of 1974–79, and the 1992–97 British General Election Panel Study. The 1992–97 study actually included a total of eight waves; however, only five of the panel waves used in-person interviews (one was a mail-in questionnaire and two were telephone surveys). Analysis of five (or more) waves of data reduces the number of cases but yields results that are substantively the same as reported below. The principal investigators for the first panel were David Butler and Donald Stokes. Ivor Crewe, Bo Sarlvik, and James Alt were the principal investigators for the 1974–79 panel. Anthony Heath, Roger Jowell, and John Curtice were the principal investigators for the 1992–97 study.

6. This survey is "The German Election Panel Study, 1990." The principal investigators were Max Kaase, H. D. Klingermann, M. Kuechler, F. U. Pappi, and H. A. Semetko.

7. This survey is titled "Political Support in Canada, 1983–1988" and was conducted by Harold D. Clarke and Allen Kornberg.

8. This change in Labour's image was not confined to the party's identifiers. In 1992, 61% of Liberal Democrats and 74% of Tory identifiers claimed that Labour was good for just one class, whereas a mere 28% of Liberals and 15% of Tories viewed Labour as good for all classes. Five years later, 14% of Liberals and 29% of Tories viewed Labour as good for one class, compared with the 73% of Liberals and 54% of Tories who viewed Labour as good for all classes. This suggests that the population as a whole shifted its perception of Labour.

9. The standard error for each R-squared value was computed by bootstrapping the data with five hundred replications and calculating the R-squared value for each replication. The standard error reported is the standard deviation of the R-squared estimates across these replications. In estimating the stability of partisanship, we constrained the measurement error variance to be nonnegative, and the R-squared for wave three to be less than or equal to 1.0.

10. For Great Britain, we coded Labour and the Tories as occupying the extremes, with the Liberals in the middle. In Canada, the NDP and Progressive Conservatives were coded as one and three, respectively, with Liberals in the middle. In Germany, we constructed a three-point scale with the CDU/CSU and SPD on either end, with the FDP in the middle. The Greens were omitted from the German three-point scale because it is not clear that they can be placed alongside the other major parties on a common single dimension.

11. Because the unemployment item was not asked in 1974, the inflation item alone was used as the instrument for the inflation and unemployment index in 1979. The results

were the same when the inflation item was analyzed in both waves, without the inclusion of the unemployment variable.

12. To correct for the ordinal measurement of party identification and short-term forces, we analyzed polychoric correlations using a weighted least-squares fit function (Joreskog and Sorbom 1993). Following the methodology described in Green and Palmquist (1990), reliabilities were stipulated for the party identification measures on the basis of an initial estimation of the measurement error characteristics of these items (see Chapter 3). The nonrecursive models were structured so that party identification was predicted by contemporaneous short-term forces and lagged partisanship. Short-term forces were predicted by contemporaneous partisanship and lagged short-term forces.

13. We also assessed the effects of voting behavior on party identification for the two four-wave surveys (Schickler and Green 1997). The results again show no statistically significant estimates for the effects of the vote on party identification.

14. This is the case when party identification and leadership evaluations in wave one are used as an instrument for these two variables in wave three; there is less evidence for an effect when the same instruments are instead drawn from wave two.

15. These estimates are based on stipulating a reliability of 0.950 for the partisanship measures.

16. Identification with the Progressive Conservatives remained at 12% as late as 1999. Only in 2000, after the Reform Party's transformation from a regional party into the more nationally oriented Alliance, did the PC finally lose its ability to command social identification. This change in party imagery allowed the Reform Party to nearly double its share of identifiers while identification with the PC slid to 8% (Political Support in Canada Study: The 2000 Federal Election Survey; principal investigators Harold D. Clarke and Allan Kornberg; see also Clarke, Kornberg, and Wearing 2000).

CHAPTER 8: HOW PARTISAN ATTACHMENTS STRUCTURE POLITICS

1. The same holds for other variables, such as evaluations of the candidates' personal traits. If Republicans prefer candidates who are former business executives and Democrats prefer candidates with a legal background, the direct effect of party identification may become negligible when we control for perceptions of the candidate's attributes. Yet in this instance party identification (and group identification more generally) expresses itself by shaping what voters look for in their candidates.

2. In theory, there is no end to the list of potential variables that one could include in a regression model to derive a lower bound. But variables that are highly proximal to the vote decision itself, such as evaluations of the candidates' personal traits, are not plausible determinants of party identification.

3. In surveys such as the NES and Gallup Poll, one finds a fairly strong correlation between party and economic assessments. This relationship is weaker in surveys that focus on topics other than politics, such as the General Social Survey. Presumably, surveys of consumer behavior elicit even lower levels of partisan cheering, although we know of no such surveys that try to measure party identification. To argue that partisanship alters economic perceptions—not just partisan spin reported to pollsters—means that con-

sumption patterns in Democratic and Republican states move in opposite directions when elections change the party in power. Thus, the perceptual bias argument has a testable, potentially lucrative, but deeply implausible empirical implication.

4. We stop short of including in our models survey questions that assess the candidates' personal traits, as these seem likely to be subject to rationalizations by those who have already made up their minds about whom they intend to vote for.

5. The results are not changed materially if one discards the small number of people who cast votes for the Green Party candidate, Ralph Nader, rather than classifying them as non-Bush voters. We also discarded from the analysis three respondents who voted for Pat Buchanan.

6. The natural log of 50/50 is zero. The natural log of 91/9 is 2.3. Thus, the movement from 50% to 91% represents a change in log-odds of 2.3

7. One could argue that the upper bound should in fact be slightly higher on the grounds that the three-point party identification scale contains some measurement error.

8. Regressing the seven-point party identification scale on the demographic items produces an R-squared value of 0.15, which rises to 0.43 when all of the issues scales are added as predictors.

9. This conclusion follows from the assumption that vote probabilities conform to a logistic distribution (or any similarly peaked distribution). We do not require as an axiom (see Converse 1966: 22) that partisans are by their nature less responsive to short-term forces than nonpartisans.

10. The estimate of 36.9 has a standard error of 4.0 ($p < .01$). Adding a dummy variable for region raises this slope to 41.0, with a standard error of 6.6 ($p < .01$). In both cases, the adjusted R-squared value is 0.90.

11. The declining comity of the U.S. House during the 1980s and early 1990s is aptly described in these terms. Those in the supposedly "permanent" Democratic majority increasingly used their parliamentary advantages to strong-arm their Republican adversaries, who became increasingly restive in their personal attacks on the Democratic leadership, eventually forcing Jim Wright, the speaker of the House, into retirement. In 1995, when the Republicans believed themselves to be presiding over a new era of Republican ascendancy, the tables were reversed, and it was the Democrats who worked to discredit and oust the speaker, Newt Gingrich.

References

Abramowitz, Alan I. 1994. "Issue Evolution Reconsidered: Racial Attitudes and Partisanship in the U.S. Electorate." *American Journal of Political Science* 38 (1): 1–24.

Abramson, Paul R. 1979. "Developing Party Identification: Further Examination of Life-Cycle, Generational, and Period Effects." *American Journal of Political Science* 23 (1): 78–96.

Abramson, Paul R., and Charles W. Ostrom Jr. 1991. "Macropartisanship: An Empirical Reassessment." *American Political Science Review* 85: 181–92.

———. 1992. "Question Wording and Macropartisanship." *American Political Science Review* 86: 475–86.

———. 1994. "Question Form and Context Effects in the Measurement of Partisanship: Experimental Tests of the Artifact Hypothesis." *American Political Science Review* 88: 955–58.

Abramson, Paul R., John H. Aldrich, and David W. Rohde. 1982. *Change and Continuity in the 1980 Elections.* Washington, D.C.: CQ Press.

———. 1995. *Change and Continuity in the 1992 Elections.* Washington, D.C.: CQ Press.

Achen, Christopher. 1992. "Social Psychology, Demographic Variables, and Linear Regression: Breaking the Iron Triangle in Voting Research." *Political Behavior* 14:195–211.

Aldrich, John H. 1995. "Why Parties?" In *The Origin and Transformation of Political Parties in America.* Chicago: University of Chicago Press.

Alwin, Duane F., and Jon A. Krosnick. 1991. "Aging, Cohorts, and the Stability of Sociopolitical Orientations over the Life Span." *American Journal of Sociology* 97: 169–95.

Anderson, T. W., and Cheng Hsiao. 1982. "Formulation and Estimation of Dynamic Models Using Panel Data." *Journal of Econometrics* 18: 47–82.

Arellano, Manuel. 1989. "A Note on the Anderson-Hsiao Estimator for Panel Data." *Econometrics Letters* 31: 337–41.

Atkeson, Lonna Rae, and Randall W. Partin. 1995. "Economic and Referendum Voting: A Comparison of Gubernatorial and Senatorial Elections." *American Political Science Review* 89: 99–107.

Babakus, Emin, Carl E. Ferguson Jr., and Karl G. Jöreskog. 1987. "The Sensitivity of Confirmatory Maximum Likelihood Factor Analysis to Violations of Measurement Scale and Distributional Assumptions." *Journal of Marketing Research* 24: 222–28.

Bartels, Larry M. 2000. "Partisanship and Voting Behavior, 1952–1996." *American Journal of Political Science* 44: 35–50.

Bartle, John. 1999. "Improving the Measurement of Party Identification in Britain." In *British Elections and Parties Review,* vol. 9, edited by Justin Fisher, Philip Cowley, David Denver, and Andrew Russell, 119–35. London: Frank Cass.

Beck, Paul Allen. 1977. "Partisan Dealignment in the Post-War South." *American Political Science Review* 71: 477–96.

Berelson, Bernard R., Paul F. Lazarsfeld, and William N. McPhee. 1954. *Voting.* Chicago: University of Chicago Press.

Bishop, George F., Alfred J. Tuchfarber, and Andrew E. Smith. 1994. "Question Form and Context Effects in the Measurement of Partisanship: Experimental Tests of the Artifact Hypothesis." *American Political Science Review* 88: 945–58.

Black, Earl, and Merle Black. 1987. *Politics and Society in the South.* Cambridge, Mass: Harvard University Press.

Box-Steffensmeier, Janet M., and Renee M. Smith. 1997. "Heterogeneity and Individual Party Identification." Paper presented at the annual meeting of the Midwest Political Science Association, Chicago.

Brady, Henry E., and Paul M. Sniderman. 1985. "Attitude Attribution: A Group Basis for Political Reasoning." *American Political Science Review* 79 (4): 1061–78.

Brody, Richard A., and Lawrence S. Rothenberg. 1988. "The Instability of Partisanship: An Analysis of the 1980 Presidential Election." *British Journal of Political Science* 18: 445–65.

Brown, Robert D., and James A. Woods. 1991. "Toward a Model of Congressional Elections." *Journal of Politics* 53 (2): 454–73.

Brown, Thad A. 1981. "On Contextual Change and Partisan Attitudes." *British Journal of Political Science* 11: 427–48.

Bruce, J. M, and J. A. Clark. 1998. "Segmented Partisanship in a Southern Political Elite." *Polity* 30 (4): 627–44.

Budge, Ian, and Dennis Farlie. 1976. "A Comparative Analysis of Factors Correlated with Turnout and Voting Choice." In *Party Identification and Beyond,* edited by Ian Budge, Ivor Crewe, and Dennis Farlie. New York: John Wiley and Sons.

Burnham, Walter Dean. 1965. "The Changing Shape of the American Political Universe." *American Political Science Review* 59: 7–28.

————. 1970. *Critical Elections and the Mainsprings of American Politics*. New York: Norton.

Butler, David, and Donald Stokes. 1969. *Political Change in Britain*. London: Macmillan.

————. 1974. *Political Change in Britain,* 2nd ed. London: Macmillan.

Cain, Bruce E., and John Ferejohn. 1981. "Party Identification in the United States and Britain." *Comparative Political Studies* 14: 31–47.

Campbell, Angus, Philip E. Converse, Warren E. Miller, and Donald E. Stokes. 1960. *The American Voter*. New York: John Wiley and Sons.

————. 1966. *Elections and the Political Order*. New York: John Wiley and Sons.

Campbell, James E., Mary Munro, John R. Alford, and Bruce A. Campbell. 1986. "Partisanship and Voting." In *Research in Micropolitics,* vol. 1, edited by Samuel Long. Greenwich, Conn.: JAI Press.

Carmines, Edward G., and James A. Stimson. 1989. *Issue Evolution: Race and the Transformation of American Politics*. Princeton, N.J.: Princeton University Press.

Chaffee, S. H., and Y. Miyo. 1983. "Selective Exposure and the Reinforcement Hypothesis: An Intergenerational Panel Study of the 1980 Presidential Campaign." *Communications Research* 10: 3–36.

Clarke, Harold D., and Allan Kornberg. 1992. "Risky Business: Partisan Volatility and Electoral Choice in Canada, 1988." *Electoral Studies* 11: 138–56.

Clarke, Harold D., Allan Kornberg, and Peter Wearing. 2000. *A Polity on the Edge: Canada and the Politics of Fragmentation*. Toronto: Broadview Press.

Clarke, Harold D., and Marianne C. Stewart. 1984. "Dealignment of Degree: Partisan Change in Britain, 1974–83." *Journal of Politics* 46: 689–718.

————. 1987. "Partisan Inconsistency and Partisan Change in Federal States: The Case of Canada." *American Journal of Political Science* 31 (2): 383–407.

————. 1998. "The Decline of Parties in the Minds of Citizens." *Annual Review of Political Science* 1: 357–78.

Clarke, Harold D., Marianne C. Stewart, and Paul Whiteley. 1994. "Tory Trends: The Dynamics of Conservative Party Support, 1992–1994." Paper presented at the Annual Elections, Public Opinion and Parties Conference, University of Cardiff, Cardiff, Wales, September 27–29. This was published in 1997 with a slightly different title: "Tory Trends: Party Identification and Conservative Support since 1992." *British Journal of Political Science* 26: 299–318.

Converse, Philip E. 1964. "The Nature of Belief Systems in Mass Publics." In *Ideology and Discontent,* edited by David Apter. Glencoe, Ill.: Free Press.

————. 1966a. "The Concept of a Normal Vote." In *Elections and the Political Order,* edited by Angus Campbell, Philip E. Converse, Warren E. Miller, and Donald E. Stokes. New York: John Wiley and Sons.

————. 1966b. "On the Possibility of Major Political Realignment in the South." In *Elections and the Political Order,* edited by Angus Campbell, Philip E. Converse, Warren E. Miller, and Donald E. Stokes. New York: John Wiley and Sons.

————. 1976. *The Dynamics of Party Support*. Beverly Hills, Calif.: Sage.

Converse, Philip E., and Roy Pierce. 1986. *Political Representation in France.* Cambridge, Mass.: Belknap Press of Harvard University Press.

———. 1992. "Partisanship and the Party System." *Political Behavior* 14: 239–59.

Cowden, Jonathan A., and Rose M. McDermott. 2000. "Short-Term Forces and Partisanship." *Political Behavior* 22 (3): 197–222.

Cox, Gary W., and Mathew D. McCubbins. 1993. *Legislative Leviathan: Party Government in the House.* Berkeley: University of California Press.

Crewe, Ivor. 1983. "Partisan Dealignment Ten Years On." In *Issues and Controversies in British Electoral Behavior,* edited by David Denver and Gordon Hands. New York: Harvester Wheatsheaf.

Dalton, Russell J. 2000. "The Decline of Party Identifications." In *Parties without Partisans,* edited by Russell J. Dalton and Martin P. Wattenberg. New York: Oxford University Press.

Dalton, Russell J., and Martin P. Wattenberg, eds. 2000. *Parties without Partisans: Political Change in Advanced Industrial Democracies.* New York: Oxford University Press.

Dalton, Russell J., Ian McAllister, and Martin P. Wattenberg. 2000. "The Consequences of Partisan Dealignment." In *Parties without Partisans,* edited by Russell J. Dalton and Martin P. Wattenberg. New York: Oxford University Press.

Davidson, Roger H. 1980. "Subcommittee Government: New Channels for Policy Making." In *The New Congress,* edited by Thomas Mann and Norman Ornstein. Washington, D.C.: AEI Press.

Devine, P. G., M. J. Monteith, J. R. Zuwerink, and A. J. Elliot. 1991. "Prejudice With and Without Compunction." *Journal of Personality and Social Psychology* 60 (6): 817–30.

Dowd, Daniel Vincent. 1999. "Understanding Partisan Change and Stability in the Late Twentieth Century." Ph.D. diss., Yale University.

Downs, Anthony. 1957. *An Economic Theory of Democracy.* New York: Harper.

Edwards, George C. 1990. *Presidential Approval: A Sourcebook.* Baltimore: Johns Hopkins University Press.

Enelow, James M., and Melvin J. Hinich. 1984. *The Spatial Theory of Voting: An Introduction.* New York: Cambridge University Press.

Enelow, James M., James W. Endersby, and Michael C. Munger. 1993. "A Revised Probabilistic Spatial Model of Elections: Theory and Evidence." In *Information, Participation, and Choice: An Economic Theory of Democracy in Perspective,* edited by Bernard Grofman. Ann Arbor: University of Michigan Press.

Erikson, Robert S., Gerald C. Wright, and John P. McIver. 1993. *Statehouse Democracy: Public Opinion and Policy in the American States.* New York: Cambridge University Press.

Erikson, Robert S., Michael B. MacKuen, and James A. Stimson. 1996. "Party Identification and Macropartisanship: Resolving the Paradox of Micro-level Stability and Macro-level Dynamics." Paper presented at the Annual Meeting of the Political Methodology Section of the American Political Science Association, Ann Arbor, Mich.

———. 1998. "What Moves Macropartisanship? A Response to Green, Palmquist, and Schickler." *American Political Science Review* 92: 901–12.

Fiorina, Morris P. 1981. *Retrospective Voting in American National Elections.* New Haven and London: Yale University Press.

Flanigan, William H., Wendy M. Rahn, and Nancy H. Zingale. 1989. "Political Parties as Objects of Identification and Orientation." University of Minnesota.

Franklin, Charles H. 1992. "Measurement and the Dynamics of Party Identification." *Political Behavior* 14: 297–309.

Franklin, Charles H., and John E. Jackson. 1983. "The Dynamics of Party Identification." *American Political Science Review* 77: 957–73.

Gerber, Alan. 1996. "African Americans' Congressional Careers and the Democratic House Delegation." *Journal of Politics* 58 (3): 831–45.

Gerber, Alan, and Donald P. Green. 1998. "Rational Learning and Partisan Attitudes." *American Journal of Political Science* 42: 794–818.

———. 1999. "Misperceptions about Perceptual Bias." *Annual Review of Political Science* 2: 189–210.

Gerber, Elisabeth R., and John E. Jackson. 1993. "Endogenous Preferences and the Study of Institutions." *American Political Science Review* 87 (3): 639–56.

Gimpel, James G. 1999. *Separate Destinations: Migration, Immigration, and the Politics of Places*. Ann Arbor: University of Michigan Press.

Green, Donald P. 1988. "On the Dimensionality of Public Sentiment toward Partisan and Ideological Groups." *American Journal of Political Science* 32: 758–80.

———. 1991. "The Effects of Measurement Error on Two-Stage, Least Squares Estimates." In *Political Analysis,* vol. 2, edited by James A. Stimson. Ann Arbor: University of Michigan Press.

Green, Donald P., Alan S. Gerber, and Suzanna L. De Boef. 1999. "Tracking Opinion over Time: A Method for Reducing Sampling Error." *Public Opinion Quarterly* 63 (2): 178–92.

Green, Donald P., and Bradley L. Palmquist. 1990. "Of Artifacts and Partisan Instability." *American Journal of Political Science* 34: 872–902.

———. 1991. "More 'Tricks of the Trade': Reparameterizing LISREL Models Using Negative Variances." *Psychometrika* 56: 137–45.

———. 1994. "How Stable Is Party Identification?" *Political Behavior* 43: 437–66.

Green, Donald P., and David H. Yoon. 2002. "Reconciling Individual and Aggregate Evidence Concerning Partisan Stability: Applying Time-Series Models to Panel Survey Data." *Political Analysis* 10: 1–24.

Green, Donald P., and Eric Schickler. 1993. "A Multiple Method Approach to the Measurement of Party Identification." *Public Opinion Quarterly* 57: 503–35.

Green, Donald P., Bradley Palmquist, and Eric Schickler. 1998. "Macropartisanship: A Replication and Critique." *American Political Science Review* 92: 883–99.

———. 2001. "Partisan Stability Evidence from Aggregate Data." In *Controversies in Voting Behavior,* 4th ed., edited by Richard G. Niemi and Herbert F. Weisberg. Washington, D.C.: CQ Press.

Greene, Steven. 1999. "Understanding Party Identification: A Social Identity Approach." *Political Psychology* 20: 393–403.

———. 2000. "The Psychological Sources of Partisan-Leaning Independence." *American Politics Quarterly* 28 (4): 511–37.

Greenstein, Fred I. 1963. *The American Party System and the American People*. Englewood Cliffs, N.J.: Prentice-Hall.

Grofman, Bernard, Lisa Handley, and Richard G. Niemi. 1992. *Minority Representation and the Quest for Voting Equality.* New York: Cambridge University Press.

Guber, Deborah Lynn. 1998. "Rethinking Environmentalism: Ecology, Public Opinion, and Mass Political Behavior." Ph.D. diss., Yale University.

Guchteneire, Paul de, Lawrence LeDuc, and Richard G. Niemi. 1985. "A Compendium of Academic Survey Studies of Elections around the World." *Electoral Studies* 4: 159–74.

———. 1991. "A Compendium of Academic Survey Studies of Elections around the World: Update 1." *Electoral Studies* 10: 231–43.

Hadley, Charles D. 1985. "Dual Partisan Identification in the South." *Journal of Politics* 47 (1): 254–68.

Hadley, Charles D., and Lewis Bowman. 1995. *Southern State Party Organizations and Activists.* Westport, Conn.: Praeger.

Harvey, Andrew C. 1989. *Forecasting, Structural Time Series Models and the Kalman Filter.* Cambridge: Cambridge University Press.

Heard, Alexander. 1952. *A Two-Party South?* Chapel Hill: University of North Carolina Press.

Heath, Anthony, and Roy Pierce. 1992. "It Was Party Identification All Along: Question Order Effects on Reports of Party Identification in Britain." *Electoral Studies* 11: 93–105.

Heath, Anthony, and Sarah K. McDonald. 1988. "The Demise of Party Identification Theory?" *Electoral Studies* 7: 95–107.

Heise, David R. 1969. "Separating Reliability and Stability in Test-Retest Correlation." *American Sociological Review* 34: 93–101.

Hilton, James L., and William von Hippel. 1996. "Stereotypes." *Annual Review of Sociology* 47: 237–71.

Hogg, Michael A., Deborah J. Terry, and Katherine M. White. 1995. "A Tale of Two Theories: A Critical Comparison of Identity Theory with Social Identity Theory." *Social Psychology Quarterly* 58 (4): 255–69.

Jackman, Mary R., and Robert W. Jackman. 1983. *Class Awareness in the United States.* Berkeley: University of California Press.

Jackson, John E. 1975. "Issues, Party Choices, and Presidential Votes." *American Journal of Political Science* 19: 161–85.

Jennings, Kent M., and Richard G. Niemi. 1981. *Generations and Politics: A Panel Study of Young Adults and Their Parents.* Princeton, N.J.: Princeton University Press.

Jennings, Kent M., Gregory B. Markus, and Richard G. Niemi. 1991. "Youth-Parent Socialization Panel Study, 1965–1982: Three Waves Combined" [computer file]. Ann Arbor, Mich.: University of Michigan, Center for Political Studies/Survey Research Center [producers], 1983. Ann Arbor, Mich.: Inter-university Consortium for Political and Social Research [distributor].

Johnston, Richard. 1992. "Party Identification Measures in the Anglo-American Democracies: A National Survey Experiment." *American Journal of Political Science* 36: 542–59.

Jöreskog, Karl G., and Dag Sorbom. 1993. *LISREL 8: User's Reference Guide.* Chicago: Scientific Software.

Kaase, Max. 1976. "Party Identification and Voting Behavior in the West-German Election of 1969." In *Party Identification and Beyond,* edited by Ian Budge, Ivor Crewe, and Dennis Farlie. New York: John Wiley and Sons.

Keith, Bruce E., David B. Magelby, Candice J. Nelson, Elizabeth Orr, Mark C. Westlye, and Raymond E. Wolfinger. 1992. *The Myth of the Independent Voter.* Berkeley: University of California Press.

Key, V. O., Jr. 1949. *Southern Politics in State and Nation.* New York: Knopf.

———. 1961. *Public Opinion and American Democracy.* New York: Knopf.

King, Gary. 1994. "Elections to the United States House of Representatives, 1898–1992" [computer file]. ICPSR version. Cambridge, Mass.: Gary King [producer]. Ann Arbor, Mich.: Inter-university Consortium for Political and Social Research [distributor].

Koch, Jeffrey W. 1998. "Electoral Competitiveness and the Voting Decision: Evidence from the Pooled Senate Election Study." *Political Behavior* 20: 295–311.

Krasno, Jonathan S., and Daniel E. Seltz. 2000. *Buying Time: Television Advertising in the 1998 Elections.* New York: Brennan Center for Justice.

Ladd, Everett Carll. 1982. *Where Have All the Voters Gone?: The Fracturing of America's Political Parties,* 2nd ed. New York: Norton.

LaPalombara, Joseph. 1987. "Italian Elections: The Rashomon Effect." In *Italy at the Polls,* edited by Howard R. Penniman. Durham, N.C.: Duke University Press.

LeDuc, Lawrence. 1981. "The Dynamic Properties of Party Identification: A Four-Nation Comparison." *European Journal of Political Science* 9: 257–68.

LeDuc, Lawrence, Harold D. Clarke, Jane Jenson, and Jon Pammett. 1984. "Partisan Instability in Canada: Evidence from a New Panel Study." *American Political Science Review* 78: 470–84.

Lijphart, Arend. 1994. *Electoral Systems and Party Systems: A Study of Twenty-Seven Democracies, 1945–1990.* Oxford: Oxford University Press.

Lipset, Seymour Martin, and Stein Rokkan, eds. 1967. *Party Systems and Voter Alignments: Crossnational Perspectives.* New York: Free Press.

Lockerbie, Brad. 1991. "The Temporal Pattern of Economic Evaluations and Vote Choice in Senate Elections." *Public Choice* 69: 279–94.

Lodge, Milton, and Ruth Hamill. 1986. "A Partisan Schema for Political Information-Processing." *American Political Science Review* 80 (2): 505–19.

Lupia, Arthur. 1994. "Shortcuts Versus Encyclopedias: Information and Voting-Behavior in California Insurance Reform Elections." *American Political Science Review* 88 (1): 63–76.

MacKuen, Michael B., Robert S. Erikson, and James A. Stimson. 1989. "Macropartisanship." *American Political Science Review* 83: 1125–42.

———. 1992. "Question Wording and Macropartisanship." *American Political Science Review* 86: 475–86.

Mael, Fred, and Lois Tetrick. 1992. "Identifying Organizational Identification." *Educational and Psychological Measurement* 54: 813–24.

Markus, Gregory B. 1982. "Political Attitudes during an Election Year: A Report on the 1980 NES Panel Study." *American Political Science Review* 76: 538–60.

McGraw, Kathleen M., and Milton Lodge. 1996. "Political Information Processing: A Review Essay." *Political Communication* 13 (1): 131–38.

Meinhold, Richard J., and Nozer D. Singpurwalla. 1983. "Understanding the Kalman Filter." *American Statistician* 37: 123–27.

Miller, Warren E. 1966. "Party Identification and Partisan Attitudes." In *Readings in Ameri-*

can Political Behavior, edited by Raymond E. Wolfinger. Englewood Cliffs, N.J.: Prentice-Hall.

———. 1991. "Party Identification, Realignment, and Party Voting: Back to Basics." *American Political Science Review* 85: 557–68.

Miller, Warren E., and J. Merrill Shanks. 1996. *The New American Voter.* Cambridge, Mass.: Harvard University Press.

Mughan, A. 1981. "The Cross-National Validity of Party Identification: Great Britain and the United States Compared." *Political Studies* 29: 365–75.

Nesmith, Bruce. 1994. *The New Republican Coalitions: The Reagan Campaigns and White Evangelicals.* New York: P. Lang.

Newport, Frank. 1979. "The Religious Switcher in the United States." *American Sociological Review* 44 (4): 528–52.

Niemi, Richard G., and Herbert F. Weisberg. 1976. *Controversies in American Voting Behavior.* San Francisco: W. H. Freeman.

Niemi, Richard G., Stephen G. Wright, and Lynda Powell. 1987. "Multiple Party Identifiers and the Measurement of Party Identification." *Journal of Politics* 49 (4): 1093–1103.

Norpoth, Helmut. 1978. "Party Identification in West Germany: Tracing an Elusive Concept." *Political Studies* 11: 36–59.

———. 1987. "Under Way and Here to Stay: Party Realignment in the 1980s." *Public Opinion Quarterly* 51 (3): 376–91.

Oldfield, Duane M. 1996. *The Right and the Righteous : The Christian Right Confronts the Republican Party.* Lanham, Md.: Rowman and Littlefield.

Page, Benjamin I. 1978. *Choices and Echoes in Presidential Elections.* Chicago: University of Chicago Press.

Page, Benjamin I., and Calvin C. Jones. 1979. "Reciprocal Effects of Policy Preferences, Party Loyalties, and the Vote." *American Political Science Review* 73 (December): 1071–89.

Page, Benjamin I., and Robert Y. Shapiro. 1992. *The Rational Public: Fifty Years of Trends in Americans' Policy Preferences.* Chicago: University of Chicago Press.

Palmquist, Bradley, and Donald P. Green. 1992. "Estimation of Models with Correlated Measurement Errors from Panel Data." In *Sociological Methodology 1992,* edited by Peter V. Marsden. Washington, D.C.: American Sociological Association.

Patterson, Thomas E. 1982. *Presidential Campaign Impact on Voters: 1976 Panel, Erie, Pennsylvania and Los Angeles.* Ann Arbor, Mich.: Inter-university Consortium for Political and Social Research. ICPSR no. 7990.

Petrocik, John R. 1987. "Realignment: New Party Coalitions and the Nationalization of the South." *Journal of Politics* 49 (2): 347–75.

Popkin, Samuel L. 1991. *The Reasoning Voter: Communication and Persuasion in Presidential Campaigns.* Chicago: University of Chicago Press.

Putnam, Robert C. 2000. *Bowling Alone: The Collapse and Renewal of American Community.* New York: Simon and Schuster.

Richardson, Bradley M. 1991. "European Party Loyalties Revisited." *American Political Science Review* 85: 751–81.

Rigdon, Edward E., and Carl E. Ferguson Jr. 1991. "The Performance of the Polychoric Correlation Coefficient and Selected Fitting Functions in Confirmatory Factor Analysis with Ordinal Data." *Journal of Marketing Research* 28: 491–97.

Rundquist, Barry, Jeong-Hwa Lee, and Jungho Rhee. 1996. "The Distributive Politics of Cold War Defense Spending: Some State Level Evidence." *Legislative Studies Quarterly* 21: 265–81.

Schickler, Eric, and Donald P. Green. 1995. "Issue Preferences and the Dynamics of Party Identification: A Methodological Critique." In *Political Analysis,* vol. 5, edited by John R. Freeman. Ann Arbor: University of Michigan Press.

———. 1997. "The Stability of Party Identification in Western Democracies: Results from Eight Panel Surveys." *Comparative Political Studies* 30: 450–83.

Schmitt, Hermann. 1989. "On Party Attachment in Western Europe, and the Utility of Eurobarometer Data." *West European Politics* 12: 122–39.

Sears, David O., and R. E. Whitney. 1973. *Political Persuasion.* Morristown, N.J.: General Learning.

Sears, David O., Richard R. Lau, Tom R. Tyler, and Harris M. Allen Jr. 1980. "Self-Interest and Symbolic Politics in Policy Attitudes and Presidential Voting." *American Political Science Review* 74: 670–84.

Sharma, Subhash, Srinivas Durvasula, and William R. Dillon. 1989. "Some Results of the Behavior of Alternate Covariance Structure Estimation Procedures in the Presence of Nonnormal Data." *Journal of Marketing Research* 26: 214–21.

Shively, W. Phillips. 1972. "Party Identification, Party Choice, and Voting Stability: The Weimar Case." *American Political Science Review* 66: 1203–25.

Simmons, Wendy W. 2001. "Election Controversy Apparently Drove Partisan Wedge into Attitudes towards Supreme Court." http://www.gallup.com/poll/releases/pr010116.asp.

Stewart, Marianne C., and Harold D. Clarke. 1998. "The Dynamics of Party Identification in Federal Systems: The Canadian Case." *American Journal of Political Science* 42 (January): 97–116.

Stokes, Donald E. 1966. "Party Loyalty and the Likelihood of Deviating Elections." In *Elections and the Political Order,* edited by Angus Campbell, Philip E. Converse, Warren E. Miller, and Donald E. Stokes. New York: John Wiley and Sons.

Sundquist, James L. 1973. *Dynamics of the Party System: Alignment and Realignment of Political Parties in the United States.* Washington, D.C.: Brookings Institution.

Tajfel, Henri, ed. 1978. *Differentiation between Social Groups: Studies in the Social Psychology of Intergroup Relations,* edited by Henri Tajfel. London: Academic Press.

Thomassen, Jacques. 1976. "Party Identification as a Cross-national Concept: Its Meaning in the Netherlands." In *Party Identification and Beyond,* edited by Ian Budge, Ivor Crewe, and Dennis Farlie. New York: John Wiley and Sons.

Wattenberg, Martin P. 1994. *The Decline of American Political Parties, 1952–1992.* Cambridge, Mass.: Harvard University Press.

Weisberg, Herbert F. 1980. "A Multidimensional Conceptualization of Party Identification." *Political Behavior* 2: 33–60.

Weisberg, Herbert F., and Edward B. Hasecke. 1999. "What Is Partisan Strength? A Social Identity Theory Approach." Paper presented at the Annual Meeting of the American Political Science Association, Atlanta, Ga., September 2–5.

Wiley, David E., and James A. Wiley. 1970. "The Estimation of Measurement Error in Panel Data." *American Sociological Review* 35: 112–17.

Witt, Hugh, Harry Crockett Jr., and Nicholas Babchuk. 1988. "Religious Switching: An Alternative Model." *Social Science Research* 17: 206–18.

Wolfinger, Raymond, and Robert B. Arseneau. 1978. "Partisan Change in the South, 1952–1976." In *Political Parties: Development and Decay,* edited by Sandy Maisel and Joseph Cooper. Beverly Hills, Calif.: Sage.

Wolfinger, Raymond E., and Joan Heifetz Hollinger. 1971. "Safe Seats, Seniority, and Power in Congress." In *Readings on Congress,* edited by Raymond E. Wolfinger. Englewood Cliffs, N.J.: Prentice-Hall.

Wong, Janelle S. 2001. "The Effects of Age and Political Exposure on the Development of Party Identification among Asian American and Latino Immigrants in the United States." *Political Behavior* 22 (4): 341–71.

Zaller, John R. 1992. *The Nature and Origins of Mass Opinion.* Cambridge: Cambridge University Press.

Index

abortion issues, 29, 83, 158, 210

Achen, Christopher/Achen model of voter learning, 113–14, 117, 119, 121, 125, 137

affirmative action, 28

African Americans, 3, 106, 162; aid to blacks issues, 210; in Democratic Party, 3, 108, 141; partisanship of, 12, 13

Alabama, 152, 154

American National Election Study (NES), 10, 14, 40–41, 89, 91, 92–93, 169; generational replacement survey, 149; ideological categories used by, 159; panel surveys, 146, 194; research on issue stances of candidates, 209, 210; survey of self-categorization and policy opinions, 213, 214; vote preference studies, 216

American South: coalition in, 159; Deep South states, 12, 152, 154, 155; evolution of partisanship in, 141; interparty com-petition in, 6, 147; macropartisanship equilibrium in, 161; "native" white cat-egory, 146, 151; one-party system in, 141, 154, 156, 160, 162; partisan change in, 141, 142, 152, 161, 202; partisan sta-bility in, 142; party identification in, 161; political institutions in, 162; rate of partisan change in, 142–55, 149; Rim states, 152, 154, 155; two-party system in, 6, 94, 153, 202; voting age factor in population, 163. *See also* party realign-ment in American South

American Voter, The (Campbell et al.), 5, 6, 7, 8, 26, 106, 110, 158, 213

Arkansas, 152, 158

Berlusconi, Silvio, 185

Blair, Tony, 178, 183, 189

Britain, 20–21

British political parties: Conservative Party, 20–21, 178, 183, 188; Labour

Willey Library
337 College Hill
Johnson, VT 05656